THE CHINA STORY

OTHER BOOKS
BY THE SAME AUTHOR

LANCASHIRE AND THE FAR EAST
JAPAN'S FEET OF CLAY
JAPAN'S GAMBLE IN CHINA
CHINA AT WAR
THE DREAM WE LOST
LAST CHANCE IN CHINA
LOST ILLUSION
THE HIGH COST OF VENGEANCE

The China Story

BY

FREDA UTLEY

HENRY REGNERY COMPANY
CHICAGO, 1951

Copyright 1951
HENRY REGNERY COMPANY
Chicago 4, Illinois

First printing, April 1951
Second printing, May 1951
Third printing, June 1951

Manufactured in the United States of America by
American Book-Knickerbocker Press, Inc., New York

Contents

		page
	Introduction	
I.	Milestones on the Road to Korea	3
II.	Too Little Too Late—the Facts about "Aid to China"	30
III.	Four Hundred Million Lost Allies	55
IV.	How and Why War Came to Korea	87
V.	How the Communists Captured the Diplomats	103
VI.	. . . and the Secretary of State	125
VII.	. . . and the Public	139
VIII.	Senator McCarthy's Charges—and the Tydings Committee	164
IX.	The Case of Owen Lattimore	188
X.	Time for Re-examination	219
	Appendices	243
	Index	271

Introduction

IN KOREA, in 1950, the first payment in American lives was demanded for the blunders of our policy makers in the Far East. Five years after the total defeat of Japan and Germany a third world war looms on the horizon.

How did it come to pass that after so great a victory American security is today in greater jeopardy than at any time since the founding of the Republic? How and why were the fruits of victory thrown away?

These are the questions which the American people are beginning to ask as the casualty lists mount and American boys fight against overwhelming odds in a country thousands of miles away which most of them had barely heard of when they were called on to defend it.

Deluded for years by dreams of "one world" to be established by collaborating with Stalin in the United Nations, the American people now face a bitter awakening.

Surveying the frustration of their hopes, we see that all and more of the European nations that won independence in World War I lost it, together with all vestiges of freedom, in World War II. Turning our eyes to the Far East, the picture is yet blacker. China before World War II had retained a part of her territory in spite of Japanese aggression. Today, she is wholly in the camp of Soviet Russia. And all Asia trembles at the prospect of Communist domination.

What combination of circumstances and influences accounts for this tragic dénouement of military victory?

The historian sees that the basic mistake we made was our failure to remember that in international affairs, as in physics, nature abhors a vacuum. President Roosevelt's demand for the unconditional surrender of Japan and Germany left power vacuums in Europe and Asia which Soviet Russia was bound to fill unless we determined to take positive action. In Europe, we endeavored at least to build up England and France and sustain Italy and Greece to compensate for the elimination of Germany. In Asia, however, we were not concerned with creating a balance of power of any kind. We had the alternative of reconstituting Japan or backing a government in China that would be a reliable ally of the United States and a counterbalance to Soviet influences and machinations in the Far East, including Korea. We chose neither way —utterly ignoring straight and logical thinking in the realm of higher politics.

The moralist and the political philosopher will argue that it was the decay of our faith in the values which made us great and strong and free which has led the Western World close to the brink of disaster. If we had stuck by the principles of the Atlantic Charter and offered just terms of peace to the vanquished provided they overthrew their totalitarian dictators and ideology, the barriers against Communism would not have been destroyed.

As Senator Taft said in his January 5, 1951, speech in the Senate, the failure of the United Nations is due to the fact that it was "never based on law and justice to be interpreted by an impartial tribunal, but on a control of the world by the power of five great nations."

Those who wrote the first draft of the Charter did not even mention the word "justice," and in the Charter as finally drafted, the Security Council entrusted with the task of preserving peace, was not enjoined to consider justice as its guiding principle.

We are already paying, in Korea, and by the conscription of our young men and heavy taxes, for the failure of the Administration, after the last war, to insist on a just peace. Yet it was not the desire for power, but the hope that peace on earth, good will toward men, could be established by American generosity and concessions, which induced the American people to support the Administration's fatal war and postwar policies.

It is not enough to recognize the consequences of its unforgivable naïveté in believing that the men in Moscow were as well-meaning as we, thus enabling Stalin to step into Hitler's place as the scourge of Western civilization. One must seek the reasons why Communist influences were able to distort American policy, and induce the American people to believe in the peaceful intentions and "democratic" nature of the Soviet State.

In the following pages, therefore, I not only give a record of our China and Korean policy, but also endeavor to show the fallacies and misconceptions which weakened our resistance and enabled a small group of Communist sympathizers to influence the Administration and the public to our lasting detriment.

This book is not concerned with our blunders in Europe, important as it is to survey them. For in Europe our errors have been at least partially recognized and to some extent compensated for. The savage Morgenthau Plan was never fully implemented in Germany and the Marshall Plan and the Truman Doctrine followed by the Atlantic Pact and now by our attempt to enlist the German people on our side in the defense of Western civilization, have begun to compensate for the agreements made at Yalta and Potsdam. In the Far East, on the other hand, in spite of the war in Korea, fundamental errors concerning the nature and aims of Communism still weaken our will and prevent us from joining hands with the only ally in Asia ready to fight beside us: the Chinese Nationalist Government in Formosa.

If the Administration recognized its errors and made every effort to amend its former mistaken policies, then in this time of peril it would be wiser and better to remain silent concerning the immediate past. Unfortunately, those responsible for the disastrous course of United States policy toward China since Japan's defeat have neither admitted their errors nor sought to rectify them. Ignorance and wishful thinking, coupled with lingering Communist influence in high places, and the desire to "save face" still prevent America from confronting squarely and honestly the realities of the situation.

No valid judgments can be made, or intelligent policies adopted, without knowledge of the facts. So the first chapters of this book are a record of our China—and Korean—policy from Yalta to the present. Later chapters deal with the evidence in the White Paper on China *(United States Relations with China)*, in the published proceedings of the Tydings Committee, and other sources concerning the extent to which Communist influences determined Far Eastern policy.

We cannot ignore the evidence that President Roosevelt must have been aware that his policy would mean Soviet domination over Europe and perhaps a great part of the world.

Robert E. Sherwood, in his book *Roosevelt and Hopkins,* provides the most authoritative proof of this assertion. He gives documentary evidence that Roosevelt and his advisers knew that "unconditional surrender" and the elimination of Germany and Japan as independent nations would lead to Soviet Russia's becoming so strong that her demands could not be resisted. Sherwood relates how, at the August 1943 Quebec Conference, Harry Hopkins had with him a document headed "Russia's Position," which was quoted from "a very high level U.S. Military Strategic estimate." This document contained the following passages:

Russia's post-war position in Europe will be a dominant one. With Germany crushed, there is no power in Europe to oppose her tremendous military forces. It is true that Great Britain is building up a position in the Mediterranean vis-à-vis Russia that she may find useful in balancing power in Europe. However, even here she may not be able to oppose Russia unless she is otherwise supported.

The conclusions from the foregoing are obvious. Since Russia is the decisive factor in the war, she must be given every assistance and every effort must be made to obtain her friendship. Likewise, *since without question she will dominate Europe on the defeat of the Axis,* it is even more essential to develop and maintain the most friendly relations with Russia (italics added).

Finally, the most important factor the United States has to consider in relation to Russia is the prosecution of the war in the Pacific. With Russia as an ally in the war against Japan, the war can be terminated in less time and at less expense in life and resources than if the reverse were the case. Should the war in the Pacific have to be carried on with an unfriendly or a negative attitude on the part of Russia, the difficulties will be immeasurably increased and operations might become abortive.

This estimate, wrote Sherwood, "was obviously of great importance as indicating the policy which guided the making of decisions at Teheran, and, much later, at Yalta."

Robert E. Sherwood is a friendly, not a hostile, witness. He cannot be suspected of weighting the evidence against Roosevelt and his trusted advisers. It must accordingly be accepted as true that the late President, and presumably also General Marshall, decided that the military situation demanded the abandonment of the principles of the Atlantic Charter, which promised liberty and opportunity, freedom and self-determination, to all nations, including the vanquished. They decided to adhere to the demand for unconditional surrender, and agreed upon the Morgenthau Plan for Germany, realizing that this policy must lead to Soviet domination over Europe.

Sacrifices of principle for immediate gain, or for the satisfaction of vengeful impulses, are always disastrous in the long run, and sometimes in the short run. So today, only five years after the end of World War II, we are already paying for the lack of principle, or for the friendliness toward Communism of those who directed American policy during and after the war.

The opponents and protagonists of America's war and postwar foreign policy cannot be divided along party lines. Many a genuine liberal who welcomed the Roosevelt Administration's efforts to alleviate distress and salvage the American economy from the disaster of the depression years, opposed its foreign policy and deplored its partiality for Communists at home and abroad. And many Republicans who intensely disliked the domestic policies of the Administration went along with it on foreign policy, and were as willing as Roosevelt to believe that Stalin's government was "peace-loving" and "democratic," and fundamentally different from the Nazis, fascists, and the Japanese militarists.

As many liberals as conservatives opposed the demand for "unconditional surrender," which they realized would not only induce the enemy to fight to the last gasp, and therefore cause unnecessary sacrifices of American lives, but would also place Stalin in too powerful a position. But, with a few notable exceptions, neither the former isolationists nor the interventionists took a strong stand against Roosevelt's "Trust Stalin" policy. The same is true of the immediate postwar period.

Whether a man calls himself a Republican or a Democrat, a conservative, a liberal, or a socialist, is therefore comparatively unimportant. The real test of whether he is a reactionary, a fascist, a Communist, or a civilized man and a good American, is whether or not he believes in the values which made America not only great and prosperous, but also the symbol of mankind's aspirations for liberty and justice.

In presenting an analysis of Communist influence on American policy, I take account of the mixed motives of men in all parties and of all political persuasions. Only the historian of the future will be able to pronounce a definite judgment. I have attempted to evaluate from such evidence as is now available the degree to which Communist influence, as distinct from incompetence, ignorance, and ambition, determined the disastrous course of America's Far Eastern policy.

One thing is certain. Communist conquest of a large part of the world since the defeat of Germany and Japan, and the threat of even greater conquests, was not unavoidable. In the first part of this book, I shall show how what we did—and what we failed to do—in the Far East led us straight down the path to war in Korea.

THE CHINA STORY

1. Milestones on the Road to Korea

UNTIL 1945 America's traditional Far Eastern policy for more than half a century had as its aim the preservation of the integrity and independence of China. The immediate, although not the basic, cause of our entry into World War II was our refusal to recognize Japanese conquests in China, as definitely stated in the Hull "ultimatum" of November 26, 1941.

At Yalta in February 1945 the United States reversed this policy. President Roosevelt agreed to let Russia acquire what was to be in effect a permanent position of power in China. The principal terms of that agreement included:

1. the "lease" of Port Arthur to Russia as a naval base;
2. the "internationalization" of Dairen with "pre-eminent rights" for the Soviet Union in this largest of China's northeastern ports;
3. the "joint operation" of the Manchurian railways by China and Russia, with the "pre-eminent interests" of the Soviet Union safeguarded.

It was further agreed that Russia should acquire the Kurile Islands and that "the southern part of Sakhalin as well as all the islands adjacent to it shall be returned to the Soviet Union."

The text of this secret Yalta agreement is revealed in *Roosevelt and the Russians,* by Edward R. Stettinius, Jr., who attended the conference as Secretary of State. In the text (as given in this book) it was stated that:

1. the former rights of Russia violated by the treacherous attack in 1904 shall be restored;
2. the President will take measures in order to obtain [the concurrence of Chiang Kai-shek] on advice from Marshal Stalin;
3. the heads of the three Great Powers have agreed that these claims of the Soviet Union shall be unquestionably fulfilled after Japan has been defeated.

This representation of the Russo-Japanese War as having originated in a "treacherous attack" on Russia by Japan was strange in view of the fact that both President Theodore Roosevelt and the British had regarded Japan at the time as a young David challenging aggressive Russian imperialism. Nor does it seem to have entered the mind either of the President or his advisers that the "pre-eminent rights" in Manchuria promised to Russia were Chinese rights which were not ours to sign away.

To understand the import of the concessions made by Roosevelt to Russia at both China's and America's expense, one must appreciate the fact that history shows that whoever controls Manchuria controls North China, and that whoever dominates North China can conquer all of China. This was proved as early as the thirteenth century, when the Mongols conquered China, and again in 1644, when the Manchus became the emperors who ruled China from Peking. It was even more certain, in our industrial age, that the "pre-eminent rights" in Manchuria guaranteed by President Roosevelt to the Soviet dictator, would place Russia in a position to dominate China, since the only areas of China where iron and coal resources are to be found in proximity are Manchuria and North China.

It had been the refusal of the Chinese National Government to resign itself to Japanese control of Manchuria and North China that had caused the Sino-Japanese War, which began in 1937. Millions of Chinese had died in the struggle to deny Japan the "pre-eminent rights" on their soil awarded to Soviet Russia in 1945 at Yalta.

The argument has been put forward with general success that the Yalta concessions were necessary in order to secure Russia as our ally in the Pacific war. However, the fact is, America in February 1945 was at the height of her power, influence, and military strength, and it would have been to her advantage to *prevent* Russia's entering the war against Japan in order to reap a harvest she had not sown. Furthermore, there is now ample evidence available showing that Japan was ready to surrender before the Yalta Conference met.[1] By February 1945 nothing but the inane demand for Japan's "unconditional" surrender stood in the way of victory and a peace which would have ensured America's lasting security in the Pacific.

Yalta was, however, neither the beginning nor the end of the story. As early as 1943 the Far Eastern Division of the State Department was pressing for aid to be given to the Chinese Communists, then "sitting out" the war in the North, secure in the knowledge that Russia's treaties with Japan guaranteed them against attack.[2]

The recall of General Joseph Stilwell from China in 1944, and the appointment, in his place, of General Albert C. Wedemeyer as Commander-in-Chief of American forces in the China Theater, had resulted by 1945 in a temporary setback for the influences which regarded the Chinese Communists as potential friends of America. General Wedemeyer's successful co-operation with the National Government in stopping Japan's last offensive had created such confidence and uplift in morale in China that on V-J Day the Communists were in a less favorable position than they had expected.

Immediately following Japan's surrender, real assistance was given to the Chinese National Government forces, which were transported in American planes and ships to reoccupy the liberated territories ahead of the Communists. The Japanese were ordered to surrender themselves and their equipment only to the Nationalist forces.

For a brief time, therefore, American influence in China seemed secure. An effective pattern of Sino-American co-operation was established by General Wedemeyer, and we had the confidence not only of the government itself, but of all the real liberals [3] in China. If this situation had continued, it is entirely possible that the reformist elements would have gained the ascendancy in the government, and the Communists would have had no opportunity to force their way to power.

Soon, however, the policy of America toward China shifted. In the fall and winter of 1945 General Wedemeyer was restricted in the use of American sea and air transport by the officials in the Far Eastern Division of the State Department. This was the period when friendly relations with Russia took precedence over all other considerations. Thus, no effective protest was made when the Soviet Union broke the pledges it had given to China in the Sino-Soviet Treaty of August 14, 1945.

This treaty was signed by the Chinese Government, under compulsion from the United States, immediately following the defeat of Japan. According to its terms, China gave Soviet Russia vital strategic and economic rights in Manchuria in exchange for a pledge that Russia would "render to China moral support and aid in military supplies and other material resources, such support and aid to be given entirely to the National Government as the Central Government of China" (that is, the government headed by Chiang Kai-shek).

This pledge was promptly ignored. As Japan was surrendering, the Red Army poured into Manchuria ahead of Nationalist forces. As a condition of allowing the latter to reenter Manchuria, Moscow tried to get the Chinese Government to agree to joint ownership of *all* Manchuria resources and industries. Failing in this, Russia looted the area of eight hundred million dollars' worth of industrial equipment and handed over huge supplies of captured Japanese arms to the Chinese Communists, whom they had meanwhile allowed to enter Manchuria. By the time the Red Army withdrew, the Communists were in possession of Manchuria and the captured arms.

The United States accepted this violation by Russia of her treaty with China. On November 2, 1945, Vice Admiral Barbey, in command of the United States Navy ships transporting Nationalist troops to Manchuria, withdrew from the port of Yingkow after a conference with Soviet representatives ashore, and after viewing several thousand Chinese Communist troops digging trenches under Russian protection. Admiral Barbey was similarly forced to retreat from the Manchurian port of Hulutao, after Communist riflemen had fired at his launch. Manchuria's two main ports, Dairen and Port Arthur, were in Russian possession, thanks to the Yalta agreement. The Red Army's refusal to allow the Chinese Nationalists to use Dairen constituted another violation of the Sino-Soviet Treaty, according to which Dairen was supposed to be an international port. Thus Chinese Nationalist forces could not be transported by sea to Manchuria and were landed instead in North China. Thence they marched north, overland, being also denied the use of the railways by the Russians. And when they reached Manchuria, they were met by the Chinese Communist forces armed by Russia and in prepared positions.

The United States made no formal protest. Instead, in December 1945, our government sent a diplomatic mission to China, headed by General George C. Marshall, to mediate between the National Government and the Chinese Communists.

In both the personal letter and the public "Statement of United States Policy" which General Marshall carried with him from President Truman, he was specifically instructed to exert pressure on the National Government to come to terms with the Chinese Communists. In his letter, President Truman said:

In your conversations with Chiang Kai-shek and other Chinese leaders, you are authorized to speak with the utmost frankness. Particularly you may state in connection with the Chinese desire for credits, technical assistance in the economic field, and military assistance, that a China disunited and torn by civil strife could not be considered realistically as a proper place for American assistance along the lines enumerated.

In his statement of policy President Truman announced:

The United States . . . believes that peace, unity, and democratic reform in China will be furthered if the basis of this Government is broadened to include other political elements in the country.

(The "other political elements" in China meant the Communists.)

President Truman further stated his confident belief that "with the institution of a broadly representative government, autonomous armies should be eliminated as such and all armed forces in China integrated effectively into the Chinese National Army." He specified, however, that: "United States support will not extend to United States military intervention to influence the course of any Chinese internal strife."

Thus, in effect, President Truman barred China from American aid until the Chinese Communists should cease fighting the National Government. Since the Chinese Communist Party, like all other Communist parties, always and at all times, acted on Stalin's instructions, the United States Government was in reality endeavoring to force the Chinese Government to submit to Moscow.

Secretary Byrnes, in a December 9 memorandum to the War Department, which President Truman told General Marshall to consider as part of his instructions, wrote:

The problem [of 'broadening' the Chinese Government to include the Communists and other minority parties] is not an easy one.

It will not be solved by the Chinese leaders themselves. To the extent that our influence is a factor, success will depend upon our capacity to exercise that influence in the light of shifting conditions in such a way as to encourage concessions by the Central Government, by the so-called Communists, and by the other factions.

This reference to "so-called Communists" proves how completely Secretary of State Byrnes, together with President Truman, had been misled by their advisers in the State Department.

The most significant paragraph in Secretary Byrnes' memorandum concerns the instructions given to the War Department to cease transporting the Nationalist forces to take over North China in advance of the Communists. He wrote:

Pending the outcome of General Marshall's discussions with Chinese leaders in Chungking ... further transportation of Chinese troops to North China, except as North China ports may be necessary for the movement of troops and supplies into Manchuria, will be held in abeyance.

In his public statement of December 15, 1945, President Truman made his intentions equally clear. He insisted upon "fair and effective representation" for the Chinese Communists in a coalition government. He expressed his confident belief that "with the institutions of a broadly representative government," autonomous armies would be eliminated as such, and "all armed forces in China integrated effectively into the Chinese National Army."

The State Department's White Paper on China, published

in 1949, states that General Marshall was instructed to give "each side impartially and confidentially the benefit of his analysis of the situation." [4] The decisions General Marshall was to be called on to make in China were to affect vitally the future interests of the United States. But he was instructed to be "impartial."

United States policy in China, as enunciated by President Truman and implemented by General Marshall, was based on the assumption that the civil war in China was strictly an internal matter and had no connection with Soviet Russia's policy of expansion by revolution.

Thus, it was assumed that the promise of American economic aid to China as the reward for "unity," would act as a powerful inducement to *both sides* to come to an agreement. Actually, the United States had no means of exerting pressure on the Chinese Communists to come to an agreement with the National Government, or to honor their pledges if an agreement were worked out. Only Stalin was in a position to do this. *America's compulsions could be and were exerted only against the National Government.* By withholding both economic and military aid from the National Government until it came to terms with those who wrought havoc in China for their own ultimate gains, it was we who put the Communists in a position in which they could blackmail the National Government.

Following President Truman's statement of December 1945, the Chinese Communists welcomed General Marshall with open arms. They were particularly fortunate in that their leading representative in Chungking was the handsome, intelligent, and charming Chou En-lai, now Foreign Minister of the Peiping Government. Chou En-lai had for years shown a singular capacity for converting American journalists to the belief that the Chinese Communist Party was composed of liberal "agrarian reformers" who should be backed against the "despotic," "reactionary" government of Chiang Kai-shek.

Soon it became apparent to those of us who were in Chungking at the time and were frequently invited to General Marshall's residence, that Chou En-lai had succeeded in captivating him. Any doubts General Marshall may originally have had as to the truth of the State Department thesis about the "progressive" Communists and the "reactionary" Nationalist Government had obviously been dispelled. The fascinating Chou En-lai had evidently finally convinced General Marshall that the Chinese Communists were not "real" Communists, or that they could be "detached" from their Russian affiliation provided only they were helped by America to bring "democracy" to China. Marshall had long since come under the influence of his old friend, General Stilwell, who believed in the liberal professions of the Chinese Communist. Chou En-lai merely completed his conversion.

Shortly after his arrival in China General Marshall arranged a truce, effective January 13, 1946, whereby the existing positions of the Communist and Nationalist forces were "frozen." However, this truce included a proviso that the Nationalist forces were to be permitted to move into Manchuria to take it over from the Russians. On January 9 a dispute arose over Jehol, the province adjoining Manchuria which had been administered by Japan as part of "Manchukuo."

The Chinese Government insisted that since no Chinese, only Soviet, troops were in Chihfeng, a railway junction city in Jehol, it should be occupied by the Nationalist armies under the agreement covering Manchuria. The Communists insisted on a standstill agreement there as in North China, and claimed that their forces had already taken over Chihfeng from the Russians.

The Communist representative in Chungking, General Chou En-lai, was very depressed that evening, according to A. T. Steele of the *New York Herald Tribune*. He told the press that the government was insisting on its right to occupy both Chihfeng and Tolun—an important trading and communications center in Chahar, just outside Jehol's western boundary. Occupation of these two strategic points by the Nationalist forces would throw a barrier across the middle of Jehol and effectively block Communist connections with the Red Army in Manchuria, threaten the Communist stronghold at Kalgan, and sandwich Communist-held Chengteh (capital of Jehol) between government armies north and south of the Great Wall. The Communists declared they would never agree.

At ten-thirty that night General Marshall visited Chiang Kai-shek at his home and stayed there until midnight. At twelve-thirty Chou En-lai had a telephone call telling him to come to Marshall's house at eight o'clock the next morning. By ten o'clock that morning a truce draft had been worked out and given to the press. The Communists had won. Chihfeng, and with it control of Jehol, was theirs.

Soon afterward it was learned that the National Government's contention had been correct. The Red Army, not the Chinese Communists, had been in Chihfeng when the truce was signed. But the Chinese Communists kept the town until driven out in the new phase of the civil war, which began the following summer. As an official of the Chinese Foreign Office said to me in Chungking in February 1946, "General Marshall need not have forced us to give Jehol to the Communists. It was not necessary as part of the appeasement of Russia, since it was covered by the Sino-Soviet agreement."

The tentative political and military agreements sponsored by General Marshall in January and February were broken almost before the ink on the documents was dry. The civil war began again, primarily because of the refusal of the Chinese Communists to honor their promise not to oppose the Nationalists taking over Manchuria. But as Russia's armies retreated from the Chinese territory they had ravaged, they handed over towns and military supplies to the Chinese Communists.

A captured document obtained by George Weller, correspondent of the *Chicago Daily News*,[5] revealed a secret agreement between the Soviet High Command and the Chinese Communists pledging 5,000 Russian men and officers to help the Communists fight the Nationalists, and obligating the Chinese Communists to subordinate their army to the Russian command. The date on this document was January 19, 1946, just nine days after the Communists had signed the truce agreement in Chungking which persuaded General Marshall of their sincere desire to help establish a united "democratic" China.

Despite the help they received from Russia in arms and expert military advice and training, the Chinese Communists were soon in full retreat before the Nationalist forces. They appealed to General Marshall to persuade Chiang Kai-shek to another truce: "It is up to Chiang Kai-shek to yield to Marshall and negotiate." General Marshall, on his return in May from a visit to Washington, exerted the necessary pressure on Chiang to cease fire and let the Communists keep the parts of Manchuria they then occupied. The victorious offensive of the Nationalist forces was halted.

In the interval that followed General Marshall and President Truman took steps to prevent the Nationalist forces from obtaining arms and ammunition. At the end of July 1946 General Marshall clamped an embargo on the sale of arms and ammunition to China. For almost a year thereafter the Chinese Government was prevented from *buying,* and was definitely *not given,* a single round of ammunition. On August 18, 1946, President Truman issued an executive order saying that China was not to be allowed to acquire any "surplus" American weapons "which could be used in fighting a civil war," meaning a war with the Communists.

Thus when, in the summer of 1946, the Chinese Government endeavored to buy one-and-a-half billion rounds of small-arms ammunition in the United States, it was informed by the State Department that export licenses would be refused. England followed suit, and there was no other country available as a source of supply.

Thus the anti-Communist forces were thrown back on their reserves, and the limited supply of their own arsenals. These were soon to prove wholly inadequate to match the vast quantities of Japanese munitions handed over to the Chinese Communists by Russia, and later supplemented by the Mukden arsenals now working day and night to supply our Korean and Chinese enemies. For, once sure of control of Manchuria, Moscow restored some of the machinery she had removed as "war booty."

During World War II we had agreed with the Chinese Nationalist Government to train and equip a force of thirty-nine divisions. That promise was broken after General Marshall arrived in China. The few divisions that had already been trained and equipped were not permitted to acquire ammunition from the United States. In that same summer of 1946 General Marshall acceded to a Communist request to assign American officers to train the Chinese Communist armies. Sixty-nine United States officers were detailed for this task, and four hundred tons of American equipment were earmarked for the training program. It was to this Dean Acheson, then Under Secretary of State, referred when on June 19, 1946, he told the House Committee on Foreign Affairs:

The Communist leaders have asked, and General Marshall has agreed, that integration with the other forces be preceded by a brief period of United States training and by the supply of minimum quantities of equipment.

As it turned out, these officers were unable to proceed from Shanghai to their task of training the Communists on account of the civil war, which prevented their getting to their stations.

This projected aid to the Chinese Communists was the more difficult to explain at this date, since Chinese Communist hostility to America was by now being openly proclaimed. Once it became clear that the United States had been unable to exert sufficient pressure on Chiang Kai-shek to force him to become a President Beneš, the Communists had started large-scale anti-American demonstrations. They had also refused the National Government's proposal to let General Marshall have supreme arbitration powers to settle all issues in dispute. It being Moscow's policy to arouse hatred of America everywhere in the world, the Chinese Communists had started a violent anti-American campaign. They were proclaiming on the radio that "the only difference between American and Japanese imperialism is that American imperialism is stronger, and its aggressive methods appear civilized and legal on the surface."

This was also the period when there were a number of incidents in which United States Marines were shot at, killed, wounded, and imprisoned in North China.

Nevertheless, General Marshall continued to urge Chiang Kai-shek to come to some agreement with the Chinese Communists. Acheson stated the policy of the United States even more exactly when he said in a speech on June 28, 1946, in New York:

Too much stress cannot be laid on the hope that our economic assistance be carried out in China through the medium of a government fully and fairly representative of all important Chinese political elements, including the Chinese Communists.

In June 1946 General Marshall had arranged the second "truce" between Chiang Kai-shek and the Chinese Communists. At this time the Nationalist forces had succeeded in forcing the Chinese Communists to retreat as far as Harbin, which some Russian forces had not yet evacuated. The Communists having acquired the breathing space they required to rally their forces, fighting broke out again and continued through the summer and fall. The Nationalists still had some ammunition, and the Communists had not yet had time to train enough men in the use of arms supplied to them by Russia, or to benefit, as they did later, from Russian military instruction and advice. So the Nationalists continued to win battles and regain territory. They captured Kalgan and other strategic points in North China, and seemed well on their way to win the war. By November 1946, the White Paper on China states, "the Government's forces had occupied most of the areas covered by its demands to the Chinese Communists in June and during later negotiations and had reached what turned out to be the highest point of its military position after V-J Day."

Throughout this period General Marshall kept pressing for yet another truce. So in October 1946 Chiang Kai-shek welcomed the Communist representative, Chou En-lai, in Nanking for peace negotiations. On November 8, following two days in conference with General Marshall, Chiang ordered all his troops to cease fire. The Communists were invited to attend an All-China National Assembly and offered positions in a coalition government. They refused. Meanwhile, they continued to harass communications, wage guerrilla warfare, perpetuating ruin and chaos throughout the country. In this way they could gain time while preparing, with Russian aid, to mount a military offensive.

Chiang Kai-shek again offered peace, but now only on condition that the Communists evacuate the railway lines and strategic centers. He had not completely given way to those members of his government who had all along advocated solution of the Communist problem by force. But he was determined to clear the railways and make possible some economic rehabilitation. The economic situation had become so desperate that it was clear to him his government would lose all authority unless some order were restored. Moreover, he was no longer entirely without hope that America would again grant aid to China. For by now the conflict between

America and Russia was openly displayed before the eyes of the world at the Paris Conferences and in the United Nations meetings. Chiang Kai-shek was encouraged to believe, therefore, that the United States might in the near future give aid to resist Russian domination in Asia.

But on December 18, 1946, President Truman issued another statement on China almost identical with that of the previous year (December 1945). He still insisted on "peace" and "unity" as the condition of American financial aid. He declared that "China has a clear responsibility to the other United Nations to eliminate armed conflict within its territory." There was one substantial difference between the December 1945 and the December 1946 statements, however. In the latter the United States joined with Great Britain *and the Soviet Union* in insisting on a "coalition" government in China.

The President stated:

It was made clear at Moscow last year that these views are shared by our Allies, Great Britain and the Soviet Union. On December 27th, Mr. Byrnes, Mr. Molotov, and Mr. Bevin issued a statement which said, in part:

"The three Foreign Secretaries exchanged views with regard to the situation in China. They were in agreement as to the need for a unified and democratic China under the National Government for broad participation by democratic elements in all branches of the National Government, and for a cessation of civil strife. They affirmed their adherence to the policy of noninterference in the internal affairs of China."

It is somewhat difficult to imagine that as late as December 1946 the President of the United States was still sincerely convinced that Moscow's conception of what constituted "democratic elements" was the same as ours. It is also puzzling to understand why, though in Europe we had begun to say "thus far and no farther" to the further spread of Communist power, in the Far East, the old self-defeating policy was not only continued, but intensified.

In Europe we had learned that coalitions which include Communists can never establish democratic government. In China the Administration continued to look upon the Communists as "liberals" who owed no allegiance to Moscow, but were anxious only to reform China along democratic lines.

General Marshall seems to have seconded these views in every respect. In his 1946 statement the President reported:

I asked General Marshall to go to China as my representative. We had agreed upon my statement of the United States Government's views and policies regarding China as his directive. He knew full well in undertaking the mission that halting civil strife, broadening the base of the Chinese Government, and bringing about a united, democratic China were tasks for the Chinese themselves. He went as a great American to make his outstanding abilities available to the Chinese. . . .

It is a matter of deep regret that China has not yet been able to achieve unity by peaceful methods. Because he knows how serious the problem is, and how important it is to reach a solution, General Marshall has remained at his post even though active negotiations have been broken off by the Communist Party. We are ready to help China as she moves toward peace and genuine democratic government.

If one reads the White Paper on China, issued by the State Department in 1949, one is struck in particular with the fact that General Marshall apparently never conceived of the outcome of his thirteen-months' mission to China as momentous to the future of the United States. There is no indication that he realized that he was not an enlightened missionary endeavoring, out of sheer benevolence, to bring peace to a benighted country, but a representative of the United States whose security would largely depend upon the outcome of the "civil war" between a friendly government and Stalin's satellites.

Thus we read on pages 186–87 of the White Paper how, in September 1946,

General Marshall made it very clear to the Communist Party representative at Nanking at this time that in view of the vicious Communist propaganda attacks directed against his personal integrity and honesty of purpose, which were being paralleled by repeated private requests from the Communists that he continue his mediation efforts, he wished to emphasize that such a procedure would no longer be tolerated—*if the Communists doubted his impartiality as a mediator, they needed only to notify him accordingly and he would immediately withdraw from the negotiations* (italics mine).

Apparently he did not realize that these propaganda attacks of the Chinese Communists, as well as their entire course of action, were dictated from Moscow. Thus, the White Paper continues,

In discussions of the situation with high-ranking National Government representatives at this time, General Marshall impressed upon them the delicacy of the situation and the possibility that, if the situation continued to deteriorate, *the Communists would be driven to seek and be dependent upon outside support, such as Russian aid, which would make the task of peaceful settlement much more difficult* (italics added).

On numerous occasions, he threatened the National Government that he would go home if it didn't take his advice, and stop fighting the Communists. This threat of complete withdrawal of American interest in the outcome of the conflict usually forced the Generalissimo to give way and halt his victorious offensives to the benefit of the Communists.

The following passages from the White Paper illustrate General Marshall's failure to understand what was at stake for America, and his "plague on both your houses" attitude:

He felt that he could not put himself in the position of mediating during a continued series of military campaigns and that he must have positive assurances from the National Government that there was a reasonable basis for compromise which offered possibility of success.

On October 1, he wrote the Generalissimo:

> I wish merely to state that unless a basis for agreement is found to terminate the fighting without further delays of proposals and counter-proposals, I will recommend to the President that I be recalled and that the United States Government terminate its efforts of mediation.

Following such communiqués, the National Government made yet further concessions to the Communists, and as might naturally have been expected, they were of no avail.

The Communists merely became more intransigent. In order to understand clearly what follows it must be emphasized at this point that all the National Government's concessions and continued halts in its offensives at Marshall's requests were designed only to get the Communists to agree to participate in a coalition government. And this the Communists refused to do. On page 203 of the White Paper we read:

> The arguments of the Communist Party at this time were not consistent. They had insisted that the Government military leaders were determined to settle the issues by force, yet the Communists were apparently risking the continuation and expansion of the fighting in the hope that the Government would make concessions in order to obtain the list of Communist delegates to the National Assembly.

And on page 209, we read that the Communists had rejected "every overture General Marshall and Dr. Stuart had persuaded the Government to make." Yet on the same page the White Paper says:

> It seemed apparent to General Marshall that the Government military leaders were in the saddle and were thoroughly convinced that the Communists would not carry out any agreement reached. The strong political clique in the Kuomintang was firmly convinced that the Communists would merely disrupt any government in which they participated.

The National Government was arraigned for having discovered, like all European governments, that "the Communists would merely disrupt any government in which they participated." On page 210 of the White Paper it is stated:

At this time a high-ranking Government official was urging upon General Marshall the need for American financial assistance to meet the serious economic situation. General Marshall was very emphatic in stating to him that it was useless to expect the United States to pour money into the vacuum being created by the Government military leaders in their determination to settle matters by force and that it was also useless to expect the United States to pour money into a Government dominated by a completely reactionary clique bent on exclusive control of governmental power.

General Marshall's definition of a "reactionary" was similar to that used by the Communists and their "liberal" supporters, for in his farewell statement of January 7, 1947 (see Appendix A), he identified reaction with anti-Communism.

On the side of the National Government, which is in effect the Kuomintang, there is a dominant group of reactionaries who have been opposed, in my opinion, to almost every effort I have made to influence the formation of genuine coalition government. . . . They were quite frank in publicly stating that their belief that cooperation by the Chinese Communist Party in the government was inconceivable and that only a policy of force could settle the issue.

Although when he became Secretary of State, General Marshall learned in his negotiations with Molotov that it was impossible for even a democratic statesman like himself to collaborate with Communists, he has never repudiated or retracted his January 7, 1947, statement.

For on pages 211–12 of the White Paper we read that "it appeared that the Communist Party had, in effect, rejected American mediation," but are also told how General Marshall continued to insist on a "peaceful settlement." In December 1946 General Marshall had a long conference with Chiang Kai-shek in which he advocated appeasement at any price. The Communists, General Marshall insisted, were too strong a military and civil force to be eliminated by military campaigning, and "he believed, therefore, that it was imperative that efforts be made to bring them into the Government."

Chiang Kai-shek replied "that he was firmly convinced that the Communists never intended to cooperate with the National Government, and that, acting under Russian influence, their purpose was to disrupt the National Government."

The Generalissimo added that "it was necessary to destroy the Communist military forces and that he believed if this were done, there would be no difficulty in handling the Communist question."

General Marshall replied "briefly but firmly" that the National Government was not capable of destroying the Communist armed forces "before the country would be faced with a complete economic collapse."

In the State Department's account it is not mentioned here that General Marshall himself and the United States Administration could have prevented such an "economic collapse" had he not embargoed arms to China. To the end of his mission General Marshall continued to ignore Russia's backing of the Chinese Communists, and continued to believe, or spoke as if he believed, that he was mediating between two Chinese "factions." The crux of the whole conflict in his eyes was the question of "reform." The White Paper (p. 210) describes his views as follows:

The best defense against Communism in his opinion was for the existing Government in China to carry out reforms which would gain for it the support of the people. He was concerned over the destructive influence of the reactionaries in the Government and felt that the Generalissimo's own feelings were so deep and his associations of such long standing that it was most difficult to separate him from the reactionary group.

General MacArthur succinctly expressed the fallacy upon which such views are based when he said: "We confused the paramount strategic interests of the United States with an internal purification problem in China."

It seems clear that General Marshall never understood that neither agrarian reform, nor reconstruction and expansion of industries to alleviate Chinese poverty, were possible in conditions of civil war with the Communists doing their best to destroy the productive capacity within the domain of the National Government, thereby following the well-known Communist device of preventing any regime except their own from functioning. He also does not seem to have realized that a democratic government cannot be established overnight by drawing up a paper constitution.

In his January 7, 1947, statement when he left China to become Secretary of State, General Marshall admitted that "the National Assembly has adopted a democratic constitution," and he further stated that it was "unfortunate that the Communists did not see fit to participate in the Assembly, since the constitution that has been adopted seems to include every major point that they wanted." He declared:

The dyed-in-the-wool Communists do not hesitate at the most drastic measures to gain their end as, for instance, the destruction of communications in order to wreck the economy of China and produce a situation that would facilitate the overthrow or collapse of the Government, without any regard to the immediate suffering of the people involved.

But Marshall added that the Communists had "good excuse" for their distrust of the Kuomintang leaders. And in the following passage he showed that he still thought of the Chinese Communist Party as an ordinary political party, composed of men of varying views, with a goodly percentage of sincere "liberals" among them:

On the side of the Chinese Communist Party are, I believe, liberals as well as radicals, though this view is vigorously opposed by many who believe that the Chinese Communist Party discipline is too rigidly enforced to admit of such differences of viewpoint. Nevertheless, it has appeared to me that there is a definite liberal group among the Communists, especially of young men who have turned to the Communists in disgust at the corruption evident in the local governments—men who would put the interest of the Chinese people above ruthless measures to establish a Communist ideology in the immediate future.

Evidently General Marshall would not listen to those whose experiences and study had taught them that Communist parties allow no opposition, or liberal backsliding. He ended his statement with the suggestion that the "liberals" should be given the leadership in the Government and with the hope that "the door will remain open for Communists or other groups to participate."

General Marshall's refusal of aid to the National Government of China unless and until it came to terms with the Communists is inconsistent with the policy he maintained toward Greece when he became Secretary of State. Soon after taking office he recommended that $400,000,000 of aid should be given to Greece to keep the Communists out, while he continued to deny any help to the Chinese National Government unless it would take the Communists in!

Moreover, before going to the Moscow Conference in the spring of 1947, Marshall ordered the withdrawal of the United States Marines from North China, thus depriving the National Government of the limited backing which their presence had constituted. On April 2, he assured Molotov that American forces were being removed from China "as rapidly as shipping becomes available," without extracting any *quid pro quo* from Russia in Europe.

More than two years after he left China, on March 10, 1948, General Marshall, then still Secretary of State, "replied in the affirmative" to a question whether President Truman's December 15, 1945, statement, demanding inclusion of the Communists in the Chinese National Government, was "still our policy." This was naturally assumed by the press to mean that a coalition government including the Communists was still favored by the United States. Next day the State Department issued a statement which made confusion worse confounded:

In view of misunderstandings that have arisen concerning the Secretary's statements about China at his March 10 press conference, it is pointed out that the Secretary referred to President Truman's statement of December 15, 1945. That statement expressed the belief of the United States "that peace, unity and democratic reform in China will be furthered if the basis of this Government [China's] is broadened to include other political elements in the country." The Secretary said that this statement still stands. When asked specifically whether broadening the base of the Chinese Government meant we favored the inclusion of the Chinese Communist Party, he replied that the Communists were now in open rebellion against the Government and that this matter [the determination of whether the Communists should be included in the Chinese Government] was for the Chinese Government to decide, not for the United States Government to dictate.

On the same day (March 11, 1948) President Truman, at his press conference, in answer to questions "concerning the inclusion of Chinese Communists in the Chinese Government," said that his December 15, 1945, statement of policy "still stood." However, the President, like the State Department, wanted to have it both ways. So he finally contradicted himself by also stating that "we did not want any Communists in the Government of China or anywhere else if we could help it."

No American who knows the facts can read without embarrassment President Truman's ambiguous reply at this time to the appeal addressed to him by Chiang Kai-shek. Chiang had written:

The general deterioration of the military situation in China may be attributed to a number of factors. But the most fundamental is the non-observance by the Soviet Government of the Sino-Soviet Treaty of Friendship and Alliance, which, as Your Excellency will doubtless recall, the Chinese Government signed as a result of the well-intentioned advice from the United States Government. I need hardly point out that, but for persistent Soviet aid, the Chinese Communists would not have been able to occupy Manchuria and develop into such a menace.

As a co-defender of democracy against the onrush and infiltration of communism throughout the world, I appeal to you for speedy and increased military assistance and for a firm statement of American policy in support of the cause for which my Government is fighting. Such a statement would serve to bolster up the morale of the armed forces and the civilian population and would strengthen the Government's position in the momentous battle now unfolding in North and Central China.[6]

President Truman replied that he had stated at his March 11, 1948, press conference that he "did not desire Communists in the Chinese Government," that General Marshall had stated that the inclusion of the Communists in the Government was a matter for the Chinese Government to decide, not for the United States Government to dictate, and that he, Truman, believed that these statements and the China Aid Act "have made the position of the United States Government clear."

"Clarity" was about the last thing which could be claimed for these ambiguous and contradictory statements. From the Chinese point of view, they meant either that the United States Government did not know what its own policy was, or that it still favored China's submission to Soviet domination, but was endeavoring to hide this fact from the American voters. Certainly Chiang Kai-shek and his armies, now engaged in a final desperate battle against Soviet Russia's satellite forces, could derive little comfort from the clever double talk of President Truman and Secretary of State Marshall. Nor was the promised aid, voted by Congress in April 1948 and referred to in President Truman's letter forthcoming in time to save China. The State Department, as will be revealed subsequently, succeeded in thwarting the intent of the China Aid Act passed by the Republican 80th Congress in April 1948, by delaying the shipment of munitions to China until the end of that fateful year.

In September 1950, in his testimony before the Senate Armed Services Committee, which was to confirm his appointment as Secretary of Defense, General Marshall "disclaimed any personal responsibility for the policy he had sought to carry out in his 1946 mission to China." Specifically, he stated that "the policy of the United States was . . . issued while I was on the ocean, going over there."

There is considerable doubt placed on this disavowal, however, by both Admiral Leahy and former Secretary of State James F. Byrnes. According to the authorized biography of Harry Truman (*The Man of Independence,* Philadelphia, Lippincott, 1950), Admiral Leahy told the author, Jonathan Daniels:

I was present when Marshall was going to China. He said he was going to tell Chiang that he had to get on with the Communists, or without help from us. He said the same thing when he got back. I thought he was wrong then, both times.

Former Secretary of State Byrnes writes (in his memoirs, *Speaking Frankly,* New York, Harper's, 1947):

Before Ambassador Hurley's resignation, the State Department had prepared a statement of policy on China, the first draft of which I showed the Ambassador a few days before he resigned. As soon as President Truman appointed General Marshall his personal representative in China, I asked the General to study the draft so that he could help prepare the final statement for presentation to the President.

The Sunday before I left for Moscow, Under Secretary Acheson, General Marshall and members of his staff met in my office. By the end of the morning's discussion, we had agreed upon the statement of policy that subsequently was approved by the President and released to the public on December 15. Thereafter the President made no change in that policy except upon the recommendation of General Marshall or with his approval.

The *Washington Post,* a warm admirer of General Marshall and advocate of the State Department's China policy, supports Mr. Byrnes' testimony.

In an editorial headed, "Marshall on the Spot," published on September 1, 1950, the *Washington Post* said:

> General Marshall was less than candid in his testimony about China in the hearing before the Senate Armed Services Committee—so much so that in the early editions of the *New York Times* the report was captioned: Marshall Disavows China Policy. . . . He added that the policy had been proclaimed in Washington when he was en route to China. . . .
>
> General Marshall gave the Senators the impression that he simply carried out instructions without having discussed those instructions beforehand—let alone having agreed to them. Let us look at the record. General Marshall . . . carried with him not only the . . . personal letter from the President which epitomized the policy in these words:
>
>> "Specifically, I desire that you endeavor to persuade the Chinese Government to call a national conference of representatives of the major political elements to bring about the unification of China and, concurrently, to effect a cessation of hostilities, particularly in north China."
>
> Elsewhere in the letter the President said: "I understand that these documents have been shown to you and received your approval." The President restated this policy the following year, on December 18, 1946. In the course of it, he said, "I asked General Marshall to go to China as my representative. We had agreed upon my statement of the United States Government's views and policies regarding China as his directive."
>
> If all this does not mean what it says, then the President owes the public an explanation. He cannot but be embarrassed by General Marshall's incomplete statement—if not disavowal of the President's policy. What General Marshall said will be picked up, as it should be, by his Republican critics as proving

that General Marshall was merely a tool—or, as Representative Judd once put it, a "dupe." The facts are that the Marshall assignment was, in Mr. Byrnes' words when he was Secretary of State, to bring Chungking [the Nationalists] and Yenan [the Communists] together, and that, on the President's showing, General Marshall had his eyes open and his mind receptive when he accepted it.

It is hard to resist the conclusion that General Marshall must have been fully in agreement with the Administration's policy. And while in his eyes that policy envisaged the formation of a government for China after the model of a Western coalition cabinet, its outcome could only shove China straight into the lap of Moscow.

2. Too Little, Too Late—
The Facts About "Aid to China"

THE RECORD of America's China policy since 1945, as briefly outlined, shatters the myth that China was lost to the Communists simply because of the shortcomings of the National Government. Examination of the figures of "military aid" to China leads to the conclusion that it was lack of ammunition, as well as too much American interference to the benefit of the Communists, which gave the victory to Stalin.

The extent of American military aid to China is not an academic question of interest only to historians. The past determines the future. Without knowledge of the facts it is impossible for the American people to decide what should be their present policy.

If it were true that the National Government fell of its own weight, it could logically be argued that it is useless to supply its remaining forces on Formosa with arms and ammunition. If, on the other hand, the anti-Communist forces in China were defeated by superior military strength, we should not, today, refuse to accept them as allies in the struggle for the world.

No one who takes the trouble to study the records can accept Acheson's statement:[1]

The unfortunate but inescapable fact is that the ominous result of the civil war in China was beyond the control of the government of the United States. Nothing that this country did or could have done within the reasonable limits of its capabilities could have changed that result; nothing that was left undone by this country has contributed to it.

Perhaps Mr. Acheson did not study the White Paper all the way through its unindexed 1054 pages. For in the small-print annexes in the back, as will be shown, are a number of documents that glaringly contradict the words of the State Department in the main text.

In a letter to Senator Connally on March 15, 1949, Mr. Acheson stated more explicitly that United States aid to China since V-J Day totalled "over $2 billion." He wrote:

Despite the present aid program authorized by the last Congress, together with the very substantial other aid extended by the United States to China *since V-J Day, aggregating over $2 billion,* the economic and military position of the Chinese Government has deteriorated to the point where the Chinese Communists hold almost all important areas of China from Manchuria to the Yangtze River and have the military ability . . . of eventually dominating South China. . . . *The Chinese Government forces have lost no battles during the past year because of lack of ammunition and equipment,* while the Chinese Communists have captured the major portion of military supplies, *exclusive of ammunition,* furnished the Chinese Government by the United States since V-J Day. There is no evidence that the furnishing of *additional military matériel* would alter the pattern of current developments in China (italics added).

The clear implication of this statement is that America gave two billion dollars to China in *military* and economic aid to combat Communism.

Let us first break down that $2 billion total into its component parts, with a view to ascertaining the actual amounts of *military aid* given the National Government of China to resist Communist aggression.

According to the figures given on pages 1043–44 of the White Paper, Mr. Acheson's over-all figure of $2 billion of *postwar* aid to China includes a total of $799 million of "economic aid," and $797.7 million of "military aid," which together add up to something over $1.5 billion. The balance of the $2 billion is not itemized, but presumably includes the United States' share of UNRRA aid, which is calculated to have amounted to $474 million.

The largest single item in Mr. Acheson's total of $797.7 million of military aid is "services and expenses" amounting to $335.8 million, and listed under the heading "Postwar Lend-Lease." The "services" referred to consisted of the cost of repatriating the million or more Japanese soldiers in China, and of transporting the Chinese Nationalist forces to accept the surrender of the Japanese Army in the liberated territories. According to President Truman, these "services" cannot properly be regarded as "postwar" Lend-Lease, but must be included under the heading of World War II expenditures. For on December 18, 1946, he said:

While comprehensive large-scale aid has been delayed, this Government has completed its wartime lend-lease commitments to China. Lend-lease assistance was extended to China to assist her in fighting the Japanese, and later to fulfill our promise to assist in re-occupying the country from the Japanese. Assistance took the form of goods and equipment and of services. Almost half the total made available to China consisted of services, such as those involved in air and water transportation of troops. According to the latest figures reported, lend-lease assistance to China up to V-J Day totalled approximately $870,000,000. From V-J Day to the end of February, shortly after General Marshall's arrival, the total was approximately $600,000,000—mostly in transportation costs.

These transportation costs involved the repatriation of Japanese soldiers and the reoccupation of liberated territories carried out by Chinese Nationalist forces. The operation had been managed entirely by United States military authorities, and President Truman on December 15, 1945, said that these sums had been disbursed "to effect the disarmament and evacuation of Japanese troops in the liberated areas."

As Dr. Walter Judd said in Congress, "If we had not transferred the Chinese to take the surrender of the Japanese, we would have had to use Americans. We saved money in the transaction. It cost us less to transport them than it would have cost us to transport and support Americans there."

Thus, in our analysis of the actual military aid given to China after Japan's defeat, we must first deduct the $335.8 million represented by the cost of repatriating the Japanese and accepting their surrender. This leaves us with a total of $461.9 million of postwar military aid to China. This figure must be further reduced by eliminating the non-military "surplus war stocks" sold to China in 1946, which Mr. Acheson also includes in his total of "military aid." For as noted in the previous chapter reviewing General Marshall's mission to China, President Truman, in the summer of 1946, expressly prohibited any further acquisition by China of arms or ammunition which could be used to fight the Communists. So the "surplus" United States war stocks sold to China in 1946 included little of any military value to the National Government. Out of the total of $100 million worth of "surplus" United States stocks sold to China in 1946, 40 per cent consisted of quartermaster supplies, and only $3 million consisted of the small-arms and ammunition required in the war against the Communists.

It is true that some armaments, such as large-caliber artillery pieces, were included, but these were not of a kind, as I shall show later, which could be used in fighting the Communists. The same can be said of such items as the half-million gas masks, priced at $8 apiece—total $4,000,000—which the Chinese Government presumably bought for the value of the rubber to the civilian economy.

Elimination of both the "services" charges and of the $100 million or so of United States non-military "war surplus" stocks sold to China in 1946 reduces the total of postwar "military aid" to China to about $360 million. This total is disputed by the Chinese National Government. According to its calculations, China received $110 million worth of "effective military aid" prior to the 1948 China Aid Act, which, together with the $125 million allocated by that Act, brought the total to $225 million. Whichever figure is correct, the total sum is far less than the "billions" which are popularly assumed to have been squandered to no purpose.

The evidence shows also that the most of the military aid actually given to the Nationalist Chinese forces reached them too late. The $125 million of munitions allocated under the April 1948 China Aid Act was not delivered until nine months or a year later, and by that time the Communists had already conquered most of China.

Before proceeding to an account of the 1948 China Aid Act, it is necessary to examine the consequences of General Marshall's 1946–47 embargo on the shipment of arms or ammunition to China, and President Truman's insistence that no help should be given to the anti-Communist forces in the so-called "civil war."

Colonel L. B. Moody, a United States Army Ordnance Corps officer, now retired, who served with the Donald Nelson mission to China, has made an intensive and detailed study of aid to China. In a speech in Washington on April 11, 1950, he said that in China

the massive support of artillery, tanks, motor transport and aircraft to which western armies are accustomed is practically non-existent. The side which has the predominating infantry weapons, and especially the ammunition therefor, holds all the aces. You are asked to bear this in mind as this talk will endeavor to show that the foreseen and inevitable defeat of the Nationalist Armies was due to a Nationalist deficit in these items, and Communist superiority therein, resulting from persistent United States action.

He explained that a Chinese division consists of three regiments of infantry, totalling 5,000 rifles, 12 light howitzers carried on pack animals, and a complement of signal, medical, and transport troops; and that three such divisions constitute what the Chinese call an "army." United States types of weapons have all along constituted a minor fraction of Chinese armament.

Real military aid to China to combat Communism would have meant the delivery of small arms and ammunition to the Nationalists. But this was precisely what America denied to the anti-Communist forces. As Colonel Moody said:

It is obvious that "military aid" means to the Chinese infantry weapons and ammunition above all else, and it is precisely these items which the United States action has consistently denied, delayed or limited. Only passing reference will be made to the billions of moldy cigarettes, blown-up guns, junk bombs, and disabled vehicles from the Pacific Islands, which have been totalled up with other real or alleged "aid" in various State Department, Communist, and leftist statements to create the impression that we have furnished the Nationalist Government with hundreds of millions, or even billions, of dollars worth of useful fighting equipment. From the start of Japanese aggression to this evening the prime need of the Nationalist Armies has been, in the language of Joe Stilwell, "Bullets, damn it, just bullets."

Colonel Moody also drew attention to the fact that the Chinese Communist admissions concerning their own casualties disproved the popular assumption that the Nationalist forces lost because of poor morale. For the Chinese Communist command reported that in the three years of civil war from July 1946 to July 1949, the number of their killed and wounded was 1,233,600. This is greater than the total of American casualties in World War II.

General Marshall's embargo on the sale of American arms and ammunition to the Nationalist forces in China was not lifted until July 1947, when the State Department allowed the Chinese Government to purchase some three weeks' supply of 7.92 mm. ammunition—130 million rounds. Chiang Kai-shek had been endeavoring, for a year, to get permission from the State Department to be allowed to acquire this ammunition, which could not be sold to anyone else because it had been made during World War II according to Chinese specifications.

One other small boon was vouchsafed to the Nationalists in 1947. The Marines and the Navy, when ordered to leave China, gave them a six days' supply for their .30 caliber weapons.

Colonel Moody calculates that in December 1947, at the normal rate of use, the total of ammunition in possession of the Nationalists was sufficient for only twenty-two days in the case of the Chinese 7.92 mm. weapons; and for thirty-six days in the case of their .30 caliber—U.S.—guns.

General Marshall's and President Truman's arms embargo in 1946 was not the first denial of arms to the anti-Communist forces in China. Even before Japan's surrender, when abundant supplies of German arms and ammunition of the type used by the Chinese Nationalist forces became available, and could have been given them at no cost to the American taxpayer, this help was refused.

The standard Chinese Nationalist rifle ammunition was the same as the German 7.92 mm. Had the Administration desired to help create a "strong, independent and friendly China," ample ammunition could therefore have been supplied at no cost to the National Government after Germany's defeat. The supply of German light arms and ammunition to China was urgently recommended by General Wedemeyer following V-E Day, and shipment was approved by the Joint Chiefs of Staff. A first consignment of twenty thousand rifles had actually left a German port for China, but was stopped en route by an order signed by Lauchlin Currie on White House stationery, forbidding any such aid to China. Ultimately a part of what could so easily have been given to

China ended up in Russian hands in East Germany, and the rest was destroyed.

Nor is this the only evidence available of the Administration's failure from the very beginning to help China resist Russian aggression.

Following Japan's surrender, shipments of Lend-Lease supplies to China from India were stopped, and large quantities of munitions and equipment intended for China were destroyed, or thrown into the sea. Smaller caliber ammunition was blown up, and 120,000 tons of larger caliber dumped into the Indian Ocean.[2] This "Operation Destruction" cost the lives of twenty-five Americans and one hundred twenty-five Indians. Yet, these destroyed munitions are to be found included in the total of "pre-V-J Day Lend-Lease" charged to China's account.

The facts recorded above are only a small part of the record proving that neither Congress, nor the American people, have ever been permitted to know the truth about "aid to China."

The White Paper emphasizes the aid that was supplied to China early in 1948 by permitting the National Government to buy, at bargain prices, the stores which had been rotting on Pacific Islands. But it does not mention the fact that the "surplus" ammunition made available to China in January 1948 consisted mainly of types useless to the Chinese Nationalist forces. Colonel Moody's detailed analysis shows that of the total offered only 3 per cent was of the required ground-force types, and only 2 per cent of useful air-force types, and not all of this was serviceable.

Only 52,500 cartridges of the .30 caliber they required for their American rifles and machine guns were to be found, accounting for one-fortieth of one per cent of the total supplies made available to them. Certain other types of small-arms ammunition they could use brought the total tonnage to sixty-three tons, less than two-thirds of one per cent of the total shipped. This was at a time when the anti-Communist forces in China were going into battle with barely enough ammunition to fill their cartridge belts.

The Chinese contracted from their own funds for the 10,000 tons of ammunition that was made available to them at bargain prices early in 1948, because although little of it consisted of what they required, they hoped to make future use of it. For instance, they bought a stock of large-caliber shells in order to extract the explosive for mining and industrial operations, or to use in Chinese arsenals for loading the ammunition they made for themselves. But by making these purchases they enabled the State Department to claim that large supplies of munitions had been made available to fight the Communists, which was not so.

In the period December 1947 to November 1948 (when munitions voted in April 1948 in the China Aid Act began to arrive) the total of "surplus" United States ammunition sold to the Chinese provided only a month's supply for the weapons they had and could use. Chinese production could provide only 7 to 8 per cent of requirements. Colonel Moody therefore calculates that the total of Chinese-produced and American rifle and machine-gun ammunition produced or acquired in 1948 amounted to only some sixty-three days' supply in active operations.

Aside from these facts stated by an ordnance expert, dispatches to the State Department from its representatives in China in 1947 and 1948 conflict with Mr. Acheson's statement in his "Letter of Transmittal" to the White Paper that "the Nationalist armies did not lose a single battle during the crucial year 1948 through lack of arms and ammunition."

The United States Ambassador, Dr. Leighton Stuart, wrote frequently of the critical situation of the Nationalist forces and their desperate need of ammunition. Here are a few examples:

On July 1, 1947: "Persons in direct contact with the Nationalist troops in rural areas state there are insufficient small arms and ammunition to arm all combatant troops in the field."

On September 20, 1947: "Political, military and economic position of Central Government has continued to deteriorate within recent months in accordance with previous expectations. Currently, the cumulative effect of the absence of substantial financial and military assistance expected from the Wedemeyer Mission and renewed Communist military activity are intensifying the Chinese tendency to panic in times of crisis."

These dispatches in the Annexes of the White Paper do not bear out Mr. Acheson's statement on March 20, 1947, when he appeared before the House Foreign Affairs Committee to oppose military aid and advice to China, that "The Chinese Government is not in the position at the present time that the Greek Government is in. It is not approaching collapse. It is not threatened by defeat by the Communists. The war with the Communists is going on much as it has for the past twenty years."

On February 5, 1948: "The situation is very definitely one to cause pessimism. If American aid should materialize in adequate measure and palatable form, the tide may turn quickly in our favor . . . if our plans are deemed to be insufficient or unpalatable, or unlikely to be effective, it is more than likely that disaffection of some elements now in the government may ensue. Such disaffection may well result in the replacement of present dominant elements with the group desirous of effecting union with the Communists through the good offices of the Soviet Union."

On March 17, 1948: "In their despair all groups blame America for urging structural changes . . . or reforms which they feel they themselves would carry out if their immediate internal problems were not so acute, while America still delays the long promised aid upon which the survival of democratic institutions depends."

On March 31, 1948: "The Chinese people do not want to

become Communists, yet they see the tide of Communism running irresistibly onward. In the midst of this chaos and inaction the Generalissimo stands out as the only moral force capable of action."

And on August 10, 1948, panic-stricken by the imminent success of the Marshall-Acheson policy designed to establish a coalition government in China, Ambassador Stuart wrote: "Even though at present some form of coalition seems most likely, we believe that from the standpoint of the United States it would be most undesirable. We say this because the history of coalitions including Communists demonstrates all too clearly Communist ability by political means to take over complete control of the government and in the process to acquire some kind of international recognition. . . . We would recommend therefore that American efforts be designed to prevent the formation of a coalition government, and our best means to that end is continued and, if possible, increased support to the present government."

A couple of months later the Chinese delegate to the United Nations, Dr. T. F. Tsiang, appealed to Secretary of State Marshall in Paris. He asked if anything would induce the United States to help China. He offered to put United States officers in actual command of Chinese troops "under the pretense of acting as advisers." He begged for munitions. And, finally, he asked General Marshall "as to the advisability of Chinese appeal to the United Nations because of Soviet training and equipping of Japanese military and also the Koreans." [3]

General Marshall said he would refer Tsiang's requests and suggestions to Washington, but "did not offer encouragement." And he rejected the Chinese proposal to appeal to the United Nations, saying: "I thought it an inadvisable procedure and discussed possible Soviet moves to take advantage rather than to counter such a move."

Perhaps the Administration's refusal to give Chiang Kai-shek the military advice he begged for was even more helpful to the Communists than the embargo on arms and ammunition. The Chinese Nationalist armies were huge, but they had no generals capable of commanding large forces. Chiang knew this and had therefore begged America to appoint officers to China who would give the anti-Communist forces the same aid as the Russians were giving to the Communist armies. But his request—for the same kind of aid we were giving to Greece—was ignored.

As his authority for the statement that the Chinese Nationalist forces did not lose a battle in 1948 through lack of adequate arms, Mr. Acheson cited "our military observers on the spot." But our "military observers," meaning the United States Military Mission, were not in fact "on the spot"; they were sitting in Nanking, thanks to Mr. Acheson.

On August 24, 1949, in a statement to the press, he said that United States military advisers in China were not permitted to give advice in the field *because Congress refused to include* the "Greek-Turkey proviso" in the 1948 China Aid Act. In fact, however, *it was the State Department which caused this proviso to be removed from the Act.* The House had included it, but the Senate removed it at the State Department's request, and upon assurances given by the State Department that the Act would in fact be implemented as if the Greek-Turkey proviso were included.

Having induced the Senate to withdraw the House proviso for "diplomatic reasons," but with the promise that military advice would nevertheless be given to the Chinese Nationalist forces, the State Department proceeded to act within the limits set by the letter of the law, thus ignoring its promise to the Senate. In the fall of 1948, William C. Bullitt, on his return from a visit to China, reported that "the so-called mission sent to aid Chiang" had been instructed "not to advise him" with regard to the operation of his forces.

The former Ambassador and confidant of Franklin D. Roosevelt further stated that "nearly half of the 1500-man military 'mission' was composed of fellow travellers and Communist sympathizers."

Whatever the exact figures, it would seem that the Military Mission to China was never intended to be more than window dressing to satisfy the opposition in Congress. Since it was forbidden to give strategic or tactical advice to the Nationalist forces, it had no valid function.

The commander of the United States Advisory Group in Nanking was Major General David G. Barr. In April 1948 he recommended that 243 million rounds of small-arms ammunition be provided as an "immediate emergency requirement." And in his 1949 report, included in the White Paper, he refers to the "limited resources" of the Nationalists, and the difficulties thereby inherent in the defensive strategy they were compelled to adopt. Referring to the air force, he says: "There was an ever-present reluctance to take a chance on losing equipment or personnel."

General Barr, an "on the spot" military observer, was also apparently not of the opinion of the State Department and Mr. Acheson that the Nationalist Government was defeated by the Communists because of the poor morale of its troops brought about by its own corruption. . . . For in his report he speaks of the "inability" of the Nationalist forces "to realize that discretion is usually the better part of valor" as largely responsible for their huge losses. "They have been unable to be convinced," he states, "of the necessity of withdrawing from cities and prepared areas when faced with overpowering opposition and certain isolation and defeat, while the opportunity still existed to do so. In some cases their reasons for failure to withdraw were political, but in most cases they were convinced that by defensive action alone they could, through attrition if nothing else, defeat the enemy."

General Barr also emphasized the fact that the Nationalist armies were "burdened with an unsound strategy" and made the fundamental mistake of trying to get control of Manchuria, which was a task "beyond its logistic capacities." And he notes the fact that the necessity of attempting to protect railways from Communist destruction had led to many Nationalist troops degenerating "from field armies, capable of offensive conduct, to garrison troops" with an inevitable loss of offensive spirit.

In his report General Barr provides an answer to the charge so assiduously propagated that the Nationalist forces allowed their equipment to be captured by the Communists. In China, ages of lean living developed a capacity to make use in some way or another of what others would regard as refuse; thus the Chinese have acquired what General Barr calls an "inherent" inability to destroy anything of value. General Barr describes their failure to destroy equipment when forced to surrender or retreat as due to this characteristic. It should also be noted here that Mr. Acheson himself in his letter to Senator Connally quoted at the beginning of this chapter admits that ammunition was *not* captured by the Communists from the National forces. This evidence suggests that the latter surrendered because they ran out of ammunition.

Incidentally, General Barr makes a comment which disposes of the State Department's belief that the Chinese Communists are primarily Chinese and only secondarily Communists. Referring to the national characteristics which weaken the Nationalist armies, he says that the Communists have managed to "subordinate them" by making "their ideology of Communism almost a fetish."

Let us now resume our account of the record of "aid to China."

General Marshall's embargo on shipment of aid to the anti-Communist forces was, as we have already seen, lifted in the summer of 1947. The small quantity of munitions which China was then allowed to *buy* was considered by the Chinese Government as the only effective aid against the Communists which America had permitted them to obtain since General Marshall went to China.

Finally, in 1948, the Administration, as a result of the Republican control of the House of Representatives in the 80th Congress, was compelled to include a grant of $125 million of military aid to China in the China Aid Act, originally presented only as an economic aid program.

But the Chinese Government was nevertheless unable to procure the munitions it so desperately needed until nearly the end of the year.

On April 5, 1948, the Chinese Ambassador in Washington made his first request for implementation of the Act. Two months went by with the Chinese pleading in vain to be allowed to make their wants known and start procuring supplies with the funds appropriated by Congress for this purpose. At last, on June 2, President Truman (who had that same day received a strongly worded letter from Senator Bridges, the Chairman of the "Watch Dog" Committee) wrote to Secretary of State Marshall and to the Treasury advising them of the procedures to be followed in permitting China to make use of the sums appropriated. General Marshall waited over three weeks, until June 28, before so advising the Chinese Ambassador.

Even then the Chinese could not acquire arms and ammunition because the President had authorized only *commercial* transactions, and the munitions required could be obtained only from Government stocks. Another month passed before the President issued a directive authorizing United States Government departments and agencies to transfer military matériel from their own stocks, or procure it for the Chinese Government. (A year later the State Department was to point with pride to its "initiative" in having arranged the procedures for China to obtain supplies by July 28—nearly four months after the China Aid Act was passed!)

Had there been any reasonably normal expedition in handling the military aid funds made available under the Act, shipments from storage depots of at least the simpler, and most urgently required items (such as rifles, machine guns and ammunition), could have started by the end of

April. If the Administration had really wished to stem the Communist tide in China, quicker action still could have been taken. As Colonel L. B. Moody points out, a study of the American shipments to Britain made after Dunkirk shows that shipments were en route from United States ports within a week after Churchill informed Roosevelt of England's desperate need. Yet this rapid action required far more complicated procedures than was the case with the funds voted for China by Congress. For to make the shipments to England "legal," the munitions had first to be sold to a private American corporation, which in turn sold them to the British.

However small the quantities of arms and ammunitions obtainable, immediate shipments would have boosted Chinese morale tremendously. They would have provided concrete evidence of American support, and of our abandonment of the Marshall-Acheson "hands off" policy which had done so much to take the heart out of the anti-Communist forces.

As Vice Admiral Russell S. Berkey said on May 15, 1950:

The Chinese Reds would still be north of the Great Wall if specific items of arms authorized by Congress two years ago had reached the Nationalist forces in time. For some reason or other it took nine months to get specific items to China. Somewhere in the United States somebody slipped up, bogged down, or was interfered with. It has never been made plain why this material did not arrive in time.

Even at the end of July munitions did not start rolling to China. From the State Department the matter went to the Army Department, which said it could not act, or even specify the prices at which munitions would be sold, until after it had spent several weeks on "availability studies." It was not until late in September that these studies were completed. The Chinese then found that they were to be charged prices five to ten times higher than the thirty-odd other nations permitted to buy United States munitions. This drastic reduction of the total amounts they had expected to obtain under the China Aid Act necessitated the drawing up of new lists. This occasioned another, though only short, delay. The Army Department, however, now informed the Chinese that they could not expect shipment before early 1949.

In October, President Truman (influenced perhaps by the fact that the delay in getting arms to China had become an election campaign issue) issued expediting instructions, and the first substantial shipment of arms to China left Seattle on November 9, 1948. By this time the Communists had conquered the greater part of China.

The President's October directive was succeeded by more delays. "Availability studies," priorities, export licenses, and so forth, snarled deliveries once again, so that by April 30, 1949—thirteen months after Congress had voted arms aid for China—nearly a quarter of the supplies to be furnished had not yet been shipped.

In addition, the total amount of munitions China was permitted to buy with the $125 million turned out to be only about one-eighth of what had been expected. It had been assumed by Congress and the Chinese Government that the prices charged would be the same as to Greece and Turkey, not to mention the thirty-odd other nations to whom "surplus" munitions were sold at 10 per cent of list price cost. Instead, when at last on August 31, 1948, the Army had progressed far enough in its "availability studies" to give prices on some items of arms and ammunition, the Chinese discovered they would be required to pay more than double published prices, and an average of *50 per cent in excess of current commercial quotations for new manufactures.* There was no possibility of obtaining the arms or ammunition from any private sources. The Army was in fact charging the Chinese a monopoly price.

Some idea of the high prices charged to China can be obtained from the following figures:

	"Surplus" price charged to other nations	List Price	Price charged to China
Bazookas	$3.65	$36.25	$162.00
Rifles, .30 caliber	5.10	51.00	51.00
Rifle ammunition (per 1000 rounds)	4.55	45.55	85.00
Machine-gun ammunition (per 1000 rounds)	4.58	45.85	95.00

In January 1949 the Army at long last made available to China a few obsolete items at the same cheap "surplus" prices charged to other nations. For instance in 1949 armored cars, formerly priced to China at $32,154 (three times cost) were made available at the "European" price, $1,071, or 10 per cent of cost.

The fact that the delays and difficulties, and price hoists, which defeated the intent of the China Aid Act were deliberate is indicated by a letter written to Secretary of State Marshall by Ambassador Stuart from Nanking dated May 10, 1948.

"The Embassy agrees," he says, that "pressures" should now be intensified in spite of the fact that "any broad or powerful bargaining position *vis-à-vis* the Chinese Government disappeared on the date Congress passed the China Aid Act of 1948." Stuart's letter continues:

It is true, however, that we retain and should make full use of our bargaining position in the bilateral negotiations with respect to (1) methods of procurement for all commodities, (2) methods of distribution of aid commodities in China. . . . *The Embassy strongly recommends that we display no haste in the negotiation or conclusion of the bilateral agreements.* The exchange of interim letters provides an entirely satisfactory basis on which to operate in the coming weeks. . . . Delay will give time to learn at least what individuals will head the Ministries directly concerned. Finally, *it will extend the period in which our pressures can be applied.* . . . The Embassy accordingly recommends that the opening of negotiations be deferred until June 1. Meanwhile pressure for reform will be continued (italics added).

This is not the only evidence in the White Paper concerning Ambassador Stuart's discouragement of the hopes of the Chinese Government after the passage of the 1948 China Aid Act. On July 17, 1948, there is a report from Dr. Stuart recording how he had told Chiang Kai-shek not to believe that the American people favored helping the Chinese anti-Communist forces. "I told Chiang," he writes, "that Governor Dewey's announcement about increased aid to China had produced quite a bit of unfavorable editorial comment." "I had with me," continues the United States Ambassador, "the latest USIS bulletin on this subject, which I gave his secretary for reference."

Dr. Leighton Stuart, who loved the Chinese and wished them well, seems to have been unable, nevertheless, to make up his mind between the dictates of practical common sense and his "liberal" affiliations. His reports show his vacillation between his convinced belief that the National Government must reform in order to be saved, and his lively appreciation of the fact that there was little time or opportunity for it to institute a democratic form of government in view of the imminent danger of all China's being overwhelmed by the Communist totalitarian tyranny. He continued to fill his dispatches with long laments concerning the shortcomings of the National Government, while also issuing warnings of the disastrous effects to be expected from the Communist conquest of China.

Had the munitions which had been voted for China been permitted to reach the Nationalist forces at once, China might still have been saved, and Americans not have been called upon to fight Korea.

Only a brief account of the economic assistance given to China in this period is necessary, since no amount of American economic aid could have prevented a Communist victory so long as we denied arms and ammunition to the Nationalist forces.

Most of America's postwar economic aid to China consisted of immediate relief to the homeless and starving. Little was provided to remove the causes of starvation. UNRRA aid, the greater part of which was provided by the United States, consisted mainly of food and clothing. Some undertakings were financed which would have been constructive if the Communists had been prevented from destroying every dam, railway, mine, or industry reconstructed with UNRRA aid. For instance, Communist guerrillas quickly destroyed the Yellow River flood rehabilitation work of UNRRA engineers, constructed at a cost of millions of dollars. They similarly destroyed roads and railways repaired with UNRRA funds. While engaged in this deliberate destruction, they were receiving UNRRA relief supplies. For we insisted that a due proportion of UNRRA aid be furnished to Communist areas.

In Europe the Marshall Plan was quickly followed by the Truman Doctrine promising military aid to those attempting to resist the Communist aggressions which threatened to render ECA operations useless. But in China such economic aid as America furnished was futile, thanks to our refusal of arms aid to prevent Communist depredation and destruction.

In China General Marshall as Secretary of State gave evidence of being far more benevolently inclined toward the Communists than he was in Europe. It was hardly surprising, therefore, that in the spring and early summer of 1947 the Soviet Government was emboldened to give more open support to the Chinese Communists and that the latter launched a new and far more successful offensive in Manchuria.

Some details regarding the amount of Russian aid given to the Chinese Communists are specified in "China Presents Her Case to the United Nations" (see Appendix B). The evidence concerning the supply of Russian as well as Japanese arms was verified [4] by William H. Newton of the Scripps-Howard press (who was one of the ten newspapermen killed in 1949 in the crash in India of an airplane bringing them from the Dutch East Indies back to America).

The Chinese Communist forces in 1947 were reinforced by large numbers of battle-wise Japanese and Russian-trained Korean forces with a convenient base in Russia's Korean zone. The United States Government was being "neutral" now, as in the thirties, when Japan attacked China. So once again the National Government could not buy arms in America. The Nationalist forces were becoming weaker in fire power as the Communists, generously supplied by Russia, became stronger. The guns of the Nationalist First Army, originally trained and equipped in Burma by the United States and sent to Manchuria in 1946, were reported in June 1947 to be worn out, with the barrels of some machine guns so burned that "bullets fell through them to the ground." [5] But the Communist forces could count on continual replenishment of their equipment from Lend-Lease stores supplied to Russia for the war against Japan which she never fought.

The Communists by this time seemed to have been so well supplied with everything they required that they refused UNRRA relief and medical supplies, rather than allow American personnel to enter their territory. According to a *New York Times* dispatch from Peiping dated June 21, 1947, Cornelius Bodine, of Philadelphia, the UNRRA director for the Changchun area, was twice refused entry to Communist-controlled areas of Manchuria. The Communists evidently desired to prevent at all costs foreign observers from learning how much help Russia was giving them.

Had American or United Nations investigators been able to conduct the same type of investigation in Manchuria as in Greece, they might have become convinced of the truth of Chinese reports.

According to the Chinese Central News Agency, thirty thousand Japanese "prisoners" and ninety tanks were backing the Communist offensive in Manchuria. Its Mukden correspondent reported early in June that "a special bureau" of "a certain nation" had supplied the Communists with equipment for twenty divisions, and that citizens of that "certain nation"—the usual designation for Russia in the Chinese press—or Japanese were manning the tanks that were spearheading the Communist offensive. The eventuality feared all through the Sino-Japanese War had become a reality: the Communists were fighting together with the Japanese against China under Russia's orders.

In March 1947, Lieutenant General John R. Hodge, U.S. commander in Korea, stated that Chinese Communist troops were participating in the training of a Korean army of 500,000 in Russian-held North Korea. The Chinese Central News Agency stated in June that more than 100,000 Russian-trained Koreans plus a cavalry division from Outer Mongolia were in action against the Chinese Nationalist forces.

Thus early was it intimated that the fall of Nationalist China would release battle-hardened Korean veterans to fight against Americans.

The reinforcement of the Chinese Communists by Russian-trained Koreans further lengthened the odds against the Chinese Nationalists. A UP dispatch from Nanking on June 22, 1947, stated that neutral sources estimated that 200,000 Nationalist troops were up against 300,000 armed Communists, and that the latter already had control of more than three-quarters of Manchuria.

Chiang Kai-shek's persistent attempts to meet the wishes of the United States by attempting to "solve the Communist problem by political means," had thus not only failed completely, but had denied victory to the anti-Communist forces by halting their victorious offensives while the Communists were still weak. The Communists had been given the time and opportunity to rally their forces and grow strong enough, with Russian and Korean aid, to overwhelm the Nationalists.

As General Pai Chung-hsi, the Minister of Defense, stated

on May 1, 1947, the government's military progress had been blocked by the truces and peace talks of the preceding year. "Immediately after the recovery of Kalgan (October 1946)," said the Kwangsi general, who is regarded as China's foremost strategist, "we could have blasted open the whole Peiping-Hankow Railway, but our actions were deferred by intervals of negotiation. The government has suffered from an irresolute policy."

By June 1947, when prophecies were already being made in the American press that Manchuria would be lost to China, the National Government at last realized that its long silence concerning Russia's hostile acts had merely emboldened the Soviet Government to increase its aid to the Chinese Communists, and that United States help was unlikely to be forthcoming until the American people were informed of the true facts of the Far Eastern situation.

On June 25, the Chinese Ministry of Foreign Affairs issued a communiqué detailing for the first time the long record of Soviet obstruction to China's attainment of her rights under the Sino-Soviet Treaty.

"Sources close to the Generalissimo" were reported by American correspondents to be saying that Chiang Kai-shek and his advisers were framing a new policy calling for a stronger stand against Russian aggression. The policy of silence and appeasement was being abandoned, but the extent to which China would go toward a diplomatic showdown with Russia would depend upon United States support.

General Chen Cheng, the Chinese Chief of Staff, charged on June 24 that at least thirty-one Russian advisers were known to be with the Communist forces fighting at Szepingkai, the important railroad point seventy miles from Mukden.

The Chinese Nationalist commander in besieged Szepingkai said that the Communists had battered the city with 100,000 artillery shells and that Russian-trained Koreans manned the Communist guns.

Following the lifting of the siege by Nationalist forces at the end of June, the Chinese Central News Agency accused Russia of having shipped 56,635 tons of military supplies to the Chinese Communists in June, twelve Soviet ships having unloaded supplies for them at Dairen, while others ran a shuttle service between the Manchurian port and Chefoo, the Shantung port occupied by the Communists.

Even those who chose to disbelieve Chinese reports of Russian assistance to the Communists could not deny that the Soviet Government was giving aid to the Chinese Communists by its continued refusal, almost two years after V-J Day, to evacuate Dairen according to the terms of the Sino-Soviet Treaty. The denial to the Chinese Government of the use of Manchuria's principal port and the railway leading from it not only created a difficult supply problem for the Nationalist forces in Manchuria; it also put the Chinese Communists in an advantageous strategic position. As in 1937 when they had to fight the Japanese operating from an untouchable base in the International Settlement at Shanghai, so in 1946 and in 1947 the Chinese Nationalist commanders found themselves unable to crack the Communist line north of Dairen for fear of encroaching on Russia's newly established extraterritorial rights on Chinese soil. In the fall of 1946, according to Christopher Rand of the *New York Herald Tribune,* two Communist regiments had taken refuge at Port Arthur from Nationalist attack, and sheltered there until they emerged in the spring of 1947 to take part in the Communists' greatest offensive.

As Tillman Durdin of the *New York Times* reported in April 1947, the Communist forces were backed up against the Russian "defense zone" running from Port Arthur in back of Dairen, and the Chinese Government feared the "complications" which would arise if the Communists retreated into Russian-occupied territory.

On July 4, the National Government, after rallying its forces for a successful counter-offensive in Manchuria, announced its abandonment of all hope for a political solution of the Communist problem and denounced the Communists as "armed rebels" who could be dealt with only by force.

Vice President Sun Fo, so long an advocate of Sino-Soviet friendship and collaboration, was reported to be one of the leading advocates of this resolution, which marked the end of China's "Coué diplomacy" and placed her unequivocally in the world anti-Communist camp.

It was at this juncture that the United States Administration relented sufficiently to permit the Chinese Nationalists to buy 130 million rounds of ammunition in the United States. General Marshall, however, denied on July 2, 1947, that America was now supporting the National Government against the Communists. It was still the proclaimed policy of the United States to deny aid to China until the civil war ended, which meant in effect until Chiang Kai-shek came to terms with Stalin.

The Chinese were still hoping that the logic of facts would eventually convince America that there was no sense in stalling Soviet aggression in Europe while leaving our back door on the Pacific undefended. They had resisted Japan for years without our help, hoping that eventually we would become their allies. They hoped to be able to continue resisting Russia as long. But there is a limit to human endurance, and hope constantly deferred maketh the heart sick. By 1949 even inveterate enemies of the Communists saw no further possibility of resistance, in the face of United States' refusal either of aid or moral support. China went down before the overwhelming might of Soviet Russia's satellite forces, while the "Voice of America" broadcast praise of the Chinese Communists.

3. Four Hundred Million Lost Allies

TO ASCRIBE the defeat of the Chinese National Government to its "corrupt and reactionary" character is to beg the question. What is required is an examination of the causes which led to the frustration of the great national renaissance led by the Kuomintang in the 1920's and 1930's, and China's present submergence in the totalitarian sea. In General Wedemeyer's words: "The economic deterioration and the incompetence and corruption in the political and military organizations in China should be considered against an all-inclusive background."

The task which confronted the Chinese National Government when it came to power in 1927 would have been colossal in any case. It was rendered too great for China to cope with unaided, because of the interference of Japan and Russia, which both, by different means, intervened to prevent China's developing into a Western-style democracy.

The reform and reconstruction of a huge country of ancient traditions populated mainly by illiterate peasants required all the energies, talents, and patriotism of the few Chinese who had enjoyed a Western education. In the best of circumstances China would have required several generations to become prosperous and to establish the foundations of representative government in a strong middle class. By 1937 China had made some progress in this direction, but the war with Japan soon destroyed it.

The new China to which the Kuomintang had acted as midwife was stunted in childhood by too heavy burdens. While the West retreated and gave up its special privileges in China, Japan attacked, and at the same time the old Russian threat to Chinese independence was revived in a new form. The Communists, after the brief period of their collaboration with the Kuomintang from 1922–26, constituted an ever-present danger to the security of the Republic of China. Only the development of China's resources by the adoption of Western techniques could deprive the Communists of their support among the landless peasants and others whose fate was hopeless poverty. And each of the competing powers, Japan and Russia, was determined that China should not be permitted to set her house in order until it had taken possession.

Japan seized Manchuria in 1931, with the League of Nations even more powerless to stop her aggression than the United Nations is today in the case of Korea. Subsequent Japanese encroachments in North China led to the outbreak of the Sino-Japanese War in July 1937. Meanwhile the Chinese Communists, representing Russia, had been driven out of Central China, but had established themselves in the Northwest with their capital at Yenan.

In 1937 and 1938 the Chinese Communists ostensibly submitted to the National Government and fought against the Japanese with arms largely supplied by Chiang Kai-shek from those sold to China by Russia and Germany. However, even in the early stages of the Sino-Japanese War the Chinese Communists were careful to preserve their strength for future war against Chiang Kai-shek. In October 1937 Mao Tse-tung gave the following directions to the political workers of the Eighth Route Army:

The Sino-Japanese war affords our party an excellent opportunity for expansion. Our fixed policy should be seventy percent expansion, twenty percent dealing with the Kuomintang, and ten percent resisting Japan. There are three stages in carrying out this fixed policy: the first is a compromising stage, in which self-sacrifice should be made to show our outward obedience to the Central Government and adherence to the Three Principles of the People [nationality, democracy, and livelihood, as outlined by Dr. Sun Yat-sen], but in reality this will serve as camouflage for the existence and development of our party.

The second is a contending stage, in which two or three years should be spent in laying the foundation of our party's political and military powers, and developing these until we can match and break the Kuomintang, and eliminate the influence of the latter north of the Yellow River. While waiting for an unusual turn of events, we should give the Japanese invader certain concessions.

The third is an offensive stage, in which our forces should penetrate deeply into Central China, sever the communications of the Central Government troops in various sectors, isolate and disperse them until we are ready for the counteroffensive and wrest the leadership from the hands of the Kuomintang.[1]

After V-J Day the greatest problem faced by Chiang Kai-shek's government was how to restore law and order and stop the destruction of communications and disruption of economic life by the Communists and their bandit allies. Since destruction is easier than reconstruction, the Communists could be sure of ultimate victory, unless the National Government acquired the means and the authority to defeat them or contain them.

This was the situation in China at the time the United States stepped in as "mediator" and insisted that the National Government should, as the condition of American aid, both establish a thorough-going Western-style democracy and bring the Communists into the government.

This demand was, by its very nature, impossible of achievement. Communists do not, at least for long, "participate" in a government—they control it. And even if conceivably they could have been won for a time to "participate" (which they would have made the step to control), they represented concepts thoroughly antagonistic to Western-style democracy. Besides that, however, it was useless to expect that an economically backward country, exhausted from an eight-year war with Japan and currently involved in an undercover war with Russia, could, almost overnight, set up a "democratic" government. Add to these drawbacks the fact that China had no past experience of representative government.

Because of America's demands, the "Westernizers," or truly liberal reformers, in China were discredited and enjoyed less and less influence. Their social and economic basis had been all but destroyed during the Japanese occupation and the National Government's retreat to the West. During the war years the "intellectuals" had to serve the government, go over to the Communists, or starve, since there was no longer any employment for them in private industry or commerce. They might have regained influence after V-J Day, had American influence been exerted to support them instead of the Communists. The restoration of a free-enterprise economy enabling the middle class to grow and acquire influence was, in any case, practically prevented by the continuance of war. But the United States further debilitated the liberal influences in China by identifying progress with willingness to collaborate with the Communists.

There is no space in a book concerned with American policy to examine in detail the causes for the decline and fall of the National Government of China.[2] It is, however, important to realize that neither the State Department, nor most of the journalists, reporters, and radio commentators who influence public opinion, took account of the realities of China's situation. Too often it was assumed that Chiang Kai-shek, had he wished to do so, could have established a "democratic" government in China by a stroke of the pen. Little or no account was taken of the years of preparation required to establish a representative form of government, voted into office by a majority, in a country where it was first necessary to teach the people to read and write, and where the struggle for existence absorbed all the energies of the population. Another consideration generally overlooked is that no government can easily launch a program of social and economic reforms while fighting for its very existence, as the National Government was compelled to do against the Communists, who were intent on creating such disorder and misery that they would be able to seize power in a ruined land.

The most frequently heard condemnation of the National Government is its "corruption." It might be argued, of course, that corruption in China was not greater, only more conspicuous, than in some Western countries. However, the main point is that, since the Chinese Government was unable to balance its budget while endeavoring to keep huge armies in the field against the Communists, mounting inflation was inevitable, with the result that few, if any, officials could live on their salaries. Certain of our European allies tell us that they dare not lower the standard of living of their people by raising sufficient revenue to equip and maintain armies to defend Europe against Communist attack. The National Government of China, although denied American assistance for the struggle against the Communists, nevertheless continued to resist. The consequent lowering of the standard of living of the Chinese people below the subsistence level took a serious toll. For every Communist killed, more than one other Chinese was driven to become a Communist, or a bandit, by the exactions of the National Government in its endeavor to crush the Communists.

During the war with Japan the United States had assisted China in controlling inflation. But after 1945, as has been shown in the two previous chapters, this help was withdrawn. General Marshall, during his mission to China in 1946, advised Chiang Kai-shek repeatedly that since he could not afford to fight the Communists, he ought to appease them. He did not change this policy when he became Secretary of State. As late as November 28, 1947, Secretary of State Marshall wrote to our Ambassador in China, Leighton Stuart (as quoted in the White Paper):

You may rest assured premise is fully accepted here that military expenditures on present war scale are incompatible with balancing of Chinese Government budget which in turn is prerequisite to controlling of inflation. You may recall it was in anticipation of ultimate consequences for China of such a situation that as long as two years ago this Government attempted to prevent civil war in China.

As a result of Chiang Kai-shek's refusal to accept Marshall's advice—that is, to submit to Communist demands—inflation and corruption inevitably increased by leaps and bounds.

"Squeeze" was an old and accepted practice in China, as in most Eastern countries. The servant who did your marketing for you was considered to be more or less entitled to a 10 per cent cumshaw. Government officials, most of whom received very small salaries, likewise helped themselves along with a little graft upon occasion. But it was not until a runaway inflation had reduced the value of salaries almost to zero that these ancient practices became a menace.

In an effort to appear at least to be balancing its budget while military expenditures were consuming more than its total revenue, the National Government kept salaries low and printed paper money to finance the war. With prices soaring and salaries insufficient to buy food for their families, many officials and officers who had before been scrupulously honest became corrupted. Those who had private wealth, or property they could sell, could manage to get along on their salaries. But the majority faced destitution if they did not resort to graft.

When I was in China in 1946 I saw how very poorly many

a high official lived—without heat in winter, with his wife and children in patched old clothes, and with barely enough rice to eat. Certainly there were others living in comparative luxury. They were the ones who could entertain foreigners, and by doing so they gave the impression that government officials were all corrupt and lived well while the masses starved. Traditional Chinese ideas of hospitality strengthened this impression. Whereas the Communists in Yenan would serve a poor meal of rice and vegetables to American guests, even if they ate much better in private, the Kuomintang officials would serve a banquet, even if as a regular diet they had little but rice to eat.

I once heard General Wedemeyer tell a press conference in Shanghai that he very much doubted he would be incorruptible if he had to live on the salary of a Chinese general. And William Bullitt told me of how the wife of his friend, General Sun Li-jen, who now commands the Nationalist forces on Formosa, lived for months on the charity of Buddhist priests, sleeping on the floor of their temple, because her husband's salary amounted to only twenty-seven dollars a month, and he was determined they should live on it. The White Paper testifies [3] that "the men at the very top are of high integrity and continue to struggle bravely against terrific difficulties."

The situation was aggravated by the discontinuance of help from the United States, as contrasted with the generous, well-timed, and well-placed aid we gave the countries of Europe confronted with the menace of Communism. To Greece, for example, which also was involved in a "civil war" with Communist-dominated forces, the United States not only gave huge economic assistance, but the necessary American military aid and advice that saved it. China was equally threatened by Communist forces and equally unable to fight without help. Chiang Kai-shek knew he had no generals capable of commanding large armies, and he offered to place all his forces under American direction. He offered to give to an American general complete control of strategy, tactics, and supply. He urged the United States to send him that general, and a military mission to advise and help him.

All these Chinese requests were refused. China was told that the corruption in her government, and its inability to come to terms with the Communists, precluded American support. Yet as the Chinese were perfectly aware, we were also accusing the Greek government of "being corrupt and reactionary," though helping Greece just the same. We were pouring billions of dollars into France and Italy to keep the Communists from winning power without insisting on "reform."

The misapplication of American pressures on China was due not only to the State Department's evident belief that in China "progress" was synonymous with appeasement of Communists and adoption of their conception of what constitutes reform. It was evidently also due to the failure of Americans to realize the nature of the problems which confront Asiatic peoples required to jump from the Middle Ages into the twentieth century.

To the young men sent abroad to execute our policy, Europe was foreign, but not alien. Many of them were thoroughly familiar with and sympathetic to its problems. But the young Americans who went to China full of good will and good intentions had neither the experience nor the education to understand the problems they found there. The Orient was as unknown to most of them as the moon. Confronted suddenly with the primitive, semistarvation conditions of living prevalent throughout the East, they imagined that the age-old poverty of China must be due simply to bad government. They could not realize, because they did not know, that since there was little more than an acre of cultivated land per head of the population and nearly three quarters of the people lived off the land, no land reform could insure that everyone in China would have enough to eat.

The picture drawn by popular journalists and authors of a

reactionary Kuomintang preserving a "feudal" social organization for the benefit of greedy and self-seeking landowners and bureaucrats was in fact entirely misleading. The word "feudal" is today bandied about with little regard for its real meaning, thanks no doubt to Communist influences. For Stalin, by designating Chinese and other Asiatic societies as "feudal," has sought to obscure the resemblance between his own tyranny and the old Oriental despotisms in which, as in Soviet Russia today, a bureaucracy under an autocrat has absolute power. Marx carefully distinguished what he called "the Asiatic system," in which a bureaucracy was the ruling class, from the European feudal system, in which land-ownership was the basis of power. In the years I was in Russia, Stalin forbade Communist theorists to study Marx's writings on the "Asiatic system," since it was too obvious how closely the Soviet system of production resembled what Marx called the "Asiatic mode of production." Professor Karl Wittfogel of Columbia University has coined the word "hydraulic society" [4] as a better designation for the Oriental societies in which, as in ancient Egypt and Imperial China, agricultural production in huge areas depended upon public works—irrigation and flood control—and in which the state became all-powerful by "gaining control over the major portion of all land and in making possession of large estates depend upon full-time, lifelong, and unconditional government service." As Professor Wittfogel also points out, the Muscovite Tsars established the same type of Oriental despotism by creating a loyal ruling class of "serving men" whose power depended primarily not on land ownership, but government jobs. The Soviet Government, by taking over the ownership of all land and capital, has developed a modern form of the type of Oriental despotism based on control of all national resources.

Not only was the concept of a "feudal" Nationalist China completely false, since the Chinese peasant was not tied to the soil, and political power was not dependent on land ownership but rather on military force and bureaucratic privileges. An important fact, ignored by most of the critics of Chiang Kai-shek's government, is that there were few large landowners in China because primogeniture was abolished more than a thousand years ago, and estates were constantly split up among many sons.

Most landowners own only a few acres, and, as Dr. Lossing Buck has shown, more Chinese than American farmers own the land they cultivate. According to the calculations of this eminent authority, three-quarters of China's farm population own some land, be it only a fraction of an acre. The American-Chinese Agricultural Mission reported in November 1946 that overpopulation in relation to the available tillable land is China's fundamental problem. As Claude B. Hutchinson, Dean of the College of Agriculture of California University said, overpopulation is far more important in China than the ills emphasized by political writers—landlordism, high rents, usurious interest rates, and heavy taxes. The latter are the effects, not the basic cause, of Chinese agrarian conditions.

The Communist solution for rural overpopulation was simply expropriation and liquidation, terror and murder and expulsion of the landowners and richer peasants, and the redivision of the land among the survivors. No liberal government with any regard for justice or democratic practices could have emulated the Communists.

Sun Yat-sen from the beginning had recognized the necessity for land reform, but had envisioned an orderly process in which the landowners or peasants with large holdings would be compensated, and the desperate poverty of the peasants also alleviated, by industrial development. For obviously the pressure on the land could not be relieved simply by its redistribution. Industrial development, flood control, irrigation, reforestation and, in general, the application of modern scientific techniques to increase both the cultivated area and its yield, were a vital necessity. The Kuomintang had never abandoned the idea of Sun Yat-sen's project of land reform, and the National Government had some excellent laws on paper restricting rents and forbidding usurious interest rates. Unfortunately, it had never had sufficient power, or been sufficiently determined, to enforce its decrees. No doubt Chiang Kai-shek was too much under the influence of the rural gentry who clung to their local privileges as well as to their land, and whose sons constituted a large proportion of the officer corps. However, Chiang Kai-shek's failure to carry out a bold land reform in spite of the vested interests opposed to it does not constitute evidence of the autocratic nature of his government. A true autocratic government is perhaps even more capable of carrying through drastic reforms than a democratic government, which must support minority rights and interests. Actually, in this matter of land reform, it was the National Government's sins of omission rather than of commission which were the cause of its decline and fall.

Here it is relevant to recall that in 1908 Lenin was upset by Stolypin's land reform because he feared that the successful implementation of the Tsarist Minister's program might destroy peasant support for the revolution. And Stalin once said it was fortunate that Chiang Kai-shek had never thought to steal his fire by imitating Stolypin's reforms. In this connection it is interesting to note that in his testimony before the Tydings Committee Owen Lattimore said that he had never recommended anything but "mild and modest" reforms to Chiang Kai-shek.[5] Since he himself all along believed that drastic reforms were necessary, he evidently did not wish to give his best advice to the Chinese Nationalists.

Sometimes a great disaster is required to awaken men to their fundamental errors. In October 1950 Chiang Kai-shek, who cannot be cleared of the charge that he was formerly blind to the acute military, as well as political, importance of the agrarian problem, solemnly announced that he recognized the need for drastic land reform. Most important of all is the fact that he promised to recognize the bulk of the changes made by the Communists in the villages. This pronouncement is of vital importance. One need only recall how different the history of Russia might have been if the anti-Bolshevik forces in 1918–20 had promised to let the peasants keep the land they had won after the Bolshevik Revolution. The belief that the overthrow of the Bolshevik regime would have meant the return of the landlords enabled the Communists to consolidate their power.

Confronted with the complexity of China's agrarian and general economic problem Mr. Acheson in his Foreword to the White Paper makes the following superficial judgment: "In no small measure the predicament in which the National Government finds itself today is due to its failure to provide China with enough to eat."

Even if one thinks that the Chinese National Government, given the desire, could have introduced reforms in the midst of the civil war and could have eliminated corruption and graft, the United States failed to exert pressure on behalf of the liberal reformers, as distinct from the phony ones who were masquerading Communists. As I wrote in *Last Chance in China* (1947):

> The tragedy of the situation lay also in the fact that the United States could have used its influence and its pressures to aid the liberals in China instead of the Communists. Instead of insisting on a unity which could never be achieved without Stalin's permission, America could have urged and assisted Chiang Kai-shek to replace the corrupt and reactionary elements in his government by liberals and efficient administrators. Loans and technical assistance could have been given or withheld, not as a lever to hoist the Communists into a coalition government, but to bring about democratic administrative reforms and to cure abuses.

The "Westernizers" among the Chinese had been weakened by the war with Japan which had destroyed their bases in the port cities and ruined the middle class of industrialists, merchants, engineers, doctors, lawyers, and professors. American policy, by insisting that "Westernization" or "progress" meant acceptance of the materialist philosophy of the Communists, finally destroyed their influence. The reactionaries, or extreme conservatives, who still clung to old and outworn traditions, beliefs, and ways of life which had made China great and stable in ages past, but which prevented her survival in the Western world, won the ascendancy in the councils of the Kuomintang.

We made things more difficult by our "either or" attitude. No American of any authority, from the very beginning, seems ever to have conceived that we had any alternative between the National Government and the Communists. The State Department conceived of the Communists as more "progressive" than the Nationalists. Others looked upon the National Government as the only alternative to the Communists. It is conceivable that if, at the beginning, we had realized that most of the Chinese belonged to neither side, we might have helped Chiang Kai-shek emancipate himself from his wife's family—the Soongs—and to trust the more honest, courageous, and truly progressive forces that still existed in China. It is understandable that Chiang, who wanted more than anything to be friendly with the United States, relied on the advice of his American-educated wife and her brother, T. V. Soong. He might perhaps better have listened to the counsels of his old-fashioned brother-in-law, H. H. Kung, whose fortune was accumulated before he entered government service and who, in Chungking during the blockade, had performed miracles in preserving confidence in Chinese currency. But Dr. Kung was regarded as "reactionary" in America, though he was little more than a practical-minded business man with understanding of Chinese traditions who had made good. T. V. Soong, on the contrary, who had salted away a comfortable fortune by imitating American nineteenth-century tycoons, was regarded as a "liberal." Perhaps Chiang should have cut himself off from both Kung and

Soong, but as he was married to Kung's sister-in-law and Soong's sister, this was not easy.

Chiang Kai-shek's loyalty to the West [6] through the desperate years of China's single-handed struggle against Japan, and after Pearl Harbor, far from having won the friendship of America seemed only to have involved China in another war in which American aid was withheld. Many Chinese who, without being members of the Kuomintang, had supported the National Government out of patriotism and because it was an ally of the Western democracies, began to think that this alliance would result in the destruction of Chinese independence. Without believing in Communism they became convinced that China could save herself only by making her own bargain with Russia and her satellite forces. It seemed to them that "investment" in the Western democratic cause had produced few dividends and huge losses. Indeed, it seemed that the Western democracies were intent on building up the power of the rival firm: "Peoples Democracy" controlled by Moscow.

In the minds of the politically conscious Chinese, certain facts stood clear. It was the United States which had first put Soviet Russia in a position from which Stalin could expect to dominate China. At Yalta President Roosevelt broke the pledge he gave Chiang Kai-shek at Cairo to return Manchuria to China, and secretly agreed to let Russia have "special rights" in Manchuria. Shortly after V-J Day United States diplomacy and pressures were directed toward forcing China to become what John Carter Vincent of the State Department called "a buffer, or a bridge in America's relations with the Soviet Union in the Far East." The role of buffer between two irreconcilable antagonists is hardly an enviable one.

There were powerful elements in China that argued it would be better for China to make her own bargain with Russia than permit her interests to be used by America in bargaining with Stalin to America's supposed advantage. This group was headed by the "liberal" Sun Fo, son of Dr.

Sun Yat-sen. It would, if successful, have been joined by the former collaborators of Japan, and others whose guiding principle was to choose the stronger side, or the side expected to win. Since in Europe the Soviet Government accepted anyone who was anti-American, whether Nazi or fascist or collaborationist, Japan's former collaborators had little to fear from the Communists if they switched to support of Russia. Yet American "liberals" smiled benignly on Sun Fo and denounced Chiang Kai-shek, who refused to "save" China by making a bargain with Stalin.

The story of Stalin's efforts to win Chiang Kai-shek over to his side has never been made public. For reasons it regarded as diplomatic the Chinese Foreign Office was silent at a time when by shouting aloud it might have saved China.

In January 1946, just as General Marshall was launching his mission to compel the National Government to accept the Communists into its ranks on the latter's terms, Chiang Kai-shek's son, Chiang Ching-kuo, was in Moscow conferring with Marshal Stalin. At this time the Chinese National Government was facing the refusal of the Red Army in Manchuria to observe the terms of the 1945 Sino-Soviet Treaty. In this treaty the Soviet Government had not only pledged itself to non-interference in China's internal affairs, but also "to render to China moral support and aid in military supplies and other material resources, such support and aid to be given entirely to the National Government as the Central Government of China."

China had paid a high price for this Soviet promise. She had to give up Port Arthur as a naval, army, and air base; she agreed to make Dairen a free port to and from which Russia could move goods without inspection or payment of customs duties, and in which Russia would own half the harbor installations and equipment; she had also been obliged to give Russia "joint ownership" of the railways in

Manchuria. In addition, China had agreed to recognize Outer Mongolia as an "independent state."

The Soviet Government never even pretended to honor its agreement. The Soviet representatives in Manchuria declared they would transfer responsibility "to whatever existing military authorities" they found on the spot. The only "existing military authorities" were, of course, the Chinese Communist forces, which the Red Army had installed.

It was in this situation that Chiang Kai-shek sent his son to talk with Stalin. Chiang Ching-kuo had spent many years in Moscow, was married to a Russian wife, and was friendly to the Soviet Union. Stalin was not at all unfriendly to the young Chiang. He proposed that if the Nationalist Government of China would collaborate with Soviet Russia against America, he would instruct the Chinese Communists to submit to Chiang Kai-shek and enter a coalition government in which the Kuomintang would maintain its ascendance. Provided American influences and business interests were excluded from Manchuria, he would return the billion dollars of machinery removed by the Red Army from Manchuria and thus restore Manchuria as the workshop of the Far East. Specifically he proposed that all Manchurian industries be monopolized by a joint Sino-Soviet authority.

Two months before Stalin made this offer to Chiang's son, Slatekovsky, the economic adviser of the Russian Commander-in-chief in Manchuria, Marshal Malinovsky, had formally proposed such a deal. On November 24, 1945, Slatekovsky had handed to Dr. Chang Chia-ngau, the chairman of the Economic Commission of Chiang Kai-shek's headquarters in Manchuria, a list of 154 plants, comprising 80 per cent of Manchuria's heavy industry, which Stalin "suggested" should be jointly operated by Russia and China. The list also included all the airfields. The gigantic Sino-Soviet corporations to be set up, according to Stalin's proposal, were to monopolize mining, power plants, and the iron, steel, chemical, and cement industries. They were to operate for thirty years with a 50–50 share for Russia and China.

In order to force the National Government of China to agree to this Soviet proposal, Marshal Malinovsky warned China, on January 16, 1946, that if this proposal were rejected the Red Army would remain in Manchuria. His actual words were: "I would not be able to predict the date of Soviet Army withdrawal from Manchuria."

On January 21, 1946, the Soviet Ambassador to Chungking handed a statement to Chiang Kai-shek which read:

The Soviet Government, mindful of the existing friendly relations between China and the Soviet Union, proposes to the Chinese Government the formation of a Chinese-Soviet joint corporation to operate those economic enterprises in Manchuria which had served the Japanese Kwantung Army. At the same time the Soviet Government agrees to accord to the Chinese Government half of the value of the enterprises.

In the negotiations in Chungking Marshal Malinovsky said in so many words his government's proposals were put forward with the aim of eliminating American power in Western Asia entrenched in Japan. The benefit to China of accepting Russia's proposals would be an order from Moscow to the Chinese Communists to submit to Chiang Kai-shek.

If the American people had known what was going on, there might have been public pressure for support of Chiang's government. But Soviet Russia's blackmailing of China was kept secret. Chiang Kai-shek's advisers on foreign relations were too timid, or too ignorant of the democratic process, to tell the truth to the world. Instead of publishing the facts, they seem to have imagined that if they kept silent they would win favor in the eyes of the State Department, and might hope eventually to obtain American aid against Soviet aggression.

When I was in Chungking and Shanghai in this critical period, I tried to persuade the Chinese Foreign Minister,

Wang Shih-chieh, and Generalissimo Chiang Kai-shek himself, that China's one hope lay in revealing the truth to the American public. I got nowhere. Wang Shih-chieh said to me: "The Polish Government protested, and look what happened to Poland. It is better to be patient and make sacrifices than to risk extinction by protesting. Since we ourselves cannot fight Russia, we must do what America wants, hoping that the United States will restrain Russia if we do everything which America wants us to do."

China may be condemned for basing her foreign policy on faith rather than fact. But what excuse can the United States offer for failure to recognize both the faith and the fact? General Marshall could not have been unaware of the Russian pressures being exerted on Chiang Kai-shek to join with Stalin against America. Few secrets were kept in Chungking. Certainly the State Department knew, for on February 9, 1946, Secretary of State Byrnes addressed notes to Chungking and Moscow that read as follows:

Current reports of discussions between officials of the Chinese Government and the Russian Government with regard to the disposition and control of industrial enterprises in Manchuria give concern to this Government.

The Sino-Soviet Treaty and agreements signed August 14, 1945, provide for joint Sino-Soviet control over certain trunk railways in Manchuria, but these agreements exclude reference to any similar control over industrial enterprise in Manchuria. ... It is felt that negotiation of agreements between the Chinese and Russian governments with regard to industries in Manchuria would be contrary to the principle of the Open Door, would constitute clear discrimination against Americans who might wish an opportunity to participate in the development of Manchurian industry and might place American commercial interests at a distinct disadvantage in establishing future trade relations with Manchuria.

This note apparently gave Chiang Kai-shek confidence that America would support China if Moscow continued to violate the terms of the treaty. So on March 5, 1946, he rejected Stalin's offer, saying:

... the Chinese Government on its part has found it impossible to agree to this Soviet proposal because it goes far beyond the provisions of the Sino-Soviet agreement of August 14, 1945, and is contrary to the aforesaid stand of the Chinese Government regarding Japanese properties and enterprises in China.

But after General Marshall's embargo on arms aid to the Nationalist forces in August, and his repeated insistence on concessions to the Chinese Communists as the condition of any future support, Chiang Kai-shek, late in September 1946, expressed his willingness to accept Stalin's invitation to visit him. Even at this date the Generalissimo was not prepared to turn against the United States. When General Nikolai V. Roschin, the Soviet military attaché, made it clear that there could be no compromise with Russia short of agreement to exclude America from Manchuria, Chiang Kai-shek canceled his visit to Moscow. The White Paper merely records that:

The failure of the expected assistance from the Wedemeyer mission to materialize ... was intensifying a tendency to panic. ... Thinly veiled suggestions were emanating from high officials of the Chinese Government to the effect that China might have to seek assistance from the Soviet Union, and that the Soviet Ambassador to China might be asked to mediate in the civil war. Such talk was regarded as primarily for effect on the United States, and secondarily as a reflection of a feeling of desperation among Chinese leaders.[7]

Over two years later General Roschin, who had meantime been named Soviet Ambassador to China, declared that Chiang Kai-shek's failure to visit Moscow in 1946 was due to "the return of General Marshall to China with his pockets stuffed with American checks."

Because Chiang refused to agree to the exclusion of American interests from Manchuria, this territory was converted into the base for Communist operations first against China, then against America in the Korean war. Throughout this period of warfare against Nationalist China, the Communists received powerful assistance from some 65,000 Korean troops, under Li Hung-kwang, trained by Russian officers and in part veterans of Stalingrad. (The fighting abilities of the North Koreans, who killed or wounded 40,000 Americans in 1950, was due in large part to their experience in fighting our Chinese allies.)

In presenting this evidence of Chiang Kai-shek's loyalty to America, I am not endeavoring to excuse his faults and shortcomings. It would, however, appear that his refusal to compromise with the forces he knew would bring about his nation's total and lasting destruction has true greatness in it. Perhaps Chiang should have braved the consequences of carrying through a land reform to give the Chinese peasant a stake in the future of China, even if this might have entailed expropriating the officers of his army at a time when he most needed them to carry on the war. Undoubtedly he erred in clinging to old associates who had neither the vision nor the self-sacrificing character to put nation above personal advantage. He also undoubtedly too often appointed generals for their political loyalty rather than their military skill. In a word, Chiang Kai-shek is human and fallible. Yet he certainly stands out in our generation as a moral leader and a great man because of his refusal to compromise with the overwhelming force represented first by Japan then by Russian totalitarian tyranny. However far short he may have come of implementing broadly democratic principles in China, he proved himself a valiant enemy of totalitarianism on two fronts.

In his testimony before the Senate Appropriations Committee on December 17, 1947, General Wedemeyer said that Chiang Kai-shek "has endeavored to meet our every requirement" and that "if I were he, I would be quite impatient with America." As General Wedemeyer pointed out, Chiang was determined to combat Communism and try to create a democracy in China whether or not he received American aid in the task.

General Wedemeyer's recommendations when he returned from China were kept secret by General Marshall and not revealed until their publication in the annexes to the White Paper in the summer of 1949.

General Wedemeyer, who not only had a rare understanding of Communist aims and methods, but was also a student of history, had recognized in his 1947 report to the President that the only working basis on which it was possible to revitalize Chinese resistance to Soviet aggression, was "through the presently corrupt, reactionary, and inefficient Chinese National Government."

Whatever its sins of omission and commission, and however far it fell short of coming up to our conceptions of good government, the National Government had proved a most loyal ally. Moreover, it had given abundant proof of its desire to "Westernize" China. The Communists, on the other hand, were our declared enemies and, in Ambassador Stuart's words, there was no doubt "that their control will follow the invariable Communist pattern of a police state, with no freedom of thought or action and with brutal slaughter or expropriation of all who seem to be in their way."

On October 29, 1947, Ambassador Stuart had written:

The corruption and the reactionary forces pervading the Kuomintang are too familiar to call for further emphasis. It should be kept in mind, however, that single-party control always tends to be corrupt, that the period during which this party has been in power has been one of incessant conflict, that the mounting costs of living have greatly aggravated an age-long tradition in China, and that the mood of defeatism in an increasingly hopeless outlook has caused a creeping paralysis upon all creative effort. Even so the men at the very top are of high integrity and continue to struggle bravely against terrific difficulties. There are many more like them within and outside of the government.

In spite of these reports, the policy of the State Department remained unchanged. The text of the White Paper gives no weight to the arguments in the memorandum presented by the National Government of China to General Wedemeyer on his departure from China in 1947. It dismisses it as merely setting forth "an account of Kuomintang accomplishments in the thirties and a justification of the Government's position." Yet this memorandum presented a factual, and by no means exaggerated, picture of the difficulties Chiang's government had faced since V-J Day, as a result of the Moscow-directed rebellion of the Communists which had destroyed all possibility of reform and rehabilitation. The full text can be found in the annexes to the White Paper,[8] but I want to quote here a few sentences that present clearly and forcefully the exact dilemma of the Chinese National Government.

It is clear that there is no weakening of determination on the part of the present Government and the Kuomintang to face the new challenge. As to the lines of policy with which the Government will meet the challenge, several things are uppermost in the minds of its leaders. First, the Communists as an armed political party must be suppressed. No half measures should be considered. The Government fully realizes that the success or failure of this fight against the Communist peril will not only decide its own fate but also the life or death of China as a sovereign power. In fact, the outcome of the struggle is bound up with the peace and security of the whole of the Far East. . . . No real form of democracy is built in a day, and it is the consensus of opinion of the Government that the best way to achieve it is to start it as soon as you can.

There is another document included in the annexes to the White Paper of which I shall quote a paragraph.[9] In November 1948 Chiang Kai-shek gave an interview to A. T. Steele, the *New York Herald Tribune* correspondent, trusted as the most objective and best informed newspaperman in China. In the course of that interview Chiang said:

Seventeen years ago with the outbreak of the September 18 incident,[10] I signalled to Democratic nations and the League of Nations a warning confirming that the disaster of a world war had since then begun. Although this warning was not considered important by the various countries, history eventually evidenced the truth that the Northeast question was the prelude to World War II.

History is now repeating itself. If international right cannot prevail and extend its influence and if democracies maintain the same stand by watching the fire ablaze across the river, the world is bound to tread the former path of disaster. Should, unfortunately, Communist bandits control China, another world war would surely descend upon this globe. And should the Communists rule over the nine Northeastern provinces, it would mean the virtual beginning of another world catastrophe. What is more obvious is that without an integral Northeast, there will be no independent Korea, nor will there be a peaceful East Asia. This much I can firmly say, the ominous and treacherous clouds will gather with the trouble in the Northeast as their starting point.

If the White Paper had, as it claims, omitted "no available item because it contains statements critical of our policy, or which might be the basis of future criticism," it would have included some of the evidence presented to Congressional investigating committees by eminent Americans who were intelligent and well informed, but whose views clashed with those of General Marshall and the State Department.

There is, however, nowhere to be found in the White Paper such important evidence and testimony as the following:

(1) The personal plea carried by Lieutenant General A. C. Gillem to General Marshall in April 1947 from General Yu Ta-wei, the Vice Minister of Defense in charge of the Chinese arsenals, who had served as liaison officer with Marshall while he was in China, and who is one of the Chinese officials who enjoys an unchallenged reputation for honesty and capabil-

ity. This plea, which was ignored, fully explained the desperate nature of the situation with respect to ammunition.

(2) Former Ambassador Bullitt's October 13, 1947, report in *Life*, following a visit to the Manchurian front, concerning the parlous situation of the Nationalist forces there. These divisions were those which had been equipped with United States weapons during the war, and now could not obtain ammunition for them.

(3) The report made by Senator D. Worth Clark, who as consultant to the Appropriations Committee of the Senate, visited China and stated in October 1948:

Chinese Nationalist Army supplies were rapidly approaching exhaustion and Chinese officials were consequently frantic to speed up deliveries of arms and ammunition under the $125 million American Defense Grant [the April China Aid Act].

A graver omission of the facts pertinent to its subject is the White Paper's failure to include the testimony given by General Wedemeyer before the Senate Appropriations Committee on December 17, 1947.

General Wedemeyer was in a very difficult position when asked by Chairman Senator Bridges, if he would make available to the Committee his report on China which General Marshall and President Truman had suppressed. He had to obey the orders of the President, who after sending him to China in the summer of 1947 to appraise the situation and make a report, had kept Wedemeyer's recommendations secret. Yet the General also felt under an obligation to tell the truth to the elected representatives of the American people. He said:

If Chiang Kai-shek is a benevolent despot . . . or whether he is a Democrat or Republican, that is unimportant. The relevant and important facts are that the man has opposed Communism throughout his history, and he also stayed on with us as an ally in the war, containing in China one million and a half Japanese soldiers who might have been employed against our men in the

Pacific. It would have made our task more costly in lives and time in the Pacific. But, no, the Generalissimo chose to remain faithful to his allies. I personally think he is a fine character.

Senator Reed next asked if there were "anybody else in China with whom we can do business." Wedemeyer in his reply disassociated himself from the State Department's support of an imaginary "Third Force." He said:

No, sir: I think he is the logical leader of China today. I should like to state, when I speak with so much conviction about him, that I was prepared not to like him when I went over there. I had heard so many conflicting stories about him. I owe him nothing; I conducted myself over there as a theater commander, as you would have me conduct myself. I did not ingratiate myself nor placate the Chinese. I think the Generalissimo is sincere in his desire to help his people, but he needs our help, and he should get our help. He is entitled to it.

In his replies to further questioning General Wedemeyer emphatically disassociated himself from the Administration's policy of refusing arms and ammunition to the anti-Communist forces in China, and also stated that America had failed to fulfill its commitments to the Chinese National Government. The verbatim report of the proceedings of the Appropriations Committee is reproduced below:

Chairman Bridges. Would you consider, in your judgment, that it was urgent that we give military supplies and economic assistance to China at this time?
General Wedemeyer. Yes, sir; I do.
Chairman Bridges. Do you think that, in your judgment, we have kept our promises to China over the years?
General Wedemeyer. No, sir, I do not. I do not say that in a malicious way. There were conditions, Mr. Chairman, that may have precluded the fulfillment of many of our commitments. I could enumerate some of those difficulties, but I do know of a few instances wherein we have not fulfilled our commitments to China.

Finally, after Senator Bridges had asked him whether Chiang Kai-shek and the National Government had kept their promises to us, General Wedemeyer replied:

I think the Generalissimo has endeavored to meet our every requirement, sir. If I were he, I would be quite impatient with America, but he never appeared so. His parting statement when I left him last August is indicative of his character. He said: "Whether or not your country gives aid or assistance to China, I will continue to use every force at my disposal to combat Communism; and I will continue to strive to create a democracy in China but changes in government are going to take a long number of years. I may not be able to accomplish that in my lifetime. It will be contingent upon outside influences, the influence of your country and of Russia, whether or not I am able to create political and economic stability at home."

He made that statement voluntarily, just before I said goodbye to him.

For two years Republican Senators and Congressmen, and many newspapers, endeavored to force, or persuade, the Administration to let the American public know the contents of General Wedemeyer's 1947 report on China. It was generally known that Wedemeyer, the former commander of the United States forces in the China Theater, who had been sent on an exploratory mission to China in 1947, did not agree with General Marshall's policy. But Wedemeyer, as shown above, would not break the bonds of secrecy imposed upon him by the Administration. Finally, his long-suppressed report was given to the public, in August 1949, in the State Department's White Paper on China. The excuse made for having kept General Wedemeyer's report a secret for so long was that he had recommended placing Manchuria under a five-power guardianship, or United Nations trusteeship; and that this suggestion would have been "highly offensive" to Chinese susceptibilities. This is a transparent alibi. General Wedemeyer, realizing that the Chinese National Government could not hope at that date (summer of 1947) to reassert its authority over Manchuria while also fighting the Communists in North China, had proposed a solution which would have saved most of China.

Perhaps the real reason for the treatment which General Wedemeyer's proposals received is given on page 260 of the White Paper. Here it is said that the President and General Marshall "believed that to place upon the United Nations responsibility for action to implement such a recommendation [concerning Manchuria] might well seriously endanger the future of that organization."

The text of the White Paper reports his criticisms of the National Government, but not his intelligent appraisal of the basic causes for its shortcomings, nor his repudiation of the State Department thesis that the Chinese Communists were not "real" Communists, nor his dire warnings of the consequence to the United States of the Soviet domination of China which a Communist victory would entail, nor his insistence that the United States had failed to fulfill its commitments to the National Government.

Instead, the White Paper in its summary of General Wedemeyer's analysis of the situation excelled itself in misrepresentation, saying that it "was in general similar to that submitted to the Department of State in numerous reports by the American Embassy and consular offices in China and by General Marshall himself."

Since few of my readers can have had the opportunity or time to read the Wedemeyer report, given in full in small print in Annex 135 of the White Paper, I quote some of the passages from it which are ignored by Philip Jessup, or whoever else may have edited the text of the White Paper. Far from agreeing with General Marshall, or with "American Embassy and consular officials in China" as the White Paper asserts, General Wedemeyer wrote:

Indirectly, the United States facilitated the Soviet program in the Far East by agreeing at the Yalta Conference to Russian re-entry into Manchuria, and later by withholding aid from the National Government. . . .

The economic deterioration and the incompetence and corruption in the political and military organizations in China should be considered against an all-inclusive background lest there be disproportionate emphasis upon defects. Comity requires that cognizance be taken of the following:

Unlike other Powers since V-J Day, China has never been free to devote full attention to internal problems that were greatly confounded by eight years of war. The current civil war has imposed an overwhelming financial and economic burden at a time when resources and energies have been dissipated and when, in any event, they would have been strained to the utmost to meet the problems of recovery.

The National Government has consistently, since 1927, opposed Communism.

Today the same political leader and same civil and military officials are determined to prevent their country from becoming a Communist-dominated State or Soviet Satellite.

Although the Japanese offered increasingly favorable surrender terms during the course of the war, China elected to remain steadfast with her Allies. If China had accepted surrender terms, approximately a million Japanese would have been released for employment against American forces in the Pacific. (See Appendix C)

The fact that the State Department had little interest in any "liberal" Chinese except those friendly to the Communists was displayed by its attitude toward General Li Tsung-jen both before and after he assumed the Presidency of the Republic of China in 1949. No civilian could possibly have held the country together in resisting the Communists. Only another military leader could have had any hope of success. Li Tsung-jen might have been that leader if the State Department had looked around for another general more to its liking than Chiang instead of imagining that liberal professors constituted a viable "Third Force."

Prior to the Sino-Japanese War, General Li Tsung-jen

and his colleague, General Pai Chung-si, had transformed Kwangsi, in the Southwest, into a model province. Without bloodshed or terror they had carried out a program of land reform which had converted their territory into one in which the tillers of the soil enjoyed the fruits of their labors, and the whole people stood behind their government.

Although they had opposed Chiang Kai-shek until Japan attacked in 1937, the Kwangsi generals left their own territory undefended to fight side by side with Chiang's armies against Japan in Central China. Their troops were the best that fought to defend Hankow in 1938.

I knew Li Tsung-jen well in Hankow in 1938. I talked with him again in Peiping in 1946. He may not be a liberal according to General Marshall's definition. But he had a great sense of justice and an appreciation of the vital need for reform—and no illusions about the Communists. As director of Chiang Kai-shek's headquarters in Peking before and after the retreat of the Nationalist forces to Central China, Li Tsung-jen had fostered local resistance to the Communists, while also protecting academic freedom in the universities in his territory from ignorant interference by the Kuomintang's police. His colleague, Pai Chung-si, reputed the best military strategist of National China, is a Mohammedan. He enjoyed the support of his coreligionists in the Northwest who have been feared by the Communists more than any other forces opposed to them.

Li Tsung-jen had the backing of the democratic-minded liberals, or reformers, in the National Government when he was elected Vice President and when he later (January 21, 1949) became President after Chiang Kai-shek had retired to Formosa. The situation was by then so desperate that Li Tsung-jen took the lead in trying to come to such terms with the Chinese Communists as might save at least part of China from Soviet domination by establishing a *modus vivendi* with Soviet Russia. He invited the Soviet Ambassador, Roschin, to a conference. The Communists were at the gates of Nanking, and America seemed determined to do nothing to hinder their advance. It must have seemed that China's last hope lay in abandoning the American connection for the sake of an understanding with Russia. At this conference the Chinese proposed a Sino-Soviet agreement guaranteeing Chinese neutrality in the event of war between Russia and America. The Chinese pointed out that such an agreement would prevent China from becoming "an American colony" exploited by the United States and used as a base for American designs against Russia. All that China asked in return was an order from Moscow stopping the Chinese Communist advance.

Roschin was receptive to these proposals, but he doubted whether China could remain "neutral" unless under a Communist government. He said that the Chinese National Government, even without Chiang Kai-shek, had become too dependent upon America to remain aloof from a Russian-American war. Nothing came of the conference, presumably because the Chinese liberals were no longer worth any consideration in the Kremlin's councils. They had played their part and could now be discarded.

In spite of Soviet Russia's rebuffs, there was one important Chinese figure who persisted in the effort to come to an agreement with Moscow. General Chang Chih-chung, who was China's High Commissioner in the Northwest, had long been subject to Russian pressure because his "authority" extended over Sinkiang (Chinese Turkestan). This was the central Asian territory where Stalin had for years been endeavoring to secure complete control by playing against each other the many races which compose its population. The Soviet Government's aim in this territory was to secure complete dominance by forcing China to agree to a fifty-year Sino-Soviet government monopoly of all mineral and oil resources.

General Chang Chih-chung endeavored unsuccessfully to trade concessions in Sinkiang for Soviet co-operation with regard to China proper. By October 1949 he had nothing left to trade with, since the Soviet Government had formally recognized the Chinese Communist Government in Peiping.

Late in 1949 Li Tsung-jen came to America and made a last desperate appeal for American support. But by that time he was only an isolated individual, since he represented neither the Kuomintang nor the Communists upon whom the State Department had staked its hopes. Ground between the upper and nether millstones, the Chinese liberals he represented have been reduced to dust.

There are those who maintain that it was inevitable that China should succumb to the Communists because they pretended at least to represent the aspirations of the voiceless millions of Chinese peasants whose only desire was to acquire sufficient land to feed their families. Since so many Western officials and journalists, who had access to all the information available about Soviet Russia and its internal regime, did not realize that the liquidation of the landowners and prosperous peasants would be followed by agrarian slavery, how then could the illiterate millions of China be expected to know that support of the Communists would lead to their future enslavement to a totalitarian state?

We do know now—we have certainly had ample evidence—that Communist China is an extension of the Russian totalitarian empire. But the State Department seems unable to learn from experience. It is still continuing on its futile course of staking American security on the emergence of a Chinese Tito. Since Dean Acheson apparently feels he cannot admit his past mistakes without ruining his reputation, he clings to the outworn belief that the Chinese Communists can be expected eventually to turn into anti-Russian Communists. Hence his willingness to follow the British line of appeasing Peiping.

As Senator William F. Knowland (Calif.) so aptly stated at a news conference (as reported in the *New York Times*, November 24, 1950): "If Formosa were in unfriendly hands —and Communist hands are unfriendly—our defense line would be driven back to the Pacific Coast." Appeasement, he said, is surrender on the installment plan.

Talk of seating the Reds in the United Nations is appeasement. Talk of establishing a neutral zone in Korea is appeasement. Waiting around for Mao Tse-tung to become a Tito is appeasement. The same people who told the United States Mao was only an agrarian reformer are now telling us Mao is a Tito. They are either badly misinformed or deliberately misinforming the American people. They are as wrong now as they were before.

4. How and Why War Came to Korea

FROM THE FOREGOING it must be clear that far from having tried to help the Chinese National Government keep China on our side of the Iron Curtain, we have positively hindered it in its attempts to cope with Communist aggression. The same self-defeating course was pursued with regard to Korea.

Effective military aid was denied to the South Korean Republic after the withdrawal of American forces, although such aid had been voted by Congress. Syngman Rhee's government, like Chiang Kai-shek's, was called reactionary, tyrannical, corrupt, and undemocratic. In the case of Korea, as in the case of China, the deficiencies of our friends were given as a reason for leaving them defenseless before our enemies.

Thus, Mr. Acheson, on April 3, 1950, warned the South Korean Government that "United States aid . . . has been predicated upon the existence and growth of democratic institutions within the Republic."

What exactly was meant by "democratic" was never made clear. It must have been extremely difficult for the Koreans to know whether the United States Secretary of State was referring to Communist "democracy" or American democracy. For had they not seen the Chinese National Government abandoned by the United States Administration on account of its failure to conciliate the Communists? Moreover, to judge from the criticisms of the South Korean Republic voiced in the American press, the land reform carried out in South Korea compared unfavorably with Communist measures and more license should have been given the Communists than was permitted by the Rhee government "police state." In short, in Korea, as in China, willingness to collaborate with Communists was regarded as the hallmark of a "democrat," and repression of subversive forces as a sign of "reaction."

Owen Lattimore epitomized in his writings the views which inspired the Administration's Far Eastern policy. He endeavored to smear the South Korean Republic with the same brush with which he had so successfully tarred the Kuomintang. In 1949[1] he wrote:

America, which has in China complained of the bad luck of having inherited the Kuomintang through no fault of its own, has in Korea manufactured its own Kuomintang. To support our proclaimed policy of world-wide opposition to police states, we have in South Korea created a weak and unreliable police state of our own.

The little South Korean Republic, like the huge Republic of China, was urged to show evidence of its "democratic" aims by coming to terms with the Communists. The lead here was taken by the United Nations, rather than directly by the State Department. The 1949 United Nations commission on Korea regretfully reported that the South Korean Government had been "unco-operative." The evidence of its "unco-operative" attitude was its refusal to "participate in official discussions with the North looking to unification." In language which inevitably recalls the Truman-Marshall-Acheson attempt to foist a coalition government upon China, the United Nations committee report says: "The Commission believes that a broadening of the government's political base would . . . enable it to play a more effective part in achieving unification."

This broadening, of course, meant including Communists, or their sympathizers, in the South Korean Government.

It was, no doubt, on account of the State Department's misguided liberal sentiments and consequent distrust of the anti-Communist South Korean Government, that the Truman Administration left the South Korean Republic, like a shorn lamb, defenseless before the blast from the North.

The Administration prior to June 25, 1950, was evidently heeding the advice of Owen Lattimore who, on July 17, 1949, wrote in the *Compass:* "The thing to do is to let South Korea fall, but not to let it look as though we pushed it. Hence the recommendation of a parting gift of 150 million dollars."

In the memorandum which Lattimore wrote a month later at the request of the State Department he was more cautious, but gave substantially the same advice: "South Korea is more of a liability than an asset. [The United States should therefore] disembarrass itself as quickly as possible from its entanglements in South Korea."

Having abandoned China to the Communists, it seemed only logical that we should let South Korea fall. The tiny republic, constituting part of a small peninsula attached to a huge Communist land area, could not be expected to survive long, with or without American arms. However, to make doubly sure that "our Koreans" should meet the same fate as "our Chinese," the Administration refused to let them acquire arms for defense, on the ground that if given them they might attack the Communist colossus.

Our postwar aid program in Korea was founded on the same principle which had misguided us in China: economic assistance unsecured by substantial military assistance or an American guarantee against Communist aggression. Not only was the American Army withdrawn from Korea in the summer of 1949, the military aid voted for Korea by Congress in 1949 was not delivered.

In the Congressional investigations following our involvement in what the President was pleased to term a "police action" in Korea, it was established that, of the ten million dollars specifically earmarked for Korea in the Military Assistance Act of October 1949, only two hundred dollars, consisting of signal wire, had been delivered by June 1950! And the reason? The reason, as given by Administration spokesmen, was that we feared that if the South Korean Republic were permitted to obtain tanks and any other supplies for a modern army, they would be tempted to attack the North Korean Communist régime in an attempt to unify the country. Brigadier General William L. Roberts, who had supervised the training of the South Korean Army for two years, told a news conference on July 14, 1950, that heavy equipment had been denied to the South Korean Government because "The South Koreans believed the best defense was to attack. This placed us in a skittish position. To prevent them from attacking, we gave them no combat air force, nor tanks, and no heavy artillery."

An official report of the House Committee on Foreign Affairs shows United States assistance to Korea totaled $523 million, of which only $57 million consisted of military aid.

The total estimated aid to Korea consists of the following items:

GARIOA (Government and Relief in Occupied Areas) funds, fiscal 1946 through 1949	$356,000,000
ECA funds, fiscal 1950	110,000,000
Military assistance: Turned over to Korea under Surplus Property Act by the Office of the Foreign Liquidation Commissioner	56,000,000

Equipment turned over to Korea subsequent to withdrawal of United States forces	1,000,000
TOTAL	$523,000,000

According to this committee, the military equipment given the Koreans included 40,000 Japanese rifles and ammunition for the security forces; 100,000 small arms (rifles, pistols, and machine guns); 50,000,000 rounds of ammunition; 2,000 bazookas and more than 40,000 rounds of bazooka ammunition; more than 4,900 vehicles of all types; a large number of 57 mm. and 37 mm. antitank guns, 105 mm. howitzers, 60 mm. and 81 mm. mortars and more than 700,000 rounds of ammunition for these weapons.

This type of equipment would arm a police or constabulary force, but was far from what was needed for defense against armed attack. After the withdrawal of United States troops from Korea, the United States sent from its supplies in Japan, organizational equipment for 115,000 troops, costing a million dollars. In addition to this ground force equipment, 79 Navy-type vessels were provided—mainly yard mine sweepers, landing craft medium, landing craft infantry, and picket boats, along with $150,000 worth of spare parts.

Seeking to abjure responsibility for its mistakes, the Administration sought to blame the Republican Party for the failure to supply the South Korean Republic with the arms aid voted by Congress. Its spokesmen cited the fact that the Republicans in Congress opposed the final grant of economic aid to Korea, and omitted to say that the Republican Party's opposition was based on the argument that it was useless to supply economic assistance without the military aid required to defend South Korea from Communist aggression.[2]

On July 26, 1949, five Republican members of the House Foreign Affairs Committee had issued a minority report opposing Lattimore's "parting gift" of $150 million to Korea on the following grounds:

Every authority who has testified before the Committee on Foreign Affairs with respect to the Korean situation has acknowledged the fact that there could be no effective defense against an armed aggression originating in the northern half of the country.... Our forces, with the exception of an advisory mission, have been withdrawn from South Korea at the very instant when logic and common sense both demanded no retreat from the realities of the situation. With our forces on the scene of action, there might have been advanced substantial arguments in favor of economic assistance, but without the pressure of an adequate force to protect delivery of, and guarantee practical utilization of, the great volume of materials and supplies, it appears folly to embark upon the program.

The Korean Aid Bill of February 14, 1950, afforded only economic aid, and the $10.5 million of arms aid voted the previous October had not actually been given nine months later when the war began. As in the case of the 1948 China Aid Act, the Administration succeeded in thwarting the intent of Congress by not delivering the munitions.

President Truman on June 27, 1950, when announcing his decision to send Americans to defend Korea, admitted that the South Korean Government forces had been armed only "to prevent border raids and to preserve internal security." It is thus clear that the money appropriated by Congress had never been used to provide South Korea with the means to resist an attack by Soviet Russia's satellite, the North Korean "Democratic People's Republic."

Either the Administration was following Dr. Lattimore's advice to "let Korea fall but not to let it look as though we pushed it," or it still believed that "good works" were sufficient to stave off Communist aggression. There can be no other explanation for using the American taxpayers' money to give South Korea "economic aid" while refusing it the means to defend itself.

The South Korean Government was under no illusions about the dangers it faced. Far from desiring the removal of

American troops, it realized that it would henceforth stand defenseless against Soviet aggression. President Syngman Rhee understood that America's policy of abandoning China to the Communists meant that it was only a question of time until South Korea would also be overwhelmed. On November 19, 1949, he said that once the Soviets had secured their Far Eastern flank by victory in China, "it is believed that several well-armed divisions of Communist troops will be sent into Korea." But Rhee's pleas for American arms aid to resist the attack which he knew was coming were refused.

Thus the disastrous China policy of the Administration was paralleled by its Korean policy. In both cases it refused to face up to the realities of the situation, and insisted on regarding the Communist menace as nonexistent, provided "reforms" were instituted. And in both cases the arms aid voted by Congress was withheld, lest our side should be militarily strengthened and thus enabled to resist Communist aggression by force of arms.

We went farther even than the denial of arms to South Korea. Administration spokesmen announced quite plainly to the whole world that we did not consider the defense of Korea our responsibility. Secretary Acheson, in his famous speech before the National Press Club on January 12, 1950, was reported by the *New York Times* to have said:

For its own security the United States must and shall maintain forces in Japan, the Ryukyu Islands (Okinawa), and the Philippines. But no such line of containment could be drawn in southern and southeast Asia, where the United States had no direct responsibilities and only limited opportunities for action.

Thus Moscow was told by our own Secretary of State that neither Formosa nor Korea was included behind the line which America would defend.

In January 1950, according to Senator Connally's reports, Acheson told the Senate Foreign Relations Committee that "he strongly reaffirmed President Truman's stand [of January

5, 1950] against sending military forces or military advice to the Chinese Nationalists on Formosa, and further stated that he alone was responsible for the State Department's confidential guidance message of December 23, telling its officials abroad to prepare for the loss of Formosa to the Communists." He said that early recognition of Communist China by America was "possible." And he gave the go-ahead signal in Korea by distinctly stating that "beyond the line laid down [Japan, Okinawa, and the Philippines] the United States could not assure the rest of the Far East against attack." [3]

As late as May 5, 1950, just one month and a half before the attack on Korea, Senator Connally, speaking with all the authority of the Chairman of the Senate Foreign Relations Committee, echoed Mr. Acheson's statement of policy in an interview given to the *United States News*. Only now there were no innuendos, no implications. This is what the Senator had to say about Korea:

QUESTION: "Do you think the suggestion that we abandon South Korea is going to be seriously considered?"

CONNALLY: "I am afraid it is going to be seriously considered because I'm afraid it's going to happen, whether we want it or not. I'm for Korea. . . . But South Korea is cut right across by this line—north of it are the Communists, with access to the mainland, and Russia is over there on the mainland. So that whenever she takes a notion she can overrun Korea just like she probably will overrun Formosa when she gets ready to do it. I hope not, of course."

QUESTION: "But isn't Korea an essential part of the defense strategy?"

CONNALLY: "No. Of course, any position like that is of some strategic importance. But I don't think it is very greatly important. It has been testified before us that Japan, Okinawa, and the Philippines make the chain of defense which is absolutely necessary. And of course any additional territory along in that area would be that much more, but it's not absolutely essential."

Could Stalin have had a warmer invitation to order his Communists in North Korea to attack?

Referring to the above authoritative statements of United States policy prior to June 25, 1950, Senator Taft, in his speech to the Senate on June 28, 1950, said:

With such a reaffirmation of our Far Eastern policy, is it any wonder that the Korean Communists took us at the word given by the Secretary of State? If we were contemplating the recognition of Communist China, as the Secretary clearly indicated, then certainly they could well think that if they could once occupy Korea, they could look forward to recognition by the United States of a Communist Korea."

The Communists were not only given the green light in Korea by the Chairman of the Senate Foreign Relations Committee as well as by the Secretary of State. They were also almost invited to attack Formosa. Stalin must naturally have concluded that, since President Truman, on January 5, 1950, had announced that "no military aid or advice" would be given to the Chinese Nationalists to defend Formosa, no American opposition would be encountered to the conquest of South Korea. For whereas Formosa required only American munitions to ward off a Communist attack, South Korea required direct American military intervention and, not being an island, was in a far more vulnerable position.

In calling for Dean Acheson's resignation Senator Taft stated on June 28 that: In the President's statement there is a direct repudiation of the policies of Secretary Acheson declared in January of this year. . . . The statement that "the occupation of Formosa by Communist forces would be a direct threat to the security of the Pacific area and the United States forces performing their lawful and necessary functions in that area" is directly contrary to the statement of Secretary

Acheson that Formosa has no military value and that "we are not going to get involved militarily in any way on the Island of Formosa."

The leading Republican Senator, whom his opponents have tagged as an isolationist, had all along advocated arms aid to the National Government.

President Truman's decision to send American armed forces to fight in defense of Korea seemed to constitute a complete repudiation of the Far Eastern policy advocated by General Marshall and Dean Acheson. However, his simultaneous order to the Seventh Fleet to defend Formosa was accompanied by the proviso that the Chinese Nationalist forces were to be prevented from continuing their successful blockade of Shanghai and Tientsin. The United States Administration was evidently determined to remain "neutral" in the struggle for control of China between the Communists and their opponents, even while fighting the Communists in Korea.

The effect of President Truman's order concerning Formosa was to enable the Communists to acquire all the war materials which they had hitherto been unable to secure on account of the Chinese Nationalist naval and air blockade of Shanghai and Tientsin. Our British allies in Hong Kong made hay while the sun shone, and such American shipping firms as the Isbrandtsen Line also profited by the United States order to prevent Chinese Nationalist attacks on shipping serving the Communists. Copper, steel, and other war supplies were rushed to Communist Chinese ports by British and American businessmen anxious only to acquire profits, and indifferent to the death and mutilation of British and American soldiers in Korea. *Time* reported on January 22, 1951, that British traders in Hong Kong, during 1950, had done 400 million dollars' worth of business with Red China, supplying our enemies and theirs with rubber, gasoline, steel, and other strategic materials. The profits made by Americans who, like the Hong Kong British, considered themselves to be "just simple traders who want to get on with our daily round" are not recorded. But it was not until Senator O'Conor of Maryland, late in 1950, started to expose the amount of aid given by American traders to the Chinese Communists killing our men in Korea, that the United States Commerce Department began to hinder the export of war supplies from America to Communist China.

It is possible that the explanation of the sudden switch in the Administration's Far Eastern policy is afforded by the old adage that foreign policy is merely the extension of domestic politics. President Truman may have been impelled to defend Korea, after his Secretary of State had announced our intention of not doing so, in order to obviate the damaging repercussions at home of Senator McCarthy's charges that Communists in the State Department were responsible for our Far Eastern policy. On the other hand, it may have been a sudden realization—brought about by the unprovoked aggression of the Communists in Korea—that the Marshall-Acheson Far Eastern policy was based on false premises.

Whatever the explanation for the sudden decision to bring all America's military strength to bear to prevent the Communist conquest of South Korea, after having abandoned the huge area of China, the bold course decided upon in June was abandoned in November. After victory had been denied to us by the large-scale intervention of the Chinese Communist Army, the former Marshall-Acheson policy was partially resumed. Not only did we continue to prevent the Chinese Nationalists on Formosa from blockading and harassing the Chinese mainland, thus safeguarding the rear of the Communists we were fighting. General MacArthur was also forbidden to attack by air the enemy's supply dumps, communications, and war industries in Manchuria. Either the old illusion that the Chinese Communists could be "detached" from Moscow still influenced our policy, or fear of

Russian intervention, as previously of Chinese Communist intervention, tied MacArthur's hands.

From the outset of the war the operations of the United States, or so-called United Nations, forces were hampered by the desire both of Washington and a majority of the United Nations to wage a limited war. So after the capture of Seoul our soldiers had to stand on the 38th parallel for days, thus giving plenty of time to the Korean Communists to escape to the mountains. General MacArthur had to wait until the obstruction of the Soviet states, and of the Indian Government, had been overcome in the United Nations. America found herself in the unenviable situation of having to win victories alone and then wait for others to decide what advantages should, or should not, be taken.

Further to increase the difficulties of our outnumbered forces, the United States State Department forbade making any use of Chinese Nationalist intelligence, as well as forbidding MacArthur to use his air force to observe troop movements in Manchuria and China proper. The United States Government itself apparently had no agents in China. The Chinese Nationalists on Formosa are able to maintain an excellent espionage network on the Chinese mainland, thanks to the ever increasing opposition to Communist rule. But during the nine months prior to June 1950, American intelligence officers were precluded by a State Department directive from consulting Chinese Nationalist intelligence agencies on Formosa.

The Chinese Embassy in Washington submits intelligence reports to the State Department and to the Pentagon, but to judge from the record, little or no attention is paid to them. For instance, in May 1950, Chinese Nationalist intelligence reported to the Pentagon that crack Chinese Communist troops belonging to the army commanded by Lin Piao and equipped and trained by Russia, were moving from South China to Manchuria, and that since Lin Piao is Russia's favored Chinese general, this indicated trouble in Korea.

No notice whatsoever was taken of this accurate report. Subsequently it turned out that the divisions which led the first North Korean attack had been part of Lin Piao's army in the Communist war against Chiang Kai-shek.

Again, in July and August 1950, Chinese Nationalist intelligence informed the State Department and the Pentagon that the bulk of Lin Piao's army, and also some of General Chen-yi's forces formerly stationed in the Shanghai area, were being moved to Manchuria. It might have been expected that this information would be taken to mean that the Chinese Communists were preparing to attack us in Korea. But no. Those who hold our fate in their hands decided that this meant that China was stiffening her resistance to Russia! According to Drew Pearson, even Admiral Nimitz was deluded, and said that the mass movement of Chinese forces from the south to the north in the spring and summer of 1950 proved "China's" determination to resist Russian encroachments.

There are none so blind as those who will not see. Having staked their hopes on the emergence of a Chinese Tito, the State Department and certain military and naval authorities were determined to believe that all evidence of the co-ordination of Peiping's and Moscow's actions constituted proof of the opposite.

In February 1950 the United States had announced in advance that it would not use the veto to prevent the admission of Red China to the United Nations. On December 9, 1950, as our casualty lists were beginning to mount from thirty, to forty, to fifty thousand, as a result of the Chinese Communist attack on the UN forces, Mr. Acheson told Congress that while the United States would attempt to prevent the UN recognition of the Chinese Communists, it could not veto it. The Secretary of State explained that although the veto might legitimately be used to stop the first admission to the UN of any nation, it was not germane to passing on the question of "which faction" of such a nation should be admitted.[4] Thus even after our bitter experience in Korea the United States Secretary of State still represented the Chinese Nationalists and Stalin's puppets as just different Chinese "factions." Public knowledge of what has happened since the Chinese Communists intervened in Korea is too recent to require a detailed account. While the so-called UN forces fought and died in Korea, the United Nations itself debated endlessly whether or not to designate Communist China as an aggressor.

A Chinese Communist delegation was invited to Lake Success and left, after a violent denunciation of American "aggression" and of the UN itself. In spite of this rebuff, India took the lead in trying to work out a formula which would give the Communists all they wanted while saving a spurious reputation for the organization set up to prevent aggression and preserve peace. The so-called Asian-Arab bloc of nations tried to induce the forces of the free world led by America to capitulate and agree to "discuss" the fate of Korea and Formosa, as well as the admission of Communist China to the United Nations, in a seven-nation conference to include the leading appeasers, and to exclude both Nationalist China and the UN sponsored and duly elected Government of South Korea.

Finally, after twelve weeks of backing and firing, a majority of the United Nations, on January 31, 1951, plucked up sufficient courage to support the United States resolution branding Communist China as an aggressor. The UN, however, marred even the moral intent of its resolution by the provision that no effective action, such as economic or military sanctions, should be applied, if the "Committee of Good Offices" (provided for in paragraph 9 of the resolution) should be able to induce the Communist aggressors to cease fire and negotiate.

At the time of writing (February 1951), therefore, it is apparent that although the UN may have "saved face," there is no likelihood of any collective measures being taken to weaken the Communist aggressors.

It is also evident that there is still an acute danger that the apostles of appeasement, led by India and supported more or less openly by Canada and less obviously by Britain and France, may induce America to abandon our old ally, the Chinese National Government. As Dorothy Thompson pointed out in one of her columns, this will be equivalent to giving the canary to the cat after the cat has lost the mouse. If this happens, the young men who died, or were maimed in Korea, will have fought in vain.

Whether or not we are induced to abandon Korea, either honorably, or as the dishonorable price of a temporary accommodation with the Communists, it is obvious that the Koreans on their own have no chance at all of maintaining their independence without permanent American support, so long as China is under Communist domination.

The case of Korea constitutes a minor *motif*, or refrain, in the orchestration which blares forth the guilt of the Administration for disaster in the Far East—a disaster which cannot be remedied even by a miraculous victory in Korea.

The State Department, however, seems still to be convinced that good works are worth more than bayonets in combatting Communism. We are surely going to be told that, provided the American taxpayer pours in sufficient aid to "reconstruct" and "democratize" Korea, there will no longer be any danger to our battered little ward in Asia.

So long as the United States favors, or appeases, the Chinese Communists, there is no sense at all in "saving" South Korea, whether or not this is still possible. So long as the appearances are that the State Department is still intent on pursuing a *vendetta* against Chiang Kai-shek, it must remain as true today as on October 29, 1950, when Hanson Baldwin wrote in the *New York Times*, "that from a strictly military point of view, Russia can gobble up Korea any time she wants."

The question at this moment is: Will we continue to let Russia maintain a position of dominance in the Far East that will be a perpetual threat to what we fought so bravely and well to win in Korea? Will we make things easier for Stalin by recognizing Communist China? President Truman carefully avoided answering these questions when he returned from his interview with General MacArthur in the Pacific prior to the Chinese Communist attack. Until and unless an answer is given, the outcome of the Korean war must be inconclusive.

5. *How the Communists Captured the Diplomats*

SINCE THE DISASTER in Korea Americans are saying, almost in a chorus, "The fault is in Washington." They are right, to some extent. Any policy must be decided upon and implemented by individuals. Most of those individuals are capable men who have been well selected for their positions and have not been led astray by propaganda. I think that is true of the majority of the members of our government. I know it is not true of a minority, an important and influential minority, who during the past decade have defined and administered United States policy in the Far East.

I have been personally acquainted with some of the leading figures of that minority. Because I consider their actions to be as much a part of the China story as the events in which they participated, I shall devote the next three chapters to an examination of their records and their influence.

The China story, from the point when this minority started to take a dominant role, begins long before the account of United States policy summarized in the first part of this book. It starts in 1938 among a small band of Americans in Hankow in the summer and fall of China's second year of war against Japanese aggression.

At that time I was correspondent for the *London News*

Chronicle in Hankow. The Japanese were expected soon to capture the "Wuhan cities,"[1] where Chiang Kai-shek had established his capital after the fall of Nanking. Most American and British correspondents and diplomatic representatives had left for Chungking. We who remained called ourselves the "Hankow Last Ditchers."

The Japanese were dropping bombs almost daily on the undefended Chinese civilians in the city as they advanced slowly up the Yangtze Valley in face of the stubborn, but hopeless, resistance of the ill-equipped Chinese Nationalist armies.

Although we were comparatively safe so long as we stayed within the bounds of the former British concession in Hankow where we had our quarters, most of us felt that the Chinese cause was our own. We were united in our feelings of shame and indignation that the United States and the British Empire were together still supplying the Japanese with the sinews of war. Whenever the Japanese planes would drop their bombs on the Wuhan cities, we would climb to the top of the Lutheran Mission tower to watch, and then rush out to see and report the carnage and horror. We went on trips to the front, hid in ditches when Japanese planes machine-gunned the roads, and witnessed the courage of the Chinese armies fighting with whatever rifles and machine guns they could lay hand to against an enemy possessed of all the most modern implements of war. Our experiences drew us into the warm camaraderie engendered only by war and danger and a common sympathy.

In order to understand the motivation for America's subsequent policy in China, one must have some understanding of the 1938 Hankow outlook. It was easy then to argue concerning the good, or bad, potentialities of the Chinese Communist Party.

It was the period of the United Front, and the Chinese Communists were fighting shoulder to shoulder with the Nationalist, and obeying the orders of the Central Government. The Communists, who had a delegation in Hankow, a newspaper, and full liberty to publish their views, were represented in 1938—as again in 1946 when General Marshall came to China—by the charming and intelligent and most persuasive Chou En-lai, who has probably made more converts to the Chinese Communist cause than any other man living.

I recall with some personal detail these circumstances in order to re-create for the reader the general atmosphere that prevailed when General (then Colonel) Joseph Stilwell was in Hankow as United States Military attaché, and first conceived his warm admiration for the Communists.

Perhaps it was inevitable that so brave, politically uninformed, and romantic a character as the late Joseph Stilwell, should have fallen under the spell of those who regarded the Communists as the Light of Asia. He was honest, courageous, and a fine commander in the field. In World War II he won the loyalty of his men by his readiness to share their hardships. But politically he lacked the knowledge, the self-restraint, and the statesmanlike qualities necessary to a diplomat or a commander-in-chief in a foreign country. His horizon did not extend beyond "winning the war." He had no conception of the problems which beset the Chinese Government, since he had no knowledge of Communism.

No man was ever so misnamed as "Vinegar Joe" Stilwell. His asperity cloaked a soft heart and a sentimental political outlook which made him react blindly to suffering and injustice without seeking their cause. I knew him well in Hankow and liked him. It was in Hankow that I saw him begin to succumb to Communist influences.

Four years later, in 1942, when Stilwell was appointed American military representative and Chief of Staff to Chiang Kai-shek, the influences brought to bear upon him in the last days of Hankow bore their fatal fruit. By that time Colonel Stilwell had made up his mind that the Communists were the "white hope" of China. And all the rest of his actions and opinions stemmed from that illusion, born in those brief months of Hankow's glory as the center of resistance in the Far East to Axis aggression.

Among those fateful influences there was, first and foremost, a woman whose romantic temperament, miserable childhood, unhappy love experiences, burning sympathy for the poor, and selfless courage had many years earlier impelled to espouse the Chinese Communist cause. She was Agnes Smedley, the old campaigner, whose whole life was activated by the faith of a true believer in the possibility of establishing social justice on earth. She and I were friends in Hankow in 1938. She would, of course, not heed my warnings of the disappointments her Communist faith inevitably held in store for her. But she was gallant, and she had a sense of humor. When driven into a corner by the arguments of her opponents, she would laughingly exclaim: "But why do you try to make me lose my faith; do you want me to marry a millionaire?"

My attempts to convince Agnes that Communist movements are only self-sacrificing and incorrupt when they are struggling to obtain power did not persuade her to change her course. She sometimes admitted that her beloved Eighth Route Army [Chinese Communist] leaders would one day also be corrupted. But she felt she must devote her life to the cause of the Chinese Communists.

Agnes was warmhearted and essentially honest in spite of her tendency to apologize for the crimes of the people on her side and to condemn those whom she conceived to be the enemies of humanity, righteousness, and justice. She resembled the best of the old Bolsheviks liquidated by Stalin, and would undoubtedly have met the same fate in Russia as they did.

Agnes not only captivated "Vinegar Joe," but also completely won over the British Ambassador, Sir Archibald Clark-Kerr, subsequently Ambassador to Moscow, and later as Lord Inverchapel, appointed to Washington. "Archie" Clark-Kerr was another benevolent friend of the Chinese Communists for many years. He told me he thought Agnes was "the greatest woman" he had ever met, and their close friendship was continued in America.

There was another, perhaps even more unique, personality in Hankow that year. Like Agnes Smedley, who loved him dearly, Captain Evans Carlson, of the United States Marine Corps, was an idealist. After marching a thousand miles with the Chinese Communist forces in the North, Carlson had embraced the cause of the Chinese people with childlike fervor. He walked around Hankow in a dirty shirt with the sleeves cut short and unhemmed, endeavoring to look like a Communist guerrilla. His strange appearance and ecstatic praise for the Chinese Communists were ridiculed by the elegant West Pointer, Captain Frank ("Pinkie") Dorn, and by the sophisticated John Davies, then United States Consul in Hankow. Nevertheless, his enthusiastic praise for the Chinese Communists, whom he represented as "true Christians," had a profound effect on those who mocked him, including John Patton Davies.

Davies was also a great admirer of Agnes Smedley, whom he called one of "the pure in heart." He used to invite us all to excellent dinners at the American Consulate, at which he expressed both his admiration and affection for Agnes, his love of aesthetic beauty, his interest in art and gracious living, and his contempt for such "comic" characters as Evans Carlson. But as future events proved, John Davies had as great a faith in Carlson as in Agnes Smedley. Together with Edgar Snow and other journalists I knew in Hankow (see Chapter 7) he became one of the most potent influences in the Department furthering the cause of the Chinese Communists.

The world, as seen from Hankow in 1938, was an unreal one in which Right was clearly distinguished from Wrong. The Communists seemed to have chosen the side of "Right," since, like the forces of Chiang Kai-shek, they were then fighting the Japanese. Even I, disillusioned as I was by my six years of life in Soviet Russia, found it hard to resist the appeal of the "United Front" in China in 1938. I knew from my life in Moscow that all Communists are liars-on-principle whenever it is necessary to delude the "common man" to achieve their "higher" aims. I ought to have known that the Chinese Communists could be no different from any other Communists anywhere in the world. But I, too, was deluded by the Hankow atmosphere, and by the seemingly "liberal" attitude of the Communists I met there. I was for the moment deceived by their apparent devotion to the "United Front" against "fascist" aggression.

My mistake was largely due to the fact that, to my great surprise, I was welcomed as warmly by the Chinese Communists as by the National Government when I arrived in China in 1938. My book, *Japan's Feet of Clay,* had been translated into Chinese and had been widely sold. And I was still sufficiently gullible not to understand that the Chinese Communists could not afford to cold-shoulder me. I imagined their friendly behavior toward me betokened their basically liberal attitude. They knew, I reasoned, that my Russian husband had been arrested in the purge trials in Moscow and that I was a fugitive from Stalin's tyranny. Yet they welcomed me so warmly that I felt they must indeed be not "real" Communists.[2] Moreover, I was under the compulsion, for the sake of what I hoped would be my husband's safety, to keep quiet concerning my feelings about what I had experienced in Russia.

In digressing to explain my own feelings and motives thirteen years ago in China, my object is to explain the influences which still to some extent permeated my thoughts and were permanently to distort the judgment of others. It is hardly surprising that those who lacked the benefit of my experience in Russia were taken in by the Chinese Communists. It is harder to understand how they persisted in their error long after the "United Front" was broken by the Stalin-Hitler and Russo-Japanese pacts, and the Communists and Japanese almost ceased fighting each other.

By the time Joe Stilwell, in 1942, was appointed American military representative in China and Chief of Staff to Chiang Kai-shek, most of the "Hankow Last Ditchers" were scattered over the face of the earth. But their influence had grown enormously. Thanks to their writings and newspaper reports and to those of them who held government jobs, they had already become a potent force in determining American opinion and policy. And there were enough of them left in China, or soon to be sent back there, to form a phalanx around General Stilwell.

Joe Stilwell's "best boys"—those whom he trusted, thanks to old associations—soon acquired practical control over the United States military and civilian missions in Chungking. Moreover, the difficulties encountered in dealing with Chiang Kai-shek's government, combined with the poor public relations sense of the Chinese Nationalists, converted most Americans in China and Washington to the Stilwell-John Davies point of view.

John Davies, becoming Stilwell's political adviser, brought with him his protégés, John Stewart Service, Raymond Paul Ludden, and John Emerson.

John Emerson's preparation for service in China consisted of a year's study at the Sorbonne in Paris, followed by a period as lecturer in social science at the University of Nebraska, and subsequent service as a State Department representative in Japan and Latin America. Sent to China in 1943 as Second Secretary of the U.S. Embassy, Emerson soon became one of a group that advocated a policy of supporting the Chinese Communists as the rising power in China.

Raymond Ludden also held the post of Second Secretary at the United States Embassy in Chungking. He began his State Department career at the Consulate in Liverpool, England,

and in 1938 was assigned to Peiping. I never knew him, but according to a *Time* correspondent, he was "the explorer type—rugged, muscular, and entertaining."

Whatever their qualifications—whether such qualifications consisted of lack of knowledge of China or sympathy for the Chinese Communists—the men who surrounded General Stilwell soon pulled into their orbit other United States Foreign Service officials not previously identified with a position favorable to the Chinese Communists.

By 1943, when Moscow was turning to all-out hostility toward the Chinese National Government, the Davies-Service clique in Chungking was already exercising a quasi monopoly in the formation of United States policy. Stilwell's personal hatred and contempt of Chiang Kai-shek made it all the easier for the friends of the Chinese Communists to manipulate him.

The Davies-Service group in Chungking had almost complete control over outgoing military and civilian dispatches. The only exception was the naval attaché, who had his own system of communication. This possibly explains the fact that Admiral Leahy's advice to the President was contrary to that of the State Department. Aside from Navy intelligence, no reports went to Washington from China which were not edited by the Davies-Service group. If intelligence officers reported that the Communists were attacking the Nationalists instead of the Japanese, the news was not sent to Washington. General Pat Hurley complained that John Davies operated behind his back to sabotage official United States policy. For instance, Hurley stated that John Davies one day flew off to Yenan to tell Mao Tse-tung that Ambassador Hurley did not represent the American viewpoint.[3]

The three Johns, Carter Vincent, Davies, and Service, who had become so powerful, thanks largely to General Stilwell, were temporarily stymied in 1945 by General Hurley and General Wedemeyer. But by 1946, during the Marshall mission, they were again exerting a paramount influence.

I have already surveyed the course and consequences of General Marshall's mission to China, and of his subsequent actions as Secretary of State. He is known to have been affected by his old friendship with General Stilwell, whose recall from China in 1944 at Chiang Kai-shek's request he deeply resented. Furthermore, while in China, he was, by the pressure of events, dependent to a considerable extent on the advice of the Davies-Service group, which consequently became powerful because President Truman had such implicit confidence in Marshall. The President accepted completely the recommendations of the man he regarded as the "greatest living American."

From the evidence in the White Paper it is clear that John Davies, who today occupies a leading position in the State Department's Policy Planning Committee, represented the Chinese Communist Party as "a modern dynamic popular government." [4] According to his 1944 recommendations, the United States should have attempted to "adjust the new alignment of power in China by peaceful processes." He advised the commencement of "some cooperation with the Communists," the force which he said was "destined to control China," in order to "influence them further into an independent position friendly to the United States." [5] He urged the need for haste in establishing friendly relations with the Communists because "if the U.S.S.R. should enter the war against Japan," the Communists would be "captured by the U.S.S.R. and become Soviet satellites."

John Davies was an intelligent and not at all naïve young man. Born and brought up in China, he both speaks and reads Chinese. He cannot therefore have been totally ignorant of the voluminous mass of evidence proving that the Chinese Communist Party, by its every word and deed, had at all times proclaimed its complete subservience to Soviet Russia.

As early as November 1944 John Davies enunciated the principle which was to form the basis of the self-defeating

China policy subsequently followed by General Marshall. On November 15 of that year Davies reported as follows from Chungking:

We should not now abandon Chiang Kai-shek. To do so at this juncture would be to lose more than we could gain. We must for the time being continue recognition of Chiang's government.

But we must be realistic. . . . A coalition Chinese Government in which the Communists find a satisfactory place is the solution of this impasse most desirable to us. It provides our greatest assurance of a strong, united, democratic, independent and friendly China—our basic strategic aim in Asia and the Pacific. If Chiang and the Communists reach a mutually satisfactory agreement, there will have been achieved from our point of view the most desirable possible solution. If Chiang and the Communists are irreconcilable, then we shall have to decide which faction we are going to support.

In seeking to determine which faction we should support we must keep in mind these basic considerations: Power in China is on the verge of shifting from Chiang to the Communists.

On December 12, 1944, Davies strongly urged that America supply the Chinese Communist forces with arms, and was outlining the policy which was to be officially adopted a year later by President Truman, namely, making "it clear to Chiang Kai-shek that we expect the Chinese to settle their own political differences: that we refuse to become further involved in and party to *Chinese domestic political disputes*" (italics added).

In previous dispatches Davies had stressed the danger that America might be involved in war with the Soviets if we continued to support the National Government. Thus he had himself recognized that the struggle in China was not a "domestic political dispute." Like many of those who support the Communist side, he does not seem to consider it necessary to argue logically.

John Davies' dispatches do not reveal that he ever was a Communist. They do prove: (a) that he had no scruples in arguing on opposite sides at different times to gain an advantage for the Chinese Communists; (b) that he was, at best, totally unaware of what should have been obvious to any man of intelligence and knowledge, namely, that Communist conquest of China would endanger the security of the United States. He became one of the men in the State Department whom General Hurley, when later testifying to a Congressional committee, accused of having "sabotaged" United States policy by privately advising the Communists that "his efforts to prevent the collapse of the Nationalist Government did not represent the policy of the United States."

In so far as China at least is concerned, Davies' reports, as reproduced in the White Paper, make it abundantly clear that he favored the Communists because he believed theirs was the winning side. "The Communists are in China to stay," he reported in a dispatch dated November 7, 1944, "and China's destiny is not Chiang's but theirs. . . . If the Generalissimo neither precipitates a civil war nor reaches an understanding with the Communists, he is still confronted with defeat. . . . The Communists are already too strong for him."

John Davies is today, as a key member of the Policy Planning Committee, still in a position to foster the State Department's leaning toward the belief that the Chinese Communist Party can be "detached" from Moscow and brought over to our side.

The dispatches of John Stewart Service and of Raymond Ludden, as given in Annex 47 of the White Paper, run along the same lines as those of John Davies, who was their senior in the Foreign Service. Their reports are distinguished only by a more unreserved enthusiasm for the "democratic self-government" in Communist China, a more definite conviction that the Chinese Communists "are not Communists," and a more complete identification of democracy with Communism.

Raymond Paul Ludden appears less conspicuously than John Davies and Service in the annexes to the White Paper, but according to the evidence of Emmanuel Larsen (one of the State Department's officials involved in the *Amerasia* espionage case), he was a leading figure in the Communist sympathizing clique in the State Department's Foreign Service.

Ludden had become a language officer in Peiping in 1938, then a Vice Consul at Canton (during the Japanese occupation), and subsequently Second Secretary at the United States Embassy in Chungking and Vice Consul at Kunming. In August 1943 he was detailed to General Stilwell's staff as political adviser, and was sent to Yenan (the Chinese Communist capital) with the United States Army observer group in June 1944. Here he remained until March 1945, when General Wedemeyer reorganized the Yenan observer group and placed it under the command of Colonel Ivan Yeaton, a real expert on Communism who had formerly been military attaché in Moscow. Ludden was then sent off to the Army and Navy Staff College where he graduated in 1945. In May 1946 he became Second Secretary and consultant at the United States Embassy in Nanking, and was promoted to First Secretary in July of that year. His last job in China was Consul in Canton from February 1948.

In a dispatch dated February 14, 1945, ascribed jointly to Ludden and Service in the White Paper, they proposed the adoption of the same policy toward China as had recently been adopted toward Yugoslavia.[6] They first quoted, with approval, Winston Churchill's declaration when he abandoned the anti-Nazi and anti-Communist Serbs led by Mikhailovitch, in favor of the Communist Marshal Tito—a declaration in which the British Prime Minister said that this was "not a time for ideological preferences," and that the only criterion to follow was who was most ready to kill Germans. Ludden and Service wrote:

A similar public statement issued by the Commander in Chief with regard to China would not mean the withdrawal of recognition or the cessation of military aid to the Central Government . . . it would serve notice, however, of our preparation to make use of all available means to achieve our primary objective.

The case of John Stewart Service is both more interesting and more complicated. As I never knew him, I am unable to offer any personal impression as in the case of John Davies.

Born in China in 1909 of American missionary parents, educated in China and America, appointed Vice Consul in Yunnan in 1934, and appointed Foreign Service officer a year later, Service appears to have fallen victim to Communist propaganda, all the more readily because of his lack of knowledge of economics and politics. His reports, as given in the White Paper, display ignorance and naïveté, rather than a definite Communist orientation. He seems to have been typical of the "liberals" who fell easy victims to Communist propaganda on account of their inexperience of totalitarian methods, and lack of knowledge of the real aims of the Communists. On the basis of the questionable evidence of Americans taken on conducted tours of Communist China, Service disserted in his reports to the State Department on the contrast between "democratic" Communist China and Nationalist China, where "unprecedented" corruption reigned, and unrest was growing due to inflation, conscription, and other consequences of the war.

In his reports in the White Paper Service not only insisted that the "Communist revolution has been moderate and democratic." He represented the Chinese Communists as independent of Moscow. In a dispatch dated June 20, 1944, he wrote that "if there were civil war," it "would press the Communists back into the arms of the U.S.S.R." He also gave full credence to the good reports about Yenan given by those who went on the conducted tour arranged in 1944. For him there was no question but that there was "democratic self-government" in Communist China, and that "there is complete solidarity of army and people."

In a report not included in the White Paper, Service took a still more favorable attitude toward the Chinese Communists than in his White Paper reports. He wrote, in a document headed J 109 (a) 7 Q 307—Service to USAF—APO 879 (a copy of which was found among the documents the FBI seized in the offices of *Amerasia* in 1945):

Any orientation which the Chinese Communists may once have had toward the Soviet Union seems to be a thing of the past. The Communists have been working to make their thinking and propaganda realistically Chinese, and they are giving out democratic policies and they expect the United States to approve and sympathetically support it—they believe the U.S. rather than the Soviet Union will be the only country able to give economic assistance.

As a result of the FBI arrests in 1945, however, we know more about Service's affiliations than we know about the other members of the group in the State Department who seemed to favor the Chinese Communists.

If it had not received active support from some of President Roosevelt's closest advisers, perhaps the Davies-Service group would never have been able to drown out the voices of such experienced State Department representatives as Joseph Grew, the former United States Ambassador to Japan, who was head of the Far Eastern Division of the State Department until he was forced to resign in 1945 as a result of his attempt to bring the *Amerasia* conspirators to judgment. He was supplanted by John Carter Vincent, and from that moment the IPR-State Department-pro-Chinese Communist axis became almost all-powerful.

Vincent had been Consul in Shanghai before Pearl Harbor. Subsequently he was Counselor of the United States Embassy in Chungking from 1942 to 1943. Either then or earlier he was influenced, probably by his friend John Davies, to favor the Chinese Communists. Subsequently he rose rapidly in the State Department. In 1943 he was appointed Assistant to the Chief of the Far Eastern Division of the State Department and also became Special Assistant to the Administrator of the Foreign Economic Administration.

Lauchlin Currie, while supervisor of the Foreign Economic Administration and President Roosevelt's Administrative Assistant for Foreign Affairs, was as important in his day as any other man in determining the course of United States policy in China. In the summer of 1948 he admitted to the House Committee on Un-American Activities that he had been instrumental in saving the job of Nathan Gregory Silvermaster, subsequently exposed by Elizabeth Bentley as a Soviet agent. At this hearing Lauchlin Currie was accompanied by his friend, Dean Acheson. Currie was himself accused before this Committee by Elizabeth Bentley and Whittaker Chambers of having been a Communist agent; he denied the charge.

Lauchlin Currie had no first-hand knowledge about China when he became a White House adviser. But since he was supposed to know about economic problems, he was asked for advice on Chinese inflation, and was soon thereafter enabled to pose as a Far Eastern expert. Either because of his Communist sympathies, or because he knew little and cared less about the problems which confronted the Chinese National Government, he took the position which the Communists also took, that the ills of China were not due to the war and Japanese occupation and blockade, but to the "fascist" character of Chiang Kai-shek's government.

Lauchlin Currie's role is important because, so long as Grew was in charge of Far Eastern affairs at the State Department, the Communists had comparatively little influence there. Lauchlin Currie, who came to exercise supervision over the Foreign Economic Administration, was able to bypass the State Department by presenting to the White House economic and political reports on China favorable to the Communists.

In 1943, when Vincent became assistant to Grew at the State Department and Special Assistant to Lauchlin Currie, the Foreign Economic Administration was in process of becoming the clearinghouse for pro-Communist reports on China, which could not be passed through the State Department so long as Joseph Grew was still head of the Office of Far Eastern Affairs. Some Foreign Service officers in China sent Currie duplicates of their reports to the State Department.

In the summer of 1944 Vincent accompanied Henry Wallace on his trip to China, and he is known to have helped write Wallace's report to the President. In the White Paper on China it is stated that "the Department is not aware of any written record which Mr. Wallace himself may have made." In 1950, after Senator McCarthy challenged the State Department to produce the report, Henry Wallace himself made it public. The White Paper does not deny that Vincent made notes on conversations between Chiang Kai-shek and Wallace. It also admits that he was present when Wallace told Chiang that if "the Chinese Communists were linked with the U.S.S.R. [as Chiang had stated], then there was even greater need for settlement," that "there should be no situation in China which might lead to conflict with the U.S.S.R.," and that any "settlement with the [Chinese] Communists might prove transitory unless China reached an understanding with the U.S.S.R."

Henry Wallace was at least open in his championship of the Soviet Government. Instead of pretending that the Chinese Communists are not "real" Communists, he based his support of them on the fact that an agreement with them was necessary in order to prevent conflict with Russia.

John Carter Vincent and his friends and subordinates, John Davies and John Stewart Service, took the opposite line. They argued that Chiang should come to terms with the

Communists because the Chinese Communists were not "real" Communists. But from China's point of view it made little difference. Either way Chiang Kai-shek was being urged to put the Communists in a position to dominate China.

In 1944 John Carter Vincent had been promoted to Chief of the Division of Chinese Affairs. In 1945, he stepped into Grew's position as head of the Office of Far Eastern Affairs of the State Department. There he was in a perfect position to exercise enormous influence over our policy in China.

His opposition to the grant of American aid to countries fighting Communism was voiced in a formal address (June 28, 1946) which he gave before the National Trade Council in New York. He said:

I believe it is unsound to invest private or public capital in countries . . . where a government is wasting its substance on excessive armament, where the threat or fact of civil war exists, where tendencies toward government monopolization exclude American business, or where undemocratic concepts of government are controlling.

In September 1946, when General MacArthur issued a warning against the danger of Communism in Japan, John Carter Vincent was quoted in the *New York Herald Tribune* as having charged MacArthur with launching an anti-Soviet campaign in violation of State Department directives to use Japan for "building a bridge of friendship to the Soviet Union."

When in December 1946 an American naval vessel was ordered out of the Chinese port of Dairen by the Soviet occupation forces in violation of the Yalta agreement and the Sino-Soviet Treaty of 1945 which declared it a free port, Vincent authorized a State Department spokesman to inform the public that the Russians were acting within their rights.

As already noted, John Carter Vincent did not become head of the Division of Far Eastern Affairs at the State Department until Under Secretary of State Grew had been removed.

In 1947, in an effort by the State Department to allay Congressional suspicions concerning him, John Carter Vincent was sent off to be our Minister to Switzerland. He was succeeded as Director of the Office of Far Eastern Affairs by William Walton Butterworth, seemingly a solid career man. Indeed, in 1943 and 1944, as First Secretary of the United States Embassy in Lisbon and in Madrid Butterworth had been regarded as too conservative. After being transferred to Nanking as Minister, he seems to have been careful not to commit himself politically. Butterworth had been a Rhodes scholar at Oxford, had served in Singapore in 1942, and his specialized knowledge concerned the British Empire. This British connection may have affected his views—the British being anxious to appease the Chinese Communists—or perhaps he had learned from his experience that it is inadvisable to become known as a conservative. Whatever the explanation, Butterworth did nothing to divert American policy in China after he became Director of the State Department's Division of Far Eastern Affairs from its pro-Communist course. The relief felt in anti-Communist circles at his appointment to take John Carter Vincent's place was short-lived. Butterworth showed little disposition to oppose the John Davies–Marshall policies. The general consensus is that Walton Butterworth is a good civil servant who does what he is told. He inherited a mess which he never attempted to clear up.

Among the American figures in the wartime Chungking group who either sympathized with the Chinese Communists, or went along with the Stilwell-Davies clique in hopes of preferment, were Philip Sprouse, Arthur G. Ringwalt, and George Atcheson. Sprouse is today head of the State Department's Division of Chinese Affairs; and Ringwalt is Far Eastern expert at the United States Embassy in London. Atcheson is shown in the White Paper (pages 86–87) to have urged the

United States in 1945 to arm the Chinese Communists. However, after being appointed to Tokyo as political advisor to General MacArthur, Atcheson adopted the latter's views on Communism. This man of integrity, who had the courage to admit his mistakes, was unfortunately killed in an airplane accident before his views could influence United States policy.

It is here important to call attention to the subtle maneuvering that enabled one member of the Communist sympathizing cabal in Washington and New York to replace another whenever suspicions were aroused. When, for instance, a leakage of top secret information was traced to the Division of International Security Affairs (whose function was to service the United States representatives in the United Nations), its chief, Joseph E. Johnson, resigned. Johnson had formerly been Alger Hiss's top assistant at the State Department. He was subsequently to be appointed to the post Hiss held when he was indicted for perjury—president of the Carnegie Foundation for International Peace. Meanwhile, Dean Rusk, thanks perhaps to his former association with Hiss and Johnson, became Under Secretary of State.

Dean Rusk and Joseph E. Johnson may be wholly free from any Communist sympathies, but it is a curious fact that neither has ever questioned the *bona fides* of the Chinese Communists. Moreover, Dean Rusk has proved that he must be classified among the dupes of the Chinese Communists. For on June 14, 1950, he told the World Affairs Council Conference of the University of Pennsylvania, that the Chinese "Revolution" is "not Russian in essence" and "does not aim at dictatorship."

Neither Mao Tse-tung nor Stalin even ventured to give such a clean bill of health to the Chinese Communists as Dean Rusk. He went farther than almost any other State Department official in his desire to represent the Chinese Communists as good liberals who follow the American ideal. For he said that "the Revolution in China" is comparable "to the American revolt against the British."

Furthermore, in the Korean crisis Dean Rusk has appealed strongly in support of an appeasement policy. In a speech on November 15, 1950, he made it quite clear that if only the Communists would limit their demands, we would be happy to forget how many American soldiers they had killed and give them all the assurances they needed that the United States had no intention whatsoever of contesting Communist rule over China. He said:

We do not know what Chinese intentions are. It is of the greatest importance to find out whether the Chinese have limited objectives which are negotiable in character, or unlimited objectives which by their very nature are not negotiable. . . . Put yourself in Peiping, consider that you have been subjected to a barrage of Soviet propaganda about our alleged aggressive designs, and see whether you yourselves might not have some such misgivings.

Dismissing as of no consequence all the evidence that the Chinese Communist Party acts on Moscow's instructions, Dean Rusk said that "we do not know" whether Communist intervention in Korea is part of a pattern of "worldwide aggressiveness, we do not know the real explanation."

Of course, no one can ever know anything if all evidence contrary to his hopes is dismissed as non-existent.

The names I have mentioned, whether of those who represented the Chinese Communists as a "democratic" force, or who went along with the tide rather than risk their chances of promotion, do not include all those in the State Department who favored the Chinese Communists. I have not dealt with other lesser-known officials in the Department nor with the personnel of UNRRA, which included a high proportion of Communist sympathizers. Nor have I compiled a list of the OWI or USIS employees in China who did their bit for the Communist cause. Lastly, I have omitted consideration of the influence of certain Treasury officials who helped to undermine the National Government of China.

On the other hand, there were men in the State Department who did oppose the policy of our government. But those who dared to stand against the pro-Communist tide knew they would not be listened to and might be blacklisted. At best they could expect to be shunted off to some post where their specialized knowledge would be wasted. It must have seemed to many the part of wisdom not to oppose the powers that be but to wait for a change in the climate of opinion, and meanwhile do their best to modify the influence of the pro-Communist clique, or remedy the effect of its ill-considered actions.

One of those who rode out the storm and suffered comparatively little because of his anti-Communist views was Everett Francis Drumright, Second Secretary of the United States Embassy in Chungking, who was referred to by the Davies-Stilwell school as "the Fascist." He was not penalized. He was merely by-passed and sent off to pastures where his knowledge of China and Communism could not impede the State Department's pro-Communist "experts." In 1946 he became First Secretary and Counselor of the United States Embassy in London. In 1947 he was transferred to Tokyo.

Another more famous Foreign Service officer, Angus Ward, did not fare so well. While United States Consul in Manchuria he was imprisoned by the Communists. After his release and return to America, he was shipped off to Nairobi in Africa.

The outstanding example of the Administration's failure to utilize the services and advice of those who had proved their competence is that of Stanley Hornbeck. As Chief of the Far Eastern Division in the late thirties he had not only advocated an embargo on war supplies to Japan, but had foretold Japan's attack on America in 1941. Having been as uncompromisingly anti-Communist as anti-Axis, he is now no longer employed or consulted by the State Department.

Apart from the honorable exceptions mentioned, the State Department and Foreign Service officers discussed in this chapter were, as advisers to the Secretary of State and the President, largely responsible for the disastrous policy we have followed in China.

Whether in each case such a policy was pursued out of personal ambition, ignorance of the true aims and purpose of the Chinese Communists, or treasonable devotion to their cause, the effect is the same. Those who manipulate the policies of their own government consciously or unconsciously for the benefit of a foreign power by misinforming their own people are more dangerous than spies, even though legally they are not guilty of treason. Or, as Max Eastman stated in a recent article, "Ignorance in the executive, ignorance in the makers of our foreign policy, at such a juncture, is more dangerous than treason." [7]

6. . . . *and the Secretary of State*

IT IS NOT merely the State Department, of course, or the Administration, which is responsible for America's self-defeating policy. The fault goes much deeper, and is due to more fundamental causes than the hope of politicians to preserve a monopoly of power by continuing to pursue policies long since proved bankrupt. Nevertheless, one must place the major share of the responsibility on the Administration and in particular on the State Department.

The muddle in Dean Acheson's mind is illustrated by his published speeches. In them the Secretary of State oscillates between two contrary theses: one that "good" and "evil" are irreconcilable; the other that there is no real incompatibility between them. When one attempts to find out what he really believes, one is bogged down in his contradictory statements.

In an address to the University of California on March 16, 1950, for instance, he said:

We can see no moral compromise with the contrary theses of international Communism: that the end justifies the means, that any and all methods are therefore permissible, and that the dignity of the human individual is of no importance as against the interests of the state.

But in the same speech he said that "it does not follow from this that the two systems, theirs and ours, cannot exist concurrently," and also assured his audience that "we are not attempting to change the government or social structure of the Soviet Union."

Gently he suggested:

In general, the Soviet leaders could refrain, I think, from systematically distorting to their own peoples the picture of the world outside their borders, and of our country, in particular.

But he hastened to add in the very next sentence:

We are not suggesting that they become propagandists for any country or system other than their own.

And finally, in what presents itself as nothing more than a sad state of confusion, he confessed:

But the Soviet leaders know and the world knows with what genuine disappointment and concern the people of this country were brought to the realization that the wartime collaboration between the major Allies was not to be the beginning of a happier and freer era in the association between the peoples of the Soviet Union and other peoples.

Mr. Acheson's "selected speeches," published by the State Department under the title *Strengthening the Forces of Freedom,* show how remote he is from understanding the basis of Soviet power or the nature of Communism. It is clear from his own statements that he has swallowed hook, line, and sinker, the Communist propaganda that the Russian "people" are enthusiastic supporters of the Communist regime. He speaks always of the "Soviet *leaders,*" not of the Communist Party's dictatorship. He identifies the Russian people with the regime. Nowhere in his speeches can one find any evidence that Mr. Acheson understands that the Russian people are *subjects,* not citizens, and have no means whatsoever of voicing their views, or influencing their government. He appears to have accepted as gospel truth the specious arguments by which American Communist sympathizers justify, or condone, Soviet tyranny. Evidently the United States Secretary of State has no inkling of the fact that Soviet power does not rest on the will of the people, that their silence and acquiescence have been obtained by the fearful penalties imposed on anyone who opposes or criticizes the regime.

Mr. Acheson's ignorance may explain the policy of appeasement he followed so long. For as Anatole Shub pointed out in the *New Leader:* [1]

If—as Mr. Acheson believes—the present Soviet rulers are the leaders of the Soviet Union (that is, if they enjoy the support of the Soviet people), then the only alternatives left to America are surrender or total war.

George Kennan's thesis concerning the possibility of "containing" Communism, which was accepted as official United States policy, was based on questionable premises. Kennan assumed that if the West built up its economic and military defenses and played from strength instead of weakness, the Communist hierarchy could be induced to give up its aim of world domination, and would agree to the peaceful coexistence of two worlds, one slave and one free. President Truman evidently still believes this, for, as late as January 1951, in his sixth message on the State of the Union, he said:

If we build our strength—and we are building it—the Soviet rulers may face the facts and lay aside their plans to take over the world. That is what we hope will happen, and that is what we are trying to bring about. That is the only realistic road to peace.

Coupled with Mr. Acheson's frequent statements that he believes in the possibility of a "cooperative relationship," or "coexistence," with the Soviet rulers, this Presidential statement must be taken to mean that those who direct our destiny believe that the Communists can be induced to abandon not only their basic aims, but the basis of their power. It takes no account of the fact that the Soviet system *must* expand if it is to continue to exist, because it is economically so wasteful and inefficient that it cannot survive without loot or tribute and fresh supplies of slave labor, and because the men in the Kremlin constantly fear that those they oppress will be tempted to revolt by the influence of a free world outside the Soviet Empire.

It is hardly surprising, in view of Mr. Acheson's attitude, that the "Voice of America" confines itself to platitudes or to extolling the American way of life. It never calls upon the people of the Iron Curtain countries to overthrow the tyrants, or promises them any support if they dare to try to win freedom. This is apparently not so much because the State Department is fearful of provoking war with Russia as that it does not conceive of the possibility of a revolt among Stalin's enslaved people. For Mr. Acheson has told us that: "The followers of Karl Marx endure the dictatorship of a police state in the delusion that they are ascending to a classless society." (It is not clear whom exactly Mr. Acheson is referring to by the designation "followers of Karl Marx." The Russian people, perhaps?)

There is little doubt Mr. Acheson believes that the Soviet Government's ambitions are not the result of any lust for power, but merely the consequence of a false philosophy. He thinks that if only we can demonstrate to the "Soviet leaders" that Marx erred, we can enjoy peace in our time. He says:

As the leaders of the Soviet Union come to appreciate that their analysis of the world and their policies growing from that analysis have been incorrect, the possibility for reasonable settlements of matters affecting the stability and progress of the international comity will increase.

Thus Mr. Acheson, according to his own statements, believes that the "Soviet leaders" aim at "stability and progress" for the world, and need only to be convinced that they have not taken the right path toward this desirable end. Let us, says Mr. Acheson, demonstrate that Marx was wrong in believing that the "capitalist world" would be destroyed as the result of its own internal contradictions, and Stalin will then recognize that the best interests of his people require friendship with us. Mr. Acheson's assumption that Stalin is not a dictator out to secure and extend his own power, but a benevolent ruler with the "best interests" of his people at heart, was clearly indicated in the following passage from the speech he made to the United Nations General Assembly in September 1950, after the U.S. Army had liberated Seoul, and an American victory in Korea would have been certain, had it not been for the intervention of the Chinese Communist army.

The Soviet leaders are realists, in some respects at least. As we succeed in building the necessary economic and defensive military strength, it will become clear to them that the non-Soviet world will neither collapse nor be dismembered piecemeal. Some modification in their aggressive policies may follow, if they then recognize that the best interests of the Soviet Union require a cooperative relationship with the outside world. Time may have its effect. It is but thirty-three years since the overthrow of the Tsarist regime in Russia. This is a short time in history. Like many other social and political movements before it, the Soviet Revolution may change. In so doing it may rid itself of the policies which now prevent the Soviet Union from living as a good neighbor with the rest of the world.

This last sentence is an important key to Mr. Acheson's thinking. It is clear that he believes Communism is a force which is likely to change for the best as it rolls on into the future. As *Time* magazine remarked,

Acheson had been waiting for the "dust to settle" in China when the Reds surprised him by kicking up a lot more dust in Korea. It now appeared that one of his basic attitudes toward Russia was that the dust of the 1917 Revolution would settle one of these days. He would not believe that the Bolshevik dust was politically radioactive.

The incurable propensity of the Secretary of State, and the Administration he advises, to regard Communism, unlike Nazism, as potentially good and peace-loving, explains America's vacillating, pusillanimous, and self-defeating foreign policy.

Senator Taft seems to have put his finger on the root cause of the Administration's disastrous foreign policy when, speaking in Detroit on Washington's birthday in 1948, he said:

Throughout the world we seem to have been dominated by an inferiority complex toward Russia. The failure in foreign policy was not chance. It resulted from the character of the New Deal Administration.

The fact that an underlying belief in the "progressive" nature of Communism, and abysmal ignorance with regards to its aims and methods continued to influence the Democratic Administration and its Republican "bipartisaners" long after the true face of Communism had been clearly revealed, is proved by President Truman's cable to Edwin W. Pauley on July 16, 1948. As quoted by Pauley before the Senate Armed Services Committee on July 16, 1950, Mr. Truman said:

By making possible the formulation and execution of liberal reforms such as the nationalization of certain industries and land redistribution, which are desired by a majority of Koreans, this policy should also help to broaden the basis for an understanding with the Russians.

Clearly, President Truman, like Mr. Acheson, was under the illusion that all that is required for us to get along with "Uncle Joe," whom as late as 1948 he was calling a "good fellow," and thereby insure world peace, is for America to show evidence that its economic, social, and political policies are as "progressive" as those of the Dictator of all the Russias!

The State Department's friendly attitude toward Marshal Tito, and the willingness of the Administration to give unconditional aid to Yugoslavia, as contrasted with the denial of arms aid to Chiang Kai-shek, constitutes further proof of their faith in the progressive, or "democratic," character of Communism.

The Administration's second great illusion about Communism is a corollary of the first, and has had equally disastrous results. It consists in the belief that Communism conquers, not by force and terror, but through popular support. In his January 12, 1950, speech to the National Press Club in Washington, Mr. Acheson declared that the best way of stopping Communism in Asia is to

develop a soundness and administration of these new governments and to develop their resources and their technical skills so that they are not subject to penetration either through ignorance or because they believe these false premises, or because there is real distress in their areas. If we can help that development, if we can go forward with it, then we have brought about the best way that anyone knows of stopping this spread of Communism.

This explains the third great illusion which has caused the State Department to view Communist conquests with complacency. Mr. Acheson evidently thinks that once the Chinese, or any other people, learn that Communism does not bring the benefits expected, it can be discarded like an old shoe.

It is clear from Mr. Acheson's public statements that he has no realization of the fact that once a nation comes under Communist domination the people have no way of getting rid of the tyrants—however much they hate their oppressors—except as a result of war and outside assistance. In his speech of January 12, 1950, he showed his continuing adherence to the notion that the Chinese Communists are not "real Communists," obedient to Moscow, and his failure to understand that Communist governments are able to compel the silent submission of the peoples they rule, by the unlimited use of terror. The Chinese people would free themselves, he said, and in order to let them do so, we must leave them strictly alone.

We must not undertake to deflect from the Russians to ourselves the righteous anger and the wrath and the hatred of the Chinese people which must develop. . . . The consequences of this Russian attitude and this Russian action in China are perfectly enormous. They are saddling all those in China who are proclaiming their loyalty to Moscow, and who are allowing themselves to be used as puppets of Moscow, with the most awful responsibility which they must pay for. Furthermore, these actions of the Russians are making plainer than any speech or any utterance or any legislation can make throughout all of Asia what the true purposes of the Soviet Union are and what the true function of Communism as an agent of Russian Imperialism is. These I suggest to you are the fundamental factors, fundamental realities of attitude out of which our relations and policies must grow.

These basic fallacies explain both the Administration's China policy and the attitude adopted toward the Republic of South Korea which were to result in America's involvement in a war costing thousands of American casualties. Having first withdrawn the American Army from Korea, and denied the Korean Republic the arms with which to defend itself from Communist attack, President Truman suddenly reversed himself and ordered American forces to defend Korea and Formosa.

The war in Korea has exploded at least one of the fallacies upon which the State Department's Far Eastern policy has been based: the belief that the people on our side in Asia would not fight the Communists because of the latter's popular support, and the "reactionary" character of the governments friendly to America.

Owen Lattimore had said that the South Korean Army

"cannot be trusted to fight; the people do not trust the government; the government cannot be depended on, and does not depend on itself." [2]

It was soon demonstrated in Korea that, once given the equipment with which to fight, the forces of the "undemocratic," "corrupt," . . . South Korean Republic were eager to fight against the "progressive" Communist North Korean "People's Republic." The South Korean soldiers were praised by the United States command as excellent fighters once they had been equipped by America. Evidently their morale had not been undermined by their government's failure to carry out a sufficiently drastic "land reform."

Can it be doubted that the same would have been true of the Chinese National Government's armies, had we not refused them arms, ammunition, and political support?

Unfortunately the course of events failed to convince Mr. Acheson of his mistaken judgments. So aid and support continued to be denied to the Chinese National Government on Formosa, even after its enemies and ours were engaged in mortal combat with American soldiers and marines in Korea.

Instead of permitting the Chinese Nationalist troops to share the heat and burden of the day with us, as they wished to do, Chiang Kai-shek's offer of 30,000 troops to fight in Korea was refused. This refusal was more inexcusable since the war in Korea was supposed to be a United Nations war, and the Chinese National Government was still China's representative in the United Nations.

No other member of the United Nations offered any substantial body of armed forces to fight in Korea.

The apologists for Yalta have justified the sacrifice of America's war aims to Stalin's ambitions as necessary to "save American lives." Yet President Truman refused to reduce American casualties in Korea by accepting the aid of *anti-Communist* Chinese forces.

The consequence of the decision to refuse Chinese aid in

the Korean war was, naturally, to give substance to Moscow's assertion that America was fighting an "imperialist" war of whites against Asiatics. Had the Chinese been permitted to fight shoulder to shoulder with us in Korea, there could have been no basis for this Communist propaganda line.

Whatever may be the prejudices and misconceptions which motivate the Secretary of State, it is clear that he has no appreciation of the psychology of Asiatics. Nor, for that matter, does he appear to have any understanding of the attitudes and feelings of any people threatened by Communist conquest or already under Soviet domination.

Hence presumably the State Department's angry reaction to General MacArthur's pronouncements on the subject of Formosa and American security in his message to the Veterans of Foreign Wars, suppressed after it had already been published. "Nothing could be more fallacious," MacArthur said, "than the threadbare argument of those who advocate appeasement in the Pacific, that if we defend Formosa we alienate continental Asia. Those who speak thus do not understand the Orient."

As the *New Leader* pointed out, this was the passage which "hurt most in Washington" since it was obviously a description of Dean Acheson and his closest colleagues.

It is not only in the Orient that evidence of strength attracts and that appeasement is taken to signify weakness. But those who have directed United States policy appear to have been blind to such elementary truths. Moreover, they also seem to have adopted the Marxist view that men's beliefs are conditioned entirely by their material circumstances and "class relationships."

Far from realizing that man does not live by bread alone, Acheson's views are predicated upon the belief that it is poverty which creates Communists, and that money can buy anything.

In spite of the evidence that some of the poorest countries in the world contain the fewest Communists, and that the

United States has more than its share of Moscow's agents and dupes, Mr. Acheson evidently believes that the Communist menace will disappear, given "a chicken in every pot"— or a full rice bowl. He takes no account of the fact that there are precious few Communists in Ireland, which is one of the poorest countries in Europe, whereas prosperous Czechoslovakia had enough of them to enable Stalin to win power without an overt act of aggression. Nor has he paused to reflect on the fact that there are fewer Communists in overcrowded Western Germany, where twelve million people exist on relief payments of eleven dollars a month, than in France, which is comparatively prosperous. He has evidently never taken into consideration the fact that India, which contains more hungry people than any other country on earth, has only a small Communist party, and that the poorest Latin American countries are not those with the strongest Communist parties.

Our Secretary of State is a leading example of a particular species of American that has flourished since the early 1930's. They think of themselves as "liberal idealists," but they are, in fact, protagonists of the Marxian materialist philosophy and apologists or supporters of Communist tyranny. The main tenets of their "idealism" seem to be a profound belief in their own goodness and the conviction that poverty is the root of all evil. They have fallen into the pitfall of a mystical trust in Marxian materialist philosophy without understanding that Communists gain support by appealing to idealist impulses among the uninformed and to the desire of "intellectuals" for power or for a secular religion.

Having adopted more fervently than any Marxist the belief that material considerations are paramount, the U.S. Administration has acted on the assumption that dollars can buy anything, including such fanatics as the Chinese Communist leaders.

John Stewart Service wrote in 1944, as recorded in the White Paper on China, that the Chinese Communists could be expected to become our allies because the United States would be the only country able to give them economic assistance.

The idea that Communists will cease to be Communists if given economic aid by "capitalist" countries is yet another of the false premises upon which United States policy has been based, and will continue to be based, so long as the Administration listens to those whose philosophy must be designated, paradoxically, as "materialist idealism." This curious mixture of idealism and materialism makes it easy for the Communists to influence the policy of such men as Dean Acheson. His application of his peculiar brand of idealism was, presumably, the main cause of his having been, for a while, the preferred statesman of the Communists and their fellow travelers. In June 1945 the *Daily Worker* of New York described him as "forward looking," which is the highest praise the Communists ever give to a "bourgeois" statesman. And *PM*, on October 7 of the same year, wrote that under Acheson's direction "State Department policy will have a better appreciation of what the Soviet Union wants."

On August 30, 1948, Mr. Adolph Berle, former Assistant Secretary of State, and today Chairman of the American Liberal Party, testified as follows before the House Un-American Activities Committee concerning Mr. Acheson's attitude in 1944:

As I think many people know, in the fall of 1944, there was a difference of opinion in the State Department. I felt that the Russians were not going to be sympathetic and cooperative. Victory was then assured, but not complete, and the intelligence reports which were in my charge, among other things, indicated a very aggressive policy, not at all in line with the kind of cooperation everyone was hoping for, and I was pressing for a pretty clean-cut showdown then when our position was strongest.

The opposite group in the State Department was largely the men—Mr. Acheson's group, of course—with Mr. Hiss as a principal assistant in the matter.

... I got trimmed in that fight and, as a result, went to Brazil, and that ended my diplomatic career.

Mr. Berle was neither the first, nor the last, who "got trimmed in that fight." Those who could not forget, and would not ignore, the evidence that Stalin's government was even more tyrannical and brutal than Hitler's, and equally aggressive, were silenced and penalized during the war, and for a long time afterward. And today Mr. Acheson, who together with his assistant, Alger Hiss, headed the pro-Russian group in the State Department, is Secretary of State. His opponents have either retired to private life, or been sent off to far corners of the earth where they can do no harm to those who enabled Stalin to win the power to threaten the whole world.

As late as November 15, 1950, Secretary of State Acheson was still cherishing his fond illusions about Communist dictatorships. Speaking to representatives of two hundred organizations being briefed at the State Department, he stressed the need to remove Chinese Communist "fears," and said:

If the Chinese have any doubt that our influence in the U.N. would be used to bring about a constructive adjustment of Chinese-Korean interests in the Yalu River, they would be very much mistaken if they thought we would not do that. We, of course, would do it.

According to the *New York Times* report of his talk, Mr. Acheson "hinted" that he would welcome discussions with the Chinese Communists on their "legitimate" interests on *both sides* of the North Korea–Manchuria border, and he stated further:

One of the first things we must do is to clear away any possible misunderstanding that there may be in the minds of the Chinese. If they believe, as their propaganda states, that the United Nations, or the United States, have any ulterior designs in Manchuria, everything possible must be done to disabuse them of such an illusion because it is not true.

Obviously the Secretary of State is unable to abandon the idea that it is a "misunderstanding" of the aims of the United States which prevents friendly relations with Communists. He cannot abandon the idea that Communist regimes represent the will of the people. Throughout his speech, as in the passage quoted above, he referred to "the Chinese," instead of to the Chinese Communist leaders, or the Communist dictatorship.

Mr. Acheson's illusions are shared by a great number of Americans of all parties. For the public is by the nature of things influenced by Washington and by the newspapers and writers who take their cue from the Administration. I shall turn next to an examination of some of those influences.

7. .... *and the Public*

IN CARRYING OUT its policy in China, the Administration was greatly aided by the concurrence of the American public. China is a long way off, and most Americans know nothing about it except what they read in the papers. Most newspapers, and nearly all other media of public information, so far as China was concerned, were firmly in the hands of a minority of writers, professors, and lecturers representing the pro-Chinese Communist views of the State Department. In China throughout the 1940's it required exceptional courage and integrity for any newspaper correspondent to stand up against the prevailing political climate, especially since their home offices did not wish to publish anything either displeasing to the Administration or contrary to the wishful thinking which was popular. Even if his newspaper was prepared to publish his dispatches, any correspondent not hostile to the National Government of China after 1943 found himself a social outcast in Chungking. He would never be invited to the wonderful parties given by Madame Sun Yat-sen, who did not allow her sympathy for the Communists to interfere with her enjoyment of the financial support of her rich brother T. V. Soong.

Honest correspondents who had their doubts about "Communist democracy" were often won over by the skilled public relations officers of the Communist Party and repelled by the inept efforts of the National Government to present its case. Moreover, Yenan, the Chinese Communist capital, exerted a fatal fascination. After spending eight days there in February 1946 I understood why most of the American journalists who visited it saw it as a primitive paradise. The appearance of social equality, and the failure to take into account the fact that under a Communist dictatorship no one dares to criticize the government, led foreigners to believe that the Communists had the enthusiastic support of the people. Americans on conducted tours also failed to take into account the fact that "land reform" was comparatively easy in the sparsely populated Northwest left practically unmolested by Japan. Only a few perspicacious correspondents realized that the National Government, whose armies had to bear the main brunt of the Japanese attack, could not, even if it wished, have instituted "agrarian reforms" in the midst of war and blockade.

For a variety of reasons (including the fact that they had been the first writers and correspondents interested in the Sino-Japanese War), the American friends of the Chinese Communists got into a position to black out contrary opinions.

In China in 1938 I had the opportunity to know some of the leading correspondents who were to become the "authorities" on the China situation Americans would read and believe. Foremost among them was Edgar Snow, the clever young journalist who was winning an international reputation by his "discovery" of Communist China. In the original edition of his best-selling book, *Red Star Over China,* Ed Snow had painted a most favorable picture of the Chinese Communist régime in the Northwest. But he had also included some passages critical of the Comintern and showing the subservience of the Chinese Communists to Moscow. My Hankow impression of Snow as an honest journalist was altered when he eliminated, in the second edition of his book, a number of passages distasteful to Moscow.[1]

Edgar Snow came to exert enormous popular influence for the cause of the Chinese Communists when he became an associate editor of the *Saturday Evening Post*. He possessed a rare faculty for presenting both the Russian and Chinese Communists to the *Post*'s readers as democrats after their own hearts. While Owen Lattimore was persuading the universities and the State Department of the superior virtues of Soviet "democracy," Ed Snow was propagating the same line to the millions who read the *Saturday Evening Post*. Snow, can, however, be complimented on his even greater mental agility. Sometimes he represented the Chinese Communists both as *real* Communists and as harmless "agrarian reformers," in one and the same book or article. For instance, in an article in the *Saturday Evening Post* for May 12, 1945, under the title "Must China Go Red?" he first argued that we ought to abandon Chiang Kai-shek in order to secure friendly relations with Russia,[2] and then stated:

For the foreign reader it is somewhat confusing that this Chinese agrarian reform movement is called "Communism." . . . Communism in China is a watered down thing today. . . . Having built up their armed power long after Moscow had more or less forsaken their struggle as hopeless, the Chinese Red leaders have a strong feeling of independence.

In another previous *Post* article (June 10, 1944) called "Sixty Million Lost Allies" he had written: "The fact is, there has never been any Communism in China, even in Communist areas." And in the February 17, 1945, issue of the *Saturday Evening Post* he wrote that the Chinese Communists "happen to have renounced years ago now any intention of establishing Communism in China in the near future." But in justice to the *Saturday Evening Post* it must be noted that its editorials consistently opposed the views expounded by Edgar Snow.

Snow's 1944 book, *People On Our Side,* which fulsomely praised Soviet Russia while damning Chiang Kai-shek, enjoyed the distinction of being published in a special edition for the United States Armed Services.

Another young writer in Hankow in 1938 was Jack Belden, a former United Press correspondent, who later, as a *Time* and *Life* correspondent, was instrumental in convincing the American public that the Communists, both in Asia and Europe, were the best allies of America. In his book *China Shakes the World* (1949) he sings the praises of the tough, intrepid, and cruel Communists, and seems almost to enjoy recalling the tortures they inflicted upon their enemies, and upon the innocent or neutral victims of civil war.

In the larger outer ring, so to speak, there was the good-natured, politically inexperienced, and hard-working chief of the United Press bureau in Hankow, Francis McCracken Fisher. He was, I feel sure, never a Communist. But his liberal sympathies for the poor and oppressed won Mac over to the group which favored the Chinese Communists. After service in OWI he became Policy Information Officer for the Far Eastern Division of the State Department, where he was in a position to decide what news and views should be passed on to the higher-ups. In this job he was certainly able to influence policy indirectly but powerfully. In 1949, when Congressional pressure forced a minor housecleaning job on the Far Eastern Division of the State Department, Mac Fisher was quietly moved over to the National War College.

Agnes Smedley, whom I mentioned in Chapter Five, was correspondent of the *Manchester Guardian* in Hankow in 1938. Later, in America in 1943 she wrote a glowing eulogy of the Chinese Communists in her book, *Battle Hymn of China.* She died in England in 1950, leaving all her possessions to General Chuh Teh, the "Father of the Red Army," and requesting in her will that her ashes be buried in Peiping.

There were a few correspondents in Hankow in 1938 who were not, and never became, members of the pro-Chinese

Communist group. The thin and scholarly Tillman Durdin, then and now correspondent of the *New York Times* is politically one of the best-informed correspondents. It was Till Durdin who, in 1946 in Chungking, saw through Chou En-lai, who captivated almost everyone else. Durdin said to me: "Chou overwhelms you by the force of his personality and his clever arguments. But after hearing him month after month and year after year, you can't trust what he says. He has contradicted himself too often." It was also Durdin who gave me what is probably the fundamental reason why so many American correspondents in China fell under the Communist spell during World War II. "You must understand," he said, "how easy it was to believe in the Communists. It was so utterly hopeless in 'Free China.' The graft, the misery, the lack of will to fight any more. Even I felt that it could not be worse, and must be better in Communist China. You missed the depressing hopeless years in China following the fall of Hankow. You have got to get the feel of them, in order to understand why so many Americans fell for the Communists."

In blockaded Berlin in the summer of 1948, I remembered Till Durdin's words, as I listened to Amadora Leber speak to a crowd in Spandau Square. For Amadora Leber said: "In the depression years many of you said, 'It couldn't be worse,' but you found out later that under the Nazis it eventually became far worse. Now in spite of our terrible difficulties with food we *know* it would be even worse than now if the Russians ruled over us. We know that we would be taken away to slave-labor camps and be ruled over by the same methods as the Nazis used."

Arch Steele who at that time represented the *Chicago Daily News,* and subsequently became correspondent of the *New York Herald Tribune,* was undoubtedly the best informed, most intelligent and objective of all American correspondents in the Far East. He was so generally liked and respected that he had friends in all political camps. He alone among the correspondents in China that fateful summer in Hankow was to preserve his balance, and his unique capacity for distinguishing between appearance and reality. He was a first-class reporter with an approach grounded in fundamental American traditions, so that he never either fell for Communist propaganda or swerved from the line of accurate reporting.

Durdin and Steele, unfortunately, did not go in for being specialists on the Far East. Whereas other correspondents with far less knowledge rushed home to write books about China, neither Durdin nor Steele ever wrote one.

In America, during the 1940's, the union of the friends of the Chinese Communists enjoyed what amounted to a closed shop in the book-reviewing field. Theirs were almost the only views expressed in such important publications as the *New York Times* and *New York Herald Tribune* Sunday book supplements and the *Saturday Review of Literature*—publications which make or break books. (The Sunday *Book Review* supplement of the *New York Times* seems in recent months to have discarded many of its old reviewers in favor of others without Communist sympathies.) If one looks through their back numbers, one finds that it was rare that any book on China was not given to one of a small group of reviewers. Week after week, and year after year, most books on China, and on the Far East, were reviewed by Owen Lattimore, John K. Fairbank, Edgar Snow, Nathaniel Peffer, Theodore White, Annallee Jacoby, Richard Lauterbach, and others with the same point of view.

An outstanding example of the manner in which anti-Communist books were damned, even when written by prominent personages, is the reception of Major General Claire Lee Chennault's *Way of a Fighter* (1949). The *New York Times Book Review* gave its front page to Annallee Jacoby to condemn the hero of the Flying Tigers. Even more remarkable was the treatment accorded John B. Powell's book *My Twenty-Five Years in China* published in 1946. J. B.

Powell was a liberal American of great courage and integrity who as editor of *The China Weekly Review* won a worldwide reputation before the Japanese took Shanghai and imprisoned him. He lost both his feet in consequence and died in 1947 after a long illness. The *New York Times Book Review* editor gave his book to Annallee Jacoby, who damned Powell as a "reactionary" and was contemptuous of his contention that a "red menace" existed in China.

George Creel's *Russia's Race for Asia* was similarly handled. Creel had been head of President Wilson's Committee on Public Information in World War I and is an eminent American. Yet the *Saturday Review of Literature* allowed Edgar Snow to do a highly successful job of damning the book and misrepresenting the viewpoint of the author.

Mr. Creel's book fared no better at the hands of the *New York Times Book Review*. It was there reviewed by Professor Nathaniel Peffer of Columbia University, who has been an unremitting foe of Nationalist China.

In contrast to the condemnation of anti-Communist books, one can note the logrolling by the friends of the Chinese Communists whenever a book on China favorable to the Communists appeared. To cite only a few examples:

The *New York Times Book Review* gave Owen Lattimore's *Solution in Asia* (1945) for review to Edgar Snow. That same year (March 11, 1945) it permitted Edgar Snow to write a full-page eulogy of Harrison Forman's *Report from Red China,* which consisted largely of praise for the Chinese Communists and of views which paralleled their position. Snow praised it for its presentation of the Chinese civil war as "an internal struggle between the Kuomintang one-party regime of Chiang Kai-shek and all the anti-Japanese and antifascist people's organizations—under the general leadership of the Chinese Communist Party."

Another outstanding example of the favorable publicity afforded pro-Communist writers is the treatment of Gunther Stein's *The Challenge of Red China* (1945). Professor Nathaniel Peffer went all out in the *New York Times Book Review* to support Stein's enthusiastic eulogy of Communist China:

> The distinguishing characteristic of Communist China is not ideological, political or economical but psychological. There is something in Communist China that captures the imagination. . . . Emotional radicals, objective intellectuals, neutral correspondents, diplomatic officials, military officers . . . they all come away from Yenan ardent defenders if not enthusiasts.

(In 1949, General MacArthur's Headquarters revealed evidence secured by the Japanese and denied by both parties that Gunther Stein and Agnes Smedley had been Soviet espionage agents. These charges were questioned by the War Department.)

In 1946, as a result of its selection by the Book-of-the-Month Club, *Thunder Out of China,* by Theodore White and Annallee Jacoby, attained very wide distribution. Professor John K. Fairbank, of Harvard, reviewing it for the *New York Times,* praised it for its contention that Communism is not "an uncalled-for conspiratorial subversion." Some idea of the manner in which Teddy White deluded the American people, is best given by quoting his reply to a question addressed to him when he appeared on the Chicago Round Table radio forum on October 27th, 1946. Asked whether he meant that the Chinese Communists are no more controlled by Moscow than the Nationalist Government by Washington, he replied:

> Frankly I should say much less. . . . Since the Communists have no bureau . . . since they are independent, the Russians have no other way of making their influence felt in China except by direct armed intervention. The Russians are tired; they are weary of war; they fought too long. They would not want to assume the burden, which is huge even for us, of stepping into China.

Owen Lattimore gloried in the influence which he and his

disciples had won over American public opinion. Reviewing Israel Epstein's *Unfinished Revolution in China* in the *New York Times* in June 1947, Lattimore wrote:

From Edgar Snow's *Red Star* to Theodore White's and Annallee Jacoby's *Thunder Out of China* the list of names is distinguished. Israel Epstein has without question established a place for himself in that distinguished company. It is noteworthy that the recent and current trend of good books about China, well documented and well written, has been well to the Left of Center.

Note the word "good"—other books on China were simply not "good," and were therefore consigned to limbo.[3]

The role played by the *New York Times* Sunday magazine section equalled that of its Sunday *Book Review*. Not only did the latter, as we have seen, usually give books on China to review to those inclined to take a sympathetic attitude toward the Chinese Communists; rarely if ever did the *New York Times Magazine* publish an article not more or less favorable to the Chinese Communists and hostile to the National Government. One of its preferred writers was Nathaniel Peffer, the Columbia University Professor of International Relations who, as late as November 1950, after the Chinese Communists had attacked the UN forces in Korea, professed himself unconvinced that Peiping was acting in concert with Moscow.

Nathaniel Peffer deserves more than a brief mention. Although his sister was on the editorial board of *Amerasia*, he himself was not directly associated either with that notorious magazine, or with the Institute of Pacific Relations. Nor can he be classified among those suspected of Communist Party membership or affiliations. He is a typical representative of the shortsighted, or deluded liberals, who have never understood the nature of Communism or the Soviet menace, and who therefore imagine that all we have to do to be saved is to sponsor "reforms" among the heathen, and pour out dollars for the relief of less fortunate peoples.

For instance, in an article he wrote for the *New York Times* on October 15, 1950, he said that "the Korean affair" was not mainly a "result of the East West schism" but of poverty which America ought to alleviate. Three or four times in the same article he insists that "what is needed is money," and "the power which financial aid gives" us to put pressure upon "present governments, or those we back to supplant them."

The influence of such economic determinists as Nathaniel Peffer and others like him, who misguide our youth in the universities and delude the public by their articles, is not to be underestimated. Without knowing it they can do as much harm as Communists, if only by propagating false beliefs.

Similarly, with regard to most of the articles published in magazines of large circulation, the friends of the Chinese Communists were able to exert a paramount influence. Mark Gayn (involved in the *Amerasia* espionage case) was *Collier's* correspondent. In spite of Henry Luce's own pronounced support of the National Government, even *Time* and *Life* built up the reputations of such champions of the Chinese Communists as Teddy White and Richard Lauterbach, both of whom were their valued correspondents.

Harper's and *The Atlantic* swelled the chorus. They rarely if ever published articles on the Far East unfavorable to the Communist cause. The *Reader's Digest* stood almost alone among magazines of mass circulation. It dared to publish articles giving the other side, as the one written by Max Eastman and John B. Powell in the June 1945 issue entitled "The Fate of the World Is at Stake in China." (In this connection, it is of interest to note that among the documents presented to the Tydings Committee is a letter from John Stewart Service to a friend in which he wrote: "My breakfast was ruined this morning by reading J. B. Powell and Max Eastman in the *Reader's Digest*. What a stinker!")

I need hardly mention the *New Republic* and the *Nation,* which in spite of their small circulation exercise a profound influence on American opinion. They, of course, were for the Chinese Communists from the beginning. This was only to be expected in view of their soft attitude toward Soviet terror and Soviet aggression. In contrast to these "liberal" weeklies, the *New Leader,* an anti-totalitarian liberal weekly magazine, has been unswervingly clear-headed from the start regarding the Communists in China as well as Russia.

Most of the institutes and associations which profess to enlighten the American public on foreign affairs went along with the pro-Communist tide. The Foreign Policy Association, like the Institute of Pacific Relations, had little room in its publications for any scholars and writers who did not favor the Chinese Communists.

The close connections maintained between the Institute of Pacific Relations and its offshoot, *Amerasia,* the State Department, the Office of War Information, the *Nation,* the *New Republic,* the Foreign Policy Association, individual professors and friends of the Chinese Communists, authors, and journalists, were similar to the interlocking directorates by means of which Big Business maintains monopolies that cannot be broken up by the law.[4] This powerful combine exerted paramount influence on the press and radio and on lecture platforms. It was able to spread the gospel according to Mao Tse-tung by eliminating the competition of the few anti-Communists who dared to oppose it.

During the war one could point to evidence of a State Department—IPR (Institute of Pacific Relations) axis, so close were the personal relations between them, so identical their points of view and the policies they advocated, and so frequently were IPR members recruited to serve in agencies affiliated to the State Department, such as the OWI and Foreign Economic Administration. There were also occasional reverse interchanges of personnel in which State Department officials resigned to become leading lights of the IPR. For instance, in 1943 Philip Jessup (who is today United States Ambassador at large), resigned from the chairmanship of the American Council of the IPR to serve in the State Department, while Lawrence Salisbury resigned from the State Department (where he had been Assistant to the Chief of the Far Eastern Division), to become editor of the IPR's fortnightly publication, *Far Eastern Survey*. In this latter capacity Mr. Salisbury inaugurated the virulent anti-Kuomintang and pro-Chinese-Communist campaign, which to a large extent paralleled that of the *Daily Worker,* the *Nation,* the *New Republic,* the Foreign Policy Association, Walter Lippmann, and a host of other publicists and journalists. Meanwhile, Mr. Jessup apparently took over from Salisbury the propagating of the same views inside the State Department.[5]

Such interchanges of personnel meant merely that one member of what might be termed the "Society of Friends of the Chinese Communists" took over from another the public, as against the official, promulgation of the myth that the Chinese Communists were not "real Communists" but nice liberal agrarian reformers and democrats whom America ought to support.

Salisbury's own writings and most of the articles published in *Far Eastern Survey* under his editorship paralleled those of his former colleagues in the State Department, such as John Davies, John Stewart Service, and Raymond Paul Ludden, whose reports in the White Paper have already been quoted. Salisbury in the April 25, 1945, issue of *Far Eastern Survey* used precisely the same arguments as Service and Ludden, also urging America to treat China like Yugoslavia. He asserted that the Chinese Communists are "liberty loving" and argued that, if Chiang Kai-shek continued to refuse to embrace them, these democratic peace-loving liberals would be "pushed into the arms of the Soviet Union."

Since this was the period when the influence of the Friends of the Soviet Union and the champions of the Chinese Communists was at its height, it was hardly surprising that many well-known columnists and commentators, and editors followed the IPR-State Department line.

Walter Lippmann, for instance, advocated "a united political front" of Soviet Russia, Britain, and the United States to force a reorganization of the Chinese National Government on "a broader democratic basis" by inclusion of the Communists. He too wished us to abandon China to the Communists. For he wrote that "the formula for China is clearly indicated and in principle like that made at Yalta for Poland."

The *New York Herald Tribune*'s foreign editor from 1944-48 was Joseph Barnes.[6] It is therefore hardly surprising that the *Tribune* editorials in this era also urged the United States to show "the same degree of sanity" in its China policy, as President Roosevelt had displayed at Yalta with regard to Poland!

It would require a whole book to present all the evidence available concerning the influence of Chinese Communist sympathizers, not only in Washington, but all over America. I have mentioned most of the better known professors and writers.

Before proceeding to mention the names of a few of the minor characters who played their part in deluding the American public on the subject of Communist China, I must here deal with the case of Philip Jessup who, following years of work at the Institute of Pacific Relations, was appointed to the State Department and became our "roving Ambassador" to the Far East in 1950. The facts concerning his record were brought before the Senate and the Tydings Committee by Senator McCarthy, but have not prevented his continuing to enjoy the confidence of the Administration. Nor were they fully publicized in the press.

Jessup was closely associated with Frederick Vanderbilt Field—the angel of many Communist fronts who has never denied that he is a Communist—and with E. C. Carter, Owen

Lattimore, Gunther Stein, Bisson, Anna Louise Strong, and other stalwart supporters of the Chinese Communist cause. Under Jessup's direction, in July 1943, the IPR started its virulent smear campaign against Nationalist China and its false representation of the Chinese Communists as liberal agrarian reformers whom we ought to support. Jessup can in fact almost claim the distinction of having originated the myth of democratic Communist China, since it was while he was Research Director of the IPR that *Pacific Affairs* and the *Far Eastern Survey* started their propaganda campaign on behalf of the enemy we are now fighting in Korea.

In his bill of indictment against Philip Jessup, Senator McCarthy, in 1950, produced evidence that the State Department's roving Ambassador and adviser on Far Eastern policy had been affiliated with several outright Communist fronts. Jessup was shown to have been a sponsor, both in November 1944 and again in May 1946, of dinner meetings of the American-Russian Institute, listed in 1948 by the Attorney General as a Communist front, and earlier so designated by the Committee on Un-American Activities. Among the other sponsors were many well-known Communists and fellow travelers, so it is difficult to believe that Mr. Jessup was not aware of the company he was keeping. Moreover, he was also a member of the Faculty Advisory Board of the American Law Students Association, which was affiliated both with the League against War and Fascism and with the American Youth Congress, both of which had been designated as early as 1942 by Attorney General Biddle as Communist fronts.

Mr. Jessup was also a sponsor of the meeting held at the Raleigh Hotel in Washington in May 1939 to protest the registration and fingerprinting of aliens—a conference enthusiastically supported by the Communist press. In 1940 he was a member of the board of the sponsors of the "National Committee for Democratic Rights"—an organization cited as subversive by the Un-American Activities Committee—whose chairman was the notorious Communist fellow traveler Professor Franz Boas (now deceased).

Jessup was one of the signers of the letter published in the *New York Times* on February 16, 1946, urging the United States to suspend the manufacture of atomic bombs, in order that the discussions with Russia should proceed in an "atmosphere of good faith and confidence." Senator McCarthy furnished a good deal of other evidence concerning Philip Jessup's judgment, including the fact that he appeared as a character witness for the defense in the trial of Alger Hiss.

Among the lesser lights who successfully excused Soviet tyranny and extolled the virtues of the Chinese Communists were the following influential writers and lecturers:

Maxwell Stewart, an editor of the *Nation,* and also a frequent contributor to IPR publications. In 1944 he wrote a pamphlet for the IPR called *Wartime China,* in which he said that the Chinese Communists were a unique species which attracted all "progressive and peace-loving Chinese."

T. A. Bisson, of the Foreign Policy Association, was a leading exponent of the theory that Communist China should "more accurately be called democratic China." Bisson, on the editorial board of *Amerasia,* was an editor of *Pacific Affairs,* as well as an official of the Foreign Policy Association. He also contributed articles to *Soviet Russia Today,* and he was one of the four hundred "intellectuals" who, in August 1939, signed the famous letter whitewashing the Soviet Union a few days before the Stalin-Hitler Pact. Bisson acted as the main link between the Foreign Policy Association and the Institute of Pacific Relations. Besides contributing articles and advice to the latter he was on the research staff of the FPA, which was directed by Vera Micheles Dean, a well-known apologist for the Soviet Union. Bisson was employed as an economist by the Board of Economic Warfare 1942–43. In 1943 he became a member of the International Secretariat of the IPR, and in 1945 he was appointed adviser to General

MacArthur in Japan, where he proved a hindrance in the implementation of a liberal anti-Communist policy.

Anna Louise Strong, the Soviet propagandist who was expelled from the Soviet Union in 1949, but even then continued to write along Communist lines, was a favorite of the IPR, which frequently published her articles extolling the Chinese Communist "Peoples Democracy."

Richard Watts, Jr., who during the war was head of the News Division of the Office of War Information in Chungking, subsequently became a member of the Board of Directors of the "Committee for a Democratic Far Eastern Policy," which has been designated by the Attorney General as a Communist front.

Foster Rhea Dulles who also had a job with the OWI in China, contributes to *Spotlight,* the organ for the "Committee for a Democratic Far Eastern Policy."

Michael Greenberg, another *Spotlight* contributor, was Owen Lattimore's successor as editor of *Pacific Affairs* but transferred to the Foreign Economic Administration in 1942, and subsequently worked in Lauchlin Currie's office. Greenberg had come to the United States in 1939 from England where his sister Esther was the Lancashire organizer of the Communist Party.

William T. Stone, who is today Vice Chairman of the "Interdepartmental Committee on Scientific and Cultural Cooperation" at the State Department, and who formerly served with the Board of Economic Warfare and the FEA, was a member of the editorial board of *Amerasia.*

Gunther Stein, a German refugee who became a British citizen, was a frequent contributor to the IPR publications, prior to a report from General MacArthur's headquarters in 1949 which maintained, even though Stein denied the charges, that he had been a Soviet spy.

The above facts constitute only a preliminary sketch of the evidence available concerning the benevolent attitude of the Institute of Pacific Relations toward the friends of the Chinese Communists.

It is particularly important to note how many "experts" on the Far East the IPR supplied to government agencies during the war and afterward, and how close was its connection with the State Department and the minor government agencies which the State Department controlled or influenced.

Four IPR staff members worked for the China Section of UNRRA. Three were employed as "research" workers on Japanese reconstruction at MacArthur's headquarters. William L. Holland, a prominent IPR official, was appointed to head the Office of War Information in China. Benjamin Kizer, the Spokane lawyer who was Vice President of the IPR, was appointed head of UNRRA in China, where I found him strongly favorable in his view of the Chinese Communists.

The United States Government bought 750,000 IPR pamphlets for distribution in the Pacific and Asiatic theaters of war, thus giving its official blessing to the pro-Communist views of this organization.

Although most Americans have probably never heard of the Institute of Pacific Relations, even their children have been influenced by its propaganda. For over a million copies were sold of its Special Series for youngsters, published jointly by the IPR and the Webster Company of St. Louis. And many an editorial writer, ignorant concerning the Far East, has made use of the material furnished him by the IPR which he has had every reason to trust on account of the eminent names which appear on its masthead.

Sheppard Marley, in an article in the December 1946 issue of *Plain Talk*, quotes the following advertisement in the "Personal" column of the *Saturday Review of Literature:*

Long on curiosity—short on time? IPR popular pamphlets make you a scintillating conversationalist on the Far East. You can deftly discuss everything from Australian slang to the problems of China and the Philippines. Send for a list of Institute of Pacific Relations pamphlets today. Box 939-K.

It is, unfortunately, all too true that a synthetic "deftness" in discussing Far Eastern problems could be acquired by reading *Pacific Affairs* and *Far Eastern Survey*. The material presented in these IPR publications had a veneer of scholarship. Only an expert on Communism can easily detect the pro-Communist slant of the majority of the articles they published.

The American Council of the IPR is so conspicuously the controlling unit of this supposedly international organization, that one frequently and naturally refers to "the IPR" when meaning the American Council. Some three years ago the International Secretariat of the IPR weeded out most of its undisguised Communist members. The British branch of the IPR had before then also sent Communist sympathizers to represent it at international meetings, notably Gunther Stein. Owing to the fact that the members of the international body are scattered from Australia and New Zealand to the Netherlands and Britain, the American Council constitutes the main and most influential unit. And in the American Council, the real power is vested in an Executive Committee of the Board of Trustees, since there is hardly ever a meeting of the membership. Up to two years ago the four most influential members of the Executive Committee were Edward C. Carter, Frederick Vanderbilt Field, Kate L. Mitchell (the Buffalo heiress who was involved in the *Amerasia* case), and Owen Lattimore.

The IPR is today under the direction of a new secretary. It now occasionally publishes anti-Communist articles, but its contributors still include many old friends of the Chinese Communists. The trouble is that the foundations and individual businessmen who contribute the money to maintain the IPR have neither the necessary expert knowledge of Communism to detect the cloven hoof which proves the existence of Communists on its staff, or the time to read and perceive the significance of many of the articles published by the Institute of Pacific Relations.

If one seeks for an explanation why Communist sympathizers were able to exert so strong an influence on the American press and public, one must take into account the mixed motives which determine attitudes and actions. In many cases the primary impulse which impelled newspapermen, authors, and Foreign Service officers to espouse the Chinese Communist cause may have been sympathy for the Chinese people, and a romantic faith in Communist professions and promises. Few Americans understood that the miserable condition of the Chinese people was due to technological backwardness and ancient traditions, aggravated by war. Nor did most of them realize that Communism could not cure the ills of China, but would inevitably lead to even worse poverty and the extinction of liberty. Such a man, for instance, was Evans Carlson, the simple soldier who had been beguiled into believing that the Communists were "true Christians."

Whatever excuses can be found for the misguided and ignorant "liberals," none can be found for the careerists, who were activated neither by humanitarian sentiment, nor loyalty to anything but their own interests. Today they condemn Stalin and the Communists with the same fervor as they used to praise him during the era when it was profitable to be pink. If they openly renounced their former support of Communist tyranny, there would be no reason to include them in the roster of names of those who deceived the American public. But some of the most eminent of them have reversed themselves without a word of apology to their readers. Edgar Snow, for instance, had an article in the *Saturday Evening Post* in October 1950 called "The Venomous Dr. Vyshinsky," in which he contradicted everything he used to write before American public opinion changed.

The careerists in the government and the press naturally

never took the risk of joining the Communist Party even if they believed it was destined to win. Time-servers, lacking principles or integrity, are always safe. Today they enjoy adopting a superior attitude toward the ex-Communists who openly joined the Party with a false concept of its aims and methods and left it when they became convinced Communism is a reactionary force.

Concrete evidence of Soviet espionage is more convincing than any amount of proof of the Communist sympathies of State Department officials, employees of other government agencies, journalists and professors, and IPR and FPA members. The *Amerasia* espionage case is therefore of primary importance. It affords unassailable proof of the existence of a Communist conspiracy which included government employees who did not scruple to hand over secret documents to Stalin's agents.

On June 7, 1945, nine weeks before the first atomic bomb was dropped on Japan, the FBI arrested six persons whom it accused of violating the Espionage Act. These six persons were: John Stewart Service and Emmanuel Larsen of the State Department; Lieutenant Andrew Roth, liaison officer between the Office of Naval Intelligence and the State Department; and Philip Jacob Jaffe and Kate Louise Mitchell, who were both editors of *Amerasia,* a magazine published by a group whose members were nearly all also closely connected with the Institute of Pacific Relations. The sixth person arrested in the group was Mark Gayn, a well-known journalist mentioned above who had contributed many articles to *Collier's* and other national magazines, as well as to *Amerasia.*

The FBI revealed that it had found a hundred files in the *Amerasia* offices, containing top secret and highly confidential papers stolen from the State Department, from the War and Navy departments, the OSS and the OWI. It also found a large photo-copying department, which could not possibly have been required by *Amerasia* for publishing purposes, and was almost certainly used for the photostating of stolen papers for transmission to Moscow. The secret papers found in *Amerasia*'s offices concerned such subjects as the Navy's schedule and targets for the bombing of Japan; the disposition of the Japanese fleet; a detailed report showing the complete disposition and strength of the units of the Chinese Nationalist armies, with their exact locations and the names of their commanders.

According to the Department of Justice statement at the time the documents recovered by the FBI included "originals and copies of papers from the Departments of State, War and Navy, the Office of Strategic Services, Office of War Information and Federal Communications Commission," and "their security classification ranged from 'restricted' to 'top secret'."

Since the Scripps-Howard papers, in particular, gave a full account in 1950 of the *Amerasia* case, and published a pamphlet by Frederick Woltman on the subject, I shall give here only a brief outline of the case.

In February 1945 Archbold Van Beuren, an OSS official, happening to glance through the pages of *Amerasia,* was startled to find an article virtually identical with a secret OSS report sent to the State Department two months before. Being already worried about serious leaks of confidential information, Van Beuren went at once to Frank Brooks Bielaski, director of undercover investigations for OSS. Bielaski decided to raid the offices of *Amerasia,* an obscure but influential magazine devoted to propagating the Communist cause. He did not apply for a search warrant for fear that the *Amerasia* staff might get wind of the investigation and destroy the evidence. When, on the night of March 11, 1945, OSS representatives entered the *Amerasia* offices, after picking the lock, they found the place "literally strewn with confidential Government documents."

The desk of the editor, Philip Jaffe, was covered with

originals and freshly made photos of a mass of secret documents, some of which were so confidential they were marked "Not to be shown to the OWI."

According to Mr. Bielaski, "every one of them bore the stamp that possession of these documents was a violation of the Espionage Act."

Early next morning, Major General William J. Donovan, head of OSS, having been informed of the discovery, telephoned to Secretary of State Stettinius and arranged to see him at once. Stettinius agreed with Donovan that the matter should be turned over to the United States Attorney General, in order that a grand jury proceeding be started. Instead, the FBI was put onto the case. For three months seventy-five FBI agents worked collecting evidence in strictest secrecy. They kept a close watch on Philip Jaffe, the editor and publisher of *Amerasia,* and on his associate, Kate Mitchell. They observed Jaffe's meetings with Andrew Roth and his wife, Emmanuel Larsen, Mark Gayn, and John Stewart Service. They saw documents being passed to the *Amerasia* editor.

On May 29 the FBI laid its evidence before the Justice Department. The six suspects were arrested on charges of conspiring to violate the Espionage Statutes by theft of confidential documents. But, two days later, the FBI was told the case must be held in abeyance until the conclusion of the United Nations conference in San Francisco, the reason given being fear of offending the Soviet Government.

Thanks to Mr. Julius Holmes, an Assistant Secretary of State, the facts were laid before President Truman, who at once ordered the Department of Justice to stop delaying the arrests. The FBI thereupon entered the *Amerasia* offices, duly provided with a search warrant, and seized 1,700 secret Government documents which it found there. Jaffe, Gayn, Service, Larsen, Roth and Kate Mitchell were arrested.

Promptly the Communist press and its "liberal" friends went into action. Many newspapers and radio commentators took up the defense of the accused. Jaffe and Miss Mitchell got a favorable response to their statement to the press that "The Red-baiting character of this case is scandalous and often libelous."

Mark Gayn proclaimed that "freedom of the press," not espionage, was the issue. Some commentators accused Joseph Grew, at that time still head of the Far Eastern Division of the State Department, of attempting to "terrorize and intimidate" his critics.

Either the clamor on the left had its effect, or the defendants were connected with persons in Government upon whom they could exert the necessary pressure to stop prosecution. On August 13, J. Raymond Walsh, a notorious joiner of Communist fronts, said on the radio that Miss Mitchell "has some very powerful connections, which probably led the State Department people to wish they had never heard of her," and that Service's arrest "brought some exceedingly powerful people within the Government to his defense."

Miss Mitchell, Gayn and Service were not indicted by the grand jury. Jaffe, Larsen and Roth were indicted, but *not* on the original espionage charge. Instead they were accused only of "conspiracy to embezzle, steal and purloin" Government property. At their trial the government prosecutor failed even to mention Jaffe's established Communist record. Nor did he inform the judge concerning the pro-Communist character of *Amerasia*. He was silent concerning the evidence dug up by the FBI.

The government attorney, Mr. Hitchcock, told the judge he needed "less than five minutes" to state his case. He did not even suggest that the material found in the *Amerasia* offices had been stolen for any disloyal purpose. The defense attorney was permitted to get away with the statement that Mr. Jaffe had "transgressed the law" only "from an excess of journalistic zeal." When the judge suggested that the probation officer investigate and report—which would have meant examination of the FBI's report on the case—Mr.

Hitchcock told the court he hoped the case could be disposed of that day and not be delayed by sending a probation officer to New York.

Indeed the prosecutor appeared to be almost as anxious as the defense attorney to let Jaffe off lightly, for he said:

> The use to which they [the stolen documents] were put was, as I understand it, largely background material that Mr. Jaffe in the conduct of his *Amerasia* magazine used to assist him in publishing articles and preparing arguments that would lend to its weight and, perhaps, its circulation. The magazine, we know as a matter of fact, was a losing proposition financially.

Asked for a recommendation, the government attorney proposed "the imposition of no jail sentence but that a substantial fine be imposed."

The judge was not told the contents of the stolen documents by the prosecutor. With the defense and the prosecution agreeing to hush up the case, it was hardly surprising that the judge commiserated with Jaffe, saying:

> I regret, Mr. Jaffe, that you in your zeal to carry on your work, which was evidently for a trustworthy purpose, that you were misled to do these things which of course did tend to break down the fidelity of Government employes and officials in the performance of their work. (I have here quoted from the account of the trial given by Frederick Woltman).

Mr. Hitchcock, the "prosecutor" in the case, resigned from the Justice Department fifteen months later to become a member of the law firm of Kenefick, Cooke, Mitchell, Bess & Letchworth. The James Mitchell of the said firm is an uncle of Kate Louise Mitchell who was never brought to trial.

The charge against Roth was dismissed on motion of the Government.

Emmanuel Larsen was fined $500, which Jaffe paid for him. Jaffe himself was let off with a $2500 fine.

The case involving Service, Roth, and other government employees was buried, and there was no further investigation. John Stewart Service was reinstated in the State Department.

Darkness descended after the one flash of lightning which had revealed the existence of a Communist spy ring in Washington. It was not until 1950, when Senator McCarthy made his sensational charges, that the *Amerasia* case again became news, and was brought to the attention of a public which five years earlier had been fed too long on pro-Soviet propaganda to be greatly concerned with the evidence of a Communist conspiracy. But again, thanks to the failure of the Tydings Committee to conduct a real investigation, the truth about Communist influence on America's Far Eastern policy, as revealed by the *Amerasia* case, was obscured.

8. Senator McCarthy's Charges— and the Tydings Committee

HAD IT NOT BEEN for Senator McCarthy, the evidence of Communist influence in the determination of U.S. foreign policy might have remained buried in the annexes to the White Paper, and the forgotten files on the *Amerasia* espionage case.

For years Congressman Walter Judd, Senator Knowland, and Senator Bridges, and a few other far-sighted representatives of the American people, had been hammering away, with little effect, at the Administration's futile and self-defeating China policy. The Un-American Activities Committee and Congressmen such as Nixon and Mundt (now Senators), and Taber and Dondero, had endeavored to expose the existence of Communist sympathizers in government. But none of them had succeeded in awakening sufficient public interest to make a dent in the complacent front presented by the State Department.

Mounting popular dismay at the dangerous situation in which America now finds herself, combined with the conviction of Alger Hiss, helped McCarthy to succeed where others had failed. By 1950 the public was ready to listen when presented with facts which indicated that the influence of Soviet sympathizers during and after the war had determined the disastrous course of American foreign policy.

The Wisconsin Senator, who had fought with the Marines in World War II, knew that he would be smeared and his aims misrepresented, but went ahead in his frontal assault on the State Department. Those who criticized him for having exaggerated Communist influence in determining American foreign policy were unaware of the reality of the danger he sought to expose. It was probably necessary to paint a terrifying picture on a large canvas without much attention to detail or fine shading, if at long last the American people were to be stirred out of their apathy concerning treason in high places. McCarthy brandished an axe instead of using a scalpel, and his "indelicate" methods were displeasing to many. But it cannot be denied that he performed the vitally necessary task of awakening the American people to the clear and present danger to the Republic constituted by the Communist conspiracy in our midst. Until McCarthy started his campaign, Communist sympathizers in government employment had found little difficulty in getting themselves cleared by the Loyalty Review Board, headed by Seth Richardson.[1]

It is legitimate to fear the danger to civil liberties inherent in any attempt to expose subversive influences in government. But McCarthy himself showed he was aware of this danger when he strenuously opposed making public the names of those he suspected until they had had a chance to refute the charges against them.[2]

McCarthy did not demand a Senate investigation of his charges until after President Truman had refused his plea, in his letter of February 11, that he "demand that Acheson give you and the proper Congressional Committee the names and complete record on all of those who were placed in the department by Alger Hiss, and all of those who were listed by your [Loyalty] Board as bad security risks because of their Communist connections."

When President Truman failed to respond, McCarthy

brought up his charges on the Senate floor. He refused to give the names of his list of eighty-one suspects in government employment, concerning whom he had some evidence of Communist Party membership or Communist connections. On February 20, 1950 he said on the Senate floor that the evidence in the files of the eighty-one "ranged all the way from being bad security risks to very dangerous individuals." He went on to say that perhaps some of these individuals would be able to produce facts to offset the material in the files and "show that they were actually loyal employees," and that therefore it would be "unfair to name names in public" before the individuals had a chance to answer his charges in executive session.

He was overruled by Lucas, the Democratic Party Senate leader, who insisted that the names be made public, saying: "I want to remain here until he names them."

On April 5, 1950, Senator Hickenlooper of Iowa defended McCarthy from the charge of having smeared innocent people by reminding the Senate of what had occurred. He said:

As a member of the subcommittee of the Committee on Foreign Relations now engaged in the inquiry into the charges of the Senator from Wisconsin, I should like to say that on the day on which the Senator from Wisconsin made his speech at some length on the floor of the Senate, in which he referred to certain cases by number . . . the Senator from Wisconsin repeatedly stated and restated on the floor of the Senate that he did not want to make the names public, that he would not tell the names to the Senate in public; and, time after time, the Senator from Illinois, the majority leader, rose to demand that he give the names in public, so the whole country would know who the people were that were suspected.

The Senator from Wisconsin repeatedly said, "No, I will not make them public." The Senator from Kentucky, Mr. Withers, rose and said he wanted to see the list of names. The Senator from Wisconsin said, "Come to my office in the morning and I will show you the names." The Senator from Kentucky said,

"Can I make them public? I intend to make them public if I see them." The Senator from Wisconsin said, "No, if you are going to make them public, I shall not give you the names."

The Congressional Record is replete with such statements on the question of the publicity of the names.

It is a matter of fact also that the junior Senator from Massachusetts and I, both at the first executive meeting of the subcommittee, suggested and proposed the procedure, that the subcommittee meet in executive session, call the Senator from Wisconsin before it, and ask him to disclose the names in private, together with whatever information he had in connection with the names; but the majority of the subcommittee said no, this must be brought out in public. So they held their first hearing, requiring the Senator from Wisconsin to come, in public, to name the names. . . .

I should like to say also that so far as I am concerned, while we did not have the machinery to set up a court of inquiry such as the Canadian spy-ring case called for, we did propose and urge that an inquiry in secrecy without naming names be made with the facts collected. But we were overruled, and the Senator from Wisconsin was required, or requested, to come before the committee in public hearing, with klieg lights, television, and all the rest of the fanfare of such an emotional occasion, there to bring out his cases, name names, and produce facts.[3]

As a result of the charges of Senator McCarthy, the Senate, on February 22, 1950, appointed a sub-committee of its Foreign Relations Committee to: "Investigate whether there are employees in the State Department disloyal to the United States."[4] Senator Millard E. Tydings, Democrat of Maryland was appointed Chairman. The other Democratic members of the Committee were Theodore Francis Green of Rhode Island and Brien McMahon of Connecticut. Republican members were Bourke B. Hickenlooper of Iowa and Henry Cabot Lodge, Jr., of Massachusetts.

McCarthy asked Tydings to conduct hearings in Executive Session so that he would not be forced to publicize the name of any suspect able to prove his, or her, innocence. Tydings, supported by McMahon and Green, refused, and insisted on open hearings. It was, therefore, the Democratic majority in the Senate and on the Committee which insisted on publicizing the names of the accused before they had had a chance to answer McCarthy's charges.

McCarthy's critics have given him no credit, either, for his willingness to admit his mistakes or his wrong choice of words. For instance, on March 30, 1950, he modified his original statement that Owen Lattimore was the chief Soviet agent in America, when he said:

> I fear in the case of Lattimore, I may have perhaps placed too much stress on the question of whether or not he has been an espionage agent. In view of his position of tremendous power in the State Department as the "architect" of our Far Eastern policy, the more important aspect of his case deals with his aims and what he advocates; whether his aims are American aims or whether they coincide with the aims of Soviet Russia. Therefore, forgetting for the time being any question of membership in the Communist Party or participation in espionage, I would like to deal briefly with what this man himself advocates and what he believes in.
> It does not take any counter-espionage staff to determine what he stands for. It does not take an investigative group to determine whether he favors communism over our form of democracy. All it takes is a detailed study of his voluminous writings.

Such corrections, like his amended figures of the number of Communists, or Communist sympathizers, in government, concerning whom he had proof of Communist sympathy, far from being accepted as evidence of his *bona fides,* were used only to discredit him, and as an excuse for refusing to examine his main charges.

It seemed as if his critics thought that if they could show that the Wisconsin Senator was himself uncertain whether there were 205, or 81, or "only" 57 subversives in the State Department, they would have proved that there are none.[5] His original accusation, in his Wheeling, West Virginia, speech, that there were 205 "security risks" among State Department personnel, was based on former Secretary of State Byrnes' statement to Congressman Sabbath that nineteen persons had been discharged out of a total of 224 suspects. Nineteen from 224 leaves 205, so McCarthy was justified in the first figure he presented. The fact that the Senator could not, unaided, produce conclusive proof concerning all those suspected of Communist affiliations, although he managed to dig out evidence first concerning 57 and later about 81 of them, in no wise disproves his charges.

From the outset of the hearings Senator Tydings would not permit the Wisconsin Senator to cross-examine witnesses, and excluded him from some of the executive hearings. The minority counsel, Robert Morris, was denied the right to cross-question witnesses in any of the Committee's open hearings. Several of McCarthy's witnesses were not called. And, as will be shown later in this chapter, Senator Tydings in his conduct of the investigation showed an evident partiality for witnesses who appeared to disprove McCarthy's charges, and a prejudice against those who supported them.

Before turning to the proceedings of the Tydings Committee, it is necessary to analyze, and attempt to explain, the widely voiced disapproval, or contempt, of McCarthy in the press and on the radio.

It is not hard to understand why "McCarthyism" came to be regarded as a synonym for Reaction among the past and present friends of the Soviet Union, champions of the Chinese Communists, and other apologists and innocents. Those who supported the shortsighted policies which have delivered so large a part of the world to the Soviet dictator are naturally not receptive to attempts to expose their former friends and their own former complicity or obtuseness. McCarthy had pulled too many skeletons out of too many closets for their comfort. Too many politicians, Republicans as well as Democrats, and too many editorial writers, columnists, and commentators, had gone along with the "Love Russia" school of thought, to be easy in their minds. Many people in all parties wanted only to lock up once more, as quickly as possible, the evidence of their past errors which McCarthy had uncovered. And since it was obviously impossible for McCarthy to prove most of his charges without a large staff of investigators, or access to the FBI files (which was denied to the Senate Investigating Committee), it was all too easy to accuse him of having made wild and unsubstantiated charges.

The reasons why the chorus of disapproval of McCarthy also included the voices of conservatives and anti-Communist liberals are more complex. Among these divergent elements some suspected McCarthy's motives and condemned his methods for fear he would give a bad name to all anti-Communists by what they considered to be his imitation of the Communist smear technique. Others were just timid, knowing from experience that anyone who attempts to expose Communist subversion is likely to be smeared as a "Fascist," or at least as a Red-Baiter and a "tool of Wall Street."

The basic reason for the contemptuous hostility displayed toward McCarthy by many liberal intellectuals is no doubt their failure to appreciate the reality of the danger which the Communist conspiracy constitutes. Those who look backwards are more concerned to defend every iota of our political and intellectual freedoms than to apprehend those who would destroy all our liberties.

The problem of preserving freedom of speech and opinion, while rooting out the Communists whose aim is the establishment of tyranny, is a very difficult one. It cannot be solved simply by ignoring the Communist danger, as certain writers would have us do.[6]

America is divided by the controversy between those who would sacrifice our security in order temporarily to preserve unabridged liberty, and those whose primary concern is the clear and present danger to both our constitutional liberties and our national existence, which requires that we limit the rights of the enemies of freedom.

In the country at large, where neither the influence of the doctrinnaire champions of suicidal libertarianism, nor the unrealistic arguments of ivory-tower liberals and of Communist sympathizers, nor the fears of timid conservatives, nor an appreciation of the fine distinction between traitors and their collaborators, had much effect on public opinion, McCarthy was, generally, applauded. Native common sense had led to the conviction that our loss of the peace, and the prospect of a third world war, proved that something was seriously wrong in Washington. So when McCarthy said that the present insecurity of the United States is the result of Communist influence in high places, many people became convinced he was right, or that his charges ought at least to be fully investigated.

It should not be ignored that those who pose as martyrs, or the defenders of martyrs, are themselves most guilty of having smeared anti-Communists as "Fascists" in the days when it was fashionable to be pro-Soviet. Also, a careful perusal of the evidence McCarthy presented—inadequate as it necessarily was in many cases—shows that, while he may have mistaken some fools for villains, he accused no one concerning whom there was not some evidence of Communist sympathies.

Those whom McCarthy accused and those who sympathized with them were successful in obscuring the vital distinction between the rules of evidence established to protect those accused in a court of law and the criteria which must be applied with regard to security risks. The Constitution safeguards individual rights and freedoms, but it does not give anyone an inalienable right to government employment, no matter what his antecedents and associations may be. Unless a state has the right to demand loyalty from its public servants, it must soon cease to exist. So that whereas the concept of guilt by association is rightly regarded as a perversion of justice, it is absurd to insist that no matter how questionable the associations of a government employee, or how manifestly disloyal his conduct, he is entitled to continue to hold a position of trust. For example, whereas it would be unjust to condemn a bank clerk to prison merely because he has associated with thieves, it is only common prudence not to give him the key of the safe.

In his indictment of Philip Jessup, Senator McCarthy made clear the vital distinction between "guilt by association," and "security risk by association," when he said:

Since the beginning of this inquiry I have noted that there are those who contend that membership in communist front organizations and association with communists, is not a serious matter. There are sincere people who are disturbed because they think this is an attempt to establish guilt by association. They forget that we are dealing here with extremely sensitive positions where the individual has access to top secret material, the disclosure of which might well shove us into, or cause us even to lose, a war. They forget that it is not a question of guilt by association, but a question of bad security risk by association.

I cannot emphasize too strongly that a naive or gullible person who associates with the wrong people constantly, and thereby discloses—perhaps even unknowingly—secret information, has done the country the same damage as the party agent who divulges or obtains the same information.

It was precisely those self-styled liberals who condemned McCarthy out of hand for having applied the principle of "guilt by association" to government employees who had been most in favor of this principle when it was applied to the defeated Germans and Japanese. None of them had protested, and most of them had approved, the Administration's instructions to our Military Government in Germany, in 1945, to regard all Germans as deserving punishment for the crimes of the Nazis, and to apply the severest penalties to all who had in any way been associated with the Nazis, or related by marriage or birth to a Nazi.

Our "Law of Liberation from National Socialism," as our denazification decree was called, penalized not only all persons who had been members of associations affiliated with the Nazi Party (i.e., Nazi "fronts"), but also the wives and children of Nazis. The principle of guilt by association was thus made the law of the land in the conquered territories. Yet of the "liberal" commentators, columnists, and politicians, who today insist that no one should come under suspicion on account of his association with Communists, not one, so far as I know, ever raised his voice to condemn our "denazification" decrees. Forgetting that liberty is founded on the concept of equality before the law, they are in favor of a different set of laws for those they hate and for those they like.

In the case of those whom McCarthy named, the question was simply one of deciding whether or not their records proved them fit to be employed in government agencies. It was not necessary to prove that they were "card carrying" Communist Party members. If they had allowed themselves to be duped into serving Stalin's interests, they are obviously not good "security risks."

Had the Administration desired to protect the innocent and expose the guilty, the evidence in the FBI files would not have been withheld from the Senate Committee appointed to investigate McCarthy's charges. Nor would both the Democratic and Republican Counselors of the Tydings Committee have been denied the right to read the State Department files. Not only were the Tydings Committee Senators who were permitted to view these files forbidden to make notes concerning what they found,[7] the files concerning Lattimore, Service, Jessup, and others who were the main target of McCarthy's accusation, were kept secret by Executive order.

It was manifestly impossible for McCarthy to provide proof of all his charges in face of the Administration's determination to keep secret the evidence which would prove, or disprove, them. And such evidence as McCarthy was able to dig up, single-handed, together with that produced by his witnesses, was obscured by inadequate, or prejudiced, reporting in the press. For instance, most newspapers and radio commentators failed to report the main evidence he produced concerning Lattimore, Jessup, Service, and others, in his carefully documented speeches to the Senate on March 30 and June 2, 1950.

It may be that most of the reporters assigned to the job were not prejudiced but simply did not understand and appreciate the significance of the evidence presented. Generally, newspaper men are assigned to a job because of their ability to obtain "spot news," and write it up well. Few have the time or special interest to undertake the hard task of studying and summarizing evidence. However, Charles A. Hazen, editor of the Shreveport *Times*, suggested at the November 1950 meeting of Associated Press managing editors that the Communist-influenced Newspaper Guild was largely responsible for the prejudiced reports of McCarthy's charges and the proceedings of the Tydings Committee. With regard to my own testimony on May 1, 1950, I found that no news agency referred to a single one of the quotations from Lattimore's writings which I presented to the Tydings Committee. The reporters were able to describe my appearance, my hat, and other completely irrelevant details, but they either would not, or could not, report my argument and the evidence I had presented.

In spite of unfavorable reporting, the Gallup Poll showed that a majority of Americans believed there must be some substance to Senator McCarthy's charges. Before the November elections Bert Andrews of the *New York Herald Tribune* reported that in Wisconsin McCarthy was regarded as a "second Fighting Bob La Follette." The defeat of Senator Tydings in Maryland, like the victory of Nixon in California, indicates that the people's judgment favors McCarthy. The results of the November 1950 elections gave McCarthy a more respected status. As William S. White wrote in the

New York Times on Sunday, January 7, 1951: " 'McCarthyism,' be it an incomparable epithet, is simply today a very considerable force in the Congress of the United States."

As White also reported, those Senators who had formerly avoided or snubbed McCarthy now show him "deference." *Vox populi, vox dei:* if one believes in the democratic process, the voice of "the people," as distinct from the press, has evidently favored McCarthy's view of the danger of subversives in government.

In general, McCarthy's terrifying picture of a State Department infested by Communists, had good results. It awakened the American people to the clear and present danger constituted by the Communist conspiracy in our midst. Unfortunately, however, it alienated many of the non-Communist liberals and others who felt that civil liberties were being abrogated and some innocent persons smeared. However, it is unlikely that even if Senator McCarthy had been meticulously careful to make no charges which he could not prove without access to the FBI's files, most of his critics would have been less hostile. For the Alger Hiss case had shown that many American intellectuals could not bring themselves to condemn those whom pro-Soviet sentiments had led over the borderline from opinion to treasonable acts.

There is a species of lizard, called chameleon, which protects itself by its ability to change the color of its skin so as to become indistinguishable from its environment. According to the dictionary the chameleon also has a projectile tongue and moves slowly. Except for their ability to move fast, those whom McCarthy endeavored to track down as Communists, or Communist sympathizers, were very much like chameleons. He must often have felt that he was in a nightmare in which the quarry continually eluded him, or changed its appearance as soon as it was caught. For those who only yesterday were joining Communist fronts, advising the Administration to place its trust in Stalin, telling the public in speeches, books, and articles that the Soviet leader was an ever loving friend of peace and democracy, and in general deluding the American people as to the nature of the Soviet régime, are today quite otherwise engaged. Either they are fighting a battle of words with the Soviet representatives in the UN, or giving advice about how to "contain" Communism, or shaking their fists at the Kremlin from behind their desks in the State Department. And if a McCarthy demands that they explain their former behavior, they can evade the issue like Dorothy Kenyon, who said:

I do not deny that my name may have been used, even at times with my consent, in connection with organizations that later proved to be subversive but which, at the time, seemed to be engaged in activities or dedicated to objectives which I could and did approve.

And how can one deny the validity of this argument unless one is prepared to denounce, not only Roosevelt, Churchill, and General Marshall, but all those who followed in their train? One should recall that the American people, whether Democrats or Republicans, almost all welcomed Stalin as an ally, and rushed to give aid and comfort to the Soviet Union in its effort against Germany.

Until about four years ago "friendship" for Soviet Russia was a national attitude. The most respectable and respected people appeared on the mastheads or platforms of the multitude of organizations with democratic-sounding names founded to ensnare the gullible, the ignorant, and the vain. And many wealthy men gave huge donations to Communist causes with the idea that they were thereby proving themselves to be true "liberals."

The proceedings of the Senate Committee appointed to investigate McCarthy's charges made it clear that Senator Tydings and the other majority members of the Committee had a quite different conception of the purpose of this Committee than the Senate which had appointed it. Far from endeavoring to ascertain "whether there are employees in the State Department disloyal to the United States," their main effort seemed to be directed instead to discrediting Senator McCarthy.

The octogenarian Senator Green stated in so many words that the purpose of the Democratic majority was not to implement the Senate Resolution, which had set up the Committee, but instead to give an opportunity to those accused by Senator McCarthy to clear themselves of any Communist taint. Senator Green stated with naive frankness:

> We seem to have gotten a long way from the original purpose of these hearings. *It was to give an opportunity to those who had been charged by Senator McCarthy on the floor of the Senate with disloyalty in the State Department, and who asked to be heard, to reply to those charges* (italics added).[8]

Millard Tydings was not quite so direct. But his endeavors to extract "evidence" favorable to those accused by McCarthy, as contrasted with his reluctance to permit witnesses against them to testify, was evident throughout the proceedings of the Committee over which he presided.

With little regard for the dignity of the Senate, Tydings pleaded with the witnesses who had shown their contempt of Congress by refusing to answer questions. Take, for instance, Senator Tydings' treatment of Frederick Vanderbilt Field, the scion of the Vanderbilt family who does not deny that he is a Communist, and who appeared elegantly attired and self-confident, flanked by two lawyers. Field's contempt of Congress did not seem to concern Senator Tydings nearly so much as the possibility of extracting evidence from him favorable to the accused. For after Field had refused to reply to every question, saying with monotonous regularity: "I decline to answer on the ground that the answer might be self-incriminating," Senator Tydings besought him to answer just one question, because refusal to do so might harm the accused.[9]

Whereupon, after conferring with his counsel, Mr. Field consented to testify that he "had no knowledge whatsoever . . . that either Mr. [John S.] Service or Mr. [Haldore] Hanson is or ever has been a Communist." He testified similarly with respect to John Carter Vincent. Then Senator Tydings, beaming at his success, expressed gratitude for Field's "cooperation." But he was not yet wholly satisfied that he had cleared the accused of every last suspicion. So in even more persuasive tones, he asked "whether or not these three men . . . have committed any act of disloyalty to the Government of the United States, including the State Department." Field's reply that so far as he knew, they had not, brought a yet warmer "Thank you." [10]

Senator Tydings' interrogation of Earl Browder affords further evidence of the former Maryland Senator's partiality for the witnesses who favored those whom his Committee was supposed to be investigating. Browder, like Field, had shown his contempt of Congress by refusing to answer questions. He had also defiantly proclaimed that he would give no information either to the Senate Committee, or to the FBI, or to any Intelligence agency, concerning his former associates in the American Communist Party. When the majority counsel, Mr. Morgan, asked him: "If you did know of Communists in the State Department, would you tell us whether you did or did not?" he answered "No."

The above testimony indicated that Earl Browder was still a Communist at heart, or hoped to get back into the Party, by showing no resentment of the fact that he was made Moscow's scapegoat in 1945 when the Comintern switched from the "Popular Front" strategy to all-out hostility to America.[11] Yet greater credence was given to Browder's testimony by the Democratic majority on the Tydings Committee than to the evidence of sincere ex-Communists such as Louis Budenz, who had proved his loyalty to the United States after voluntarily leaving the Communist Party.

The clear evidence of Browder's continuing loyalty to the

Communists (in spite of his expulsion from the American Communist Party) failed to deter Senator McMahon of Connecticut, who was almost as anxious as Senator Tydings to extract "evidence" favorable to the accused. After Browder had refused to answer every question put to him by Senator Hickenlooper concerning whether or not he knew Judge Kenyon, Haldore Hanson, Silvermaster, and others, McMahon said:

It is a privilege, of course, under our Constitution, that a witness does not have to answer, if you want to plead that it may incriminate him, but there are two names Senator Hickenlooper has presented to you, namely, Miss Dorothy Kenyon, and Mr. Haldore Hanson. . . ."

It occurs to me that whatever your answer may be . . . if you are sincerely interested in not contributing to a smear campaign, your withholding an answer on them, if the answer is in the negative, is contributing to that smear.

On the other hand, if the answer is in the positive, since those cases are before the Committee, I believe you should answer.[12]

Then Senator Tydings took a hand, saying that if Browder refused to answer, "a wrong interpretation might be drawn," and that therefore "in the interests of fairness and truth," he begged Browder to reconsider and "on those two names, tell us whether or not you know or do not know they are members of the Communist Party?"

Thereupon Browder graciously acceded to Tydings' request, stating that neither Miss Kenyon nor Haldore Hanson had "any organized connection with the Communist Party." Tydings then again thanked Browder warmly for "cooperating," and said that he hoped "we can reach an understanding and at the same time try to keep you in the character you say you want to remain." Far from even attempting to cross-question Browder, as he had cross-questioned Budenz, Tydings assured Browder:

I have no idea of trapping you or involving you. I am only dealing with you in complete frankness, to try to help this case which we are ordered to investigate, and for no other reason.

Shortly after, however, Browder again became surly when asked whether or not he had ever met John Carter Vincent and John Stewart Service. Senator Tydings again became ingratiating in order to extract a statement favorable to the accused:

Returning for a moment, Mr. Browder, leaving out the association, of whether you know these people, do you feel, inasmuch as they are employees, or have been and I believe still are employees of the State Department, do you not feel that you could at least answer this question: To your knowledge, is Mr. John Carter Vincent or Mr. Service, a member of the Communist Party? Those are the only two names I shall present to you.

"Yes," snapped Mr. Browder, "before it was two other names. Now, it is two, maybe one by one we will get into a list of thousands."

Tydings then made the very revealing remark that Browder would be "defeating the purpose of this inquiry in a way you do not realize, if you allow this to be obscured," and said he would "be very grateful" if Browder would answer. Senator Hickenlooper intervened to point out this was not the original question he had put to Browder, but Tydings brushed him off and went on until he had secured the desired negative answer. A second attempt by Senator Hickenlooper to get back to his original question was again summarily dismissed by Senator Tydings.

The examination of Bella Dodd by the Tydings Committee also constituted proof of the majority's partiality for pro-Communist witnesses. Miss Dodd is rumored to have been expelled from the Communist Party for her racist, or anti-Negro, prejudices. She made it clear when she appeared as a witness that she was not an ex-Communist, but a Communist who had been expelled from the Party and hoped to get back in. She was permitted to use the Tydings Committee as a forum for the expression of Communist views.

Bella Dodd's detailed testimony concerning the high value she had placed on the Communists as allies even before she joined the Party, her description of her visit to a San Francisco night club in 1945 with the Chinese Communist delegates to the United Nations, and a mass of other irrelevant items concerning the life and times of Bella Dodd occupies three closely printed pages of the record of the proceedings of the Tydings Committee. Her version of how she came to be expelled from the Communist Party in 1949, her list of valued Republican friends or acquaintances, such as Senators Ives and Lehman, Governor Dewey and Vice Governor Hanley of New York, her eulogy of Owen Lattimore and denunciation of Louis Budenz, take up a good five pages. She was not once interrupted. Not only was she permitted by Senator Tydings to waste the Committee's time with her elaborate *apologia pro vita sua*. She was also permitted to express her opinion of Owen Lattimore and his accusers at inordinate length. She excoriated the Communists who have denounced their former associates in their efforts to atone for their past crimes. She made it quite clear that her ideas are the same today as when she joined the Communist Party. "The fact that I do not agree with the method of achieving these ends [those of the Communists] does not make me foul my own intellectual nest."

Having thus clearly stated that her "nest" is still Communist, she attempted, not without success, to enlist Senators Tydings and McMahon on her side by reminding them of their earlier speeches in favor of America's abandonment of her atom bomb monopoly.

"Senator McMahon," she said, "believes in negotiation and international control of the atom bomb. Senator Tydings believes in total disarmament. Anyone who is for disarmament—for a negotiation of peace and for a limitation of war budgets, is in danger of attack by this group."

Neither Tydings nor McMahon rejected these bouquets.

Bella Dodd dodges her way through pages and pages of the recorded testimony, never able to answer "yes" or "no" to any question. When Senator Hickenlooper and Mr. Morgan endeavored to make her state one way or the other if she is still "ideologically a Communist," she replied:

> That is a difficult question. I still believe in the things which drove me into the Communist Party. I believe in the brotherhood of man. I believe we should not have unemployment. . . . I am no longer ready to permit myself to be a part of the organizational structure such as the Communist Party has. . . . I do not however believe that people who systematically make a profession of informing on their past associates . . . is a very worthy technique.

Asked if she had ever given any Government agency information that might be pertinent concerning the Communist conspiracy in America, she replied: "I have not informed anyone of any Communist conspiracy. I was not aware of the existence of such a conspiracy."

Since she was not an ignorant woman, this last statement merely shows that she has failed to burn her bridges and hopes one day to be readmitted to the Communist Party should they appear to be winning the battle for the world. An examination of her lengthy testimony reveals that she still supports the Soviet Union, but feels that the American Communist Party is unworthy to do so. She said she wanted to correct its errors in order to transform it into a "more effective organ" for the establishment in America of the "socialism" which "is indigenous to Russia."

Senator Hickenlooper tried in vain to induce her to give an unequivocal reply to his question whether the Communist Party in America takes its orders from Moscow and is a conspiratorial organization. Senator Tydings sat silent, never intervening to attempt to extract from the witness a "yes" or "no" answer.

Practically disregarding the evidence produced by Senator McCarthy and his witnesses, the Democratic members of the Committee gave a clean bill of health to all the accused whom it was their duty to investigate without prejudice. (The Republican members of the Committee did not agree with this verdict, and Senator Lodge issued a minority report.)

For instance, having originally promised fully to investigate the *Amerasia* case, the Committee exonerated John Service in spite of the abundant evidence that he had passed secret documents to Philip Jaffe.

Philip Jessup received a handsome apology in spite of his having admittedly belonged to a number of Communist fronts. Service was also exonerated.

The Wisconsin Senator seems to have had considerable justification when, in the case of Jessup, he said:

> It may be that the government loyalty board attaches but little significance to the fact that a person is associated with one Communist front or that he is associated with one well known Communist, and that he publicly vouched for the character of one espionage agent. However, I am of the opinion that this Committee should determine and publicly announce whether, in its opinion, the continued combination of such circumstances does or does not indicate a very definite pattern of pro-Communist activity, which makes for a bad security risk.

In many cases the Democratic majority appears to have considered it sufficient proof of innocence for some eminent American, or close associate of the accused, to come forward and say he was above suspicion.

Former Senator Tydings, on the Senate floor, said that McCarthy's charges were "a fraud and a hoax." But it was clear to anyone who had followed the proceedings of the Committee that it had signally failed to perform the task for which it was appointed, namely to investigate not Senator McCarthy, nor any individual's charges, but "whether persons who are disloyal to the United States are or have been employed by the Department of State."

A full examination of the evidence produced by Senator McCarthy and his witnesses, and of the failure of the Tydings Committee to evaluate it, would require a whole book. I have not here attempted to present even a summary of all the evidence which was produced substantiating McCarthy's charges against the eighty-one persons in the State Department whom he accused of being Communists, or Communist sympathizers, or "poor security risks." I have shown only how the Tydings Committee failed to perform the duty with which it was charged by the Senate—namely, that of ascertaining whether or not there are employees in the State Department disloyal to the United States.

Perhaps the most flagrant instance of the prejudice shown by the Tydings Committee, and its failure to carry out its mandate from Congress in an honorable and trustworthy manner, is to be found in the treatment accorded to Isaac Don Levine and Ralph de Toledano, respectively editor and managing editor of *Plain Talk,* which first published, in October 1946, a comprehensive account of the *Amerasia* case by one of the six defendants, Emmanuel S. Larsen. When he appeared before the Committee in executive session, Larsen partially repudiated his *Plain Talk* article, presumably because, since he had turned against his former Communist-sympathizing or traitorous associates, he had been unable to obtain employment. The Tydings Committee, instead of calling Levine and de Toledano to testify, condemned them both in its report as "professional anti-Communists," and heaped upon them defamatory allegations in a style almost reminiscent of the *Daily Worker* and *Pravda.*

Don Levine, who can claim the distinction of having opposed and exposed Communism for three decades, challenged Senator Tydings to repeat these charges off the Senate floor. In an open letter to him, Levine said:

Seldom, if ever, in the history of Congressional investigations, have innocent and reputable and deeply patriotic citizens been subjected at the hands of a Senatorial committee to such vilification and slander and gratuitous character assassination without benefit of a hearing, without benefit of counsel, and solely upon the word of a disloyal American whose 'credibility generally is open to serious doubt,' according to your own Report.

To cap this gross abuse of justice, the voluminous Tydings report, which includes a mass of irrelevant material, could not find space either for a reference to Senator Hickenlooper's request during the hearings that Don Levine be given an opportunity to bring his documentary evidence proving "the verity or lack of verity of Larsen's testimony," or for the text of Mr. Levine's telegram to Chairman Tydings in which he offered "to submit a stack of original writings and numerous letters by Larsen which utterly refute his alleged testimony." No notice at all was taken by Senator Tydings of Don Levine's warning that the "record would be manifestly incomplete and unfair to me without reference to this documentary and conclusive evidence."

In the period of questioning which followed my own testimony, the main endeavor of the Committee seemed to be directed either to discrediting me as a witness, or to exposing evidence of the machinations of a so-called "China lobby." None of the Senators present—Hickenlooper was not there—seemed in the least interested in investigating the charges against Owen Lattimore, or examining the evidence I had produced by quotation from his writings.

Senator Tydings, who gave Lattimore the widest possible latitude in answering questions, insisted that I answer only "yes" or "no" to all the prejudiced, even foolish, questions put to me by Senator Green, who obviously had no inkling what the proceedings were about, but was determined to prove his "liberal" sympathies by acting as the mouthpiece of Lattimore and his lawyers. Thus, through Green, Lattimore was permitted the utmost license in asking me questions concerning my income and private affairs in a vain effort to prove I was a paid "China lobbyist." The Committee did not permit any similar questions to be put to Lattimore. Indeed, I was not granted the privilege of putting any questions of any kind to Lattimore through the Committee.

For some unexplained reason the Minority failed to produce its own report, although allowed by the Senate to postpone doing so until December 1. Senator Lodge, who said little during the hearings, subsequently issued a dissenting opinion in which he stated that the investigation must be set down as "superficial and inconclusive." In his "Individual Views" the Senator from Massachusetts shows conclusively the Committee's failure to reinvestigate properly the *Amerasia* case; declares that the State Department files on the eighty-one accused were "in such an unfinished state that they reveal nothing definite or conclusive"; remarks that many essential witnesses were not called and that essential questions were not answered; and concludes with the opinion that a "trained bipartisan commission" with an adequate staff is required to tackle the "exceedingly complex and difficult subject" which the Tydings Committee failed to cope with. One hopes that Senator Lodge is right in believing that it is "not beyond the bounds of American ingenuity to devise a constitutional method to ferret out disloyalty without doing injury to innocent individuals or to the interest of the whole American people in their relations with foreign nations."

The present Loyalty Review Board has been precluded by Presidential Order from performing the function which the Tydings Committee failed to perform. Executive Order No. 9835 of 1947 practically dictated the clearance of such government employees as Alger Hiss, William W. Remington, John Stewart Service, and other "security risks," since it forbids the dismissal of a government employee unless "on *all* the evidence, reasonable grounds exist for belief that the person involved is disloyal to the United States" *NOW*, and forbids the Loyalty Review Board to make an adverse report on evidence that he is a "security risk."

The Loyalty Review Board was thus precluded from dealing with the question of security. Its members perforce concluded that "while an employee's morals, or habits, or lack of discretion, or personal associations, might readily raise the issue of 'security risk,' " these could not be used to determine the issue of loyalty with which alone it was empowered to deal.

As Arthur Krock pointed out in his column in the January 23, 1951, issue of the *New York Times*, "while L.R.B. members might feel reasonable doubts of an employee's loyalty, or regard a loyal employee as a security risk just the same, or find in the remote evidence grounds for belief that disloyalty still exists, they are under Presidential direction to clear that employee when his case comes before them for review."

Thus there is no doubt that President Truman is himself responsible for the failure of his Loyalty Review Board to expose and dismiss government employees suspected, or known, to have furthered the Communist cause.

The Majority Report of the Tydings Committee shows how difficult it was even in 1950 to obtain an impartial investigation into Communist influence in America. More notorious perhaps was the Committee's complete exoneration of its star witness. It was because of my personal acquaintance with Owen Lattimore, as well as my capacity to evaluate his writings on the basis of my study and experience of Communist policy with regard to China, that I was called to testify before the Committee. In the next chapter, therefore, I shall tell as briefly as possible the story of Owen Lattimore.

9. *The Case of Owen Lattimore*

THE MAJORITY REPORT of the Tydings Committee states: "Owen Lattimore is a writer and scholar who has been charged with a record of pro-Communism going back many years. There is no legal evidence before us whatever to support this charge, and the weight of all other information indicates that it is not true."

Perhaps it is true that there was insufficient "legal" evidence to prove his proclivity to the Chinese Communists. But no one can study Mr. Lattimore's writings without being surprised that Senator Tydings and his colleagues should also have said:

A study of the writings of Lattimore has been made, and they obviously cannot be declared to approach Communist dogma. Furthermore, there appears no apparent change in his position consistent with shifts in the Party line.

Since Senator McCarthy once said his accusations concerning Communist influence in the State Department would stand or fall on the case of Owen Lattimore, and in view of the fact that the Baltimore professor is as warmly defended in "liberal" circles as Alger Hiss before his trial, it is necessary to examine his writings in some detail.

When Senator McCarthy called him "the chief architect" of America's Far Eastern policy, he may have somewhat exaggerated Owen Lattimore's importance. There can, however, be little doubt that Lattimore exerted a profound influence, not only at the State Department, but also in the press, the universities, and on the public.

Whether or not, as McCarthy alleged, Lattimore had a desk at the State Department makes little difference. It is not denied that he was called in for consultation, and selected to lecture to Foreign Service officials. He was President Roosevelt's personal appointee as adviser to Chiang Kai-shek in 1941. In 1944 he accompanied Vice President Henry Wallace on a tour to China, following which Wallace recommended that we back the Communists. Wallace paid tribute to Lattimore's invaluable assistance in drawing up his policy recommendations. As revealed by Senator McCarthy, in August 1949 Lattimore was asked by Mr. Acheson to prepare a secret memorandum "For the guidance of Ambassador-at-large Philip Jessup," in which he recommended:

1. that the United States get out of Korea;
2. that we give no support whatsoever to Chiang Kai-shek's forces on Formosa;
3. that we refuse to support any league of Asiatic countries against Communism;
4. that the United States "accept a list of countries recommended by Trygve Lie" (who had proposed admitting Communist China to the UN);
5. that the United States withdraw its forces from Japan.

Up to June 27, 1950, the Administration followed Lattimore's recommendations concerning both China and Korea, and showed the same partiality for the Chinese Communists. Indeed its former trust in Stalin, its estimate of Communism, and its Far Eastern policy were based on the same false premises as one finds in all Lattimore's writings.

Lattimore and John Davies, in particular, echoed each

other like strophe and antistrophe in a Greek chorus. As late as September 3, 1949, Lattimore praised John Davies in the *New Republic* for the latter's report in the White Paper accusing Chiang Kai-shek of wanting to "plunge China into a civil war," and proclaiming that "Chiang's feudal China cannot long exist alongside a modern dynamic popular government in North China." [1] Exultantly Lattimore went on to say that "Russian non-intervention had wiped the floor with American intervention." Furthermore, he condemned his native land for what he called its "active gunpowder-and-human blood front against Russia." Such completely unfactual opinions are stated by Mr. Lattimore with the same apparent sincerity as his report on the customs of Mongol tribes.

Lattimore's widespread influence is due to his being the cleverest, most scholarly and persuasive of all the writers who have championed the Chinese Communists and represented the Soviet Union as democratic, peace-loving, and "progressive." His position as director of the Walter Hines Page School of International Relations at Johns Hopkins University, and formerly as editor of *Pacific Affairs* and guiding spirit of the Institute of Pacific Relations, and his service as President Roosevelt's Political Adviser to Chiang Kai-shek in 1941 and as Deputy Director of the OWI from 1942 to 1944, have enabled him to promote views favorable to the Communist cause in China, while posing as a learned professor with an "objective" outlook.

Lattimore's career, incidentally, affords evidence of the advantages obtained by those who secured a reputation for "liberalism" by showing a distinct partiality for Marxist theory and Stalinist practices. He is one of the very few professors of a great university who never even obtained a bachelor's degree from any college. His listing in *Who's Who in America* records that he attended St. Bees School in Cumberland, England, from 1915 to 1919, and that from 1920 to 1926 he was engaged in "business" or "newspaper work" in

China, and that after 1926 he was "engaged in travel and writing." The only reference to any attendance at any university is the cryptic statement: "Graduate School Harvard 1929." He cannot have spent more than a few months in Harvard, since *Who's Who* tells us that in 1929–30 he was in Manchuria as a member of "the Social Science Research Council." When and how he acquired the right to call himself "*Doctor* Lattimore" is not mentioned. As Director of the Walter Hines Page School of International Relations at Johns Hopkins he has, in any case, been able to overawe his critics.

The only person who has assailed Lattimore's reputation as a scholar is his friend and protégé, John Stewart Service. In his testimony before the Tydings Committee in May 1950,[2] Service answered as follows when asked whether he considered Lattimore a well-informed person on China:

I don't think Mr. Lattimore is a profound scholar. I think he is rather superficial in his views. He has a very active mind, but his views are apt to shift a bit. I don't think his views on current affairs and China in general are particularly noteworthy.

I agree with Service about Lattimore's tendency to "shift" his views. This is particularly apparent in his appraisals of Chiang Kai-shek before, and after, Stalin switched from support of the Generalissimo to all-out hostility against him and the Chinese National Government.

In late 1942 and in 1943, when the Soviet Government was still supporting Chiang Kai-shek because of its fears of a Japanese attack on Russia, Lattimore praised the Chinese Generalissimo enthusiastically. For instance, in 1942, in a lecture he gave at Claremont College, Lattimore said that there would be little danger of civil war in China after the war, because "we have in Asia a statesman of real genius, in Chiang Kai-shek." He averred:

One of the oldest historical controversies turns on the question of whether great men create the events of their time, or are created by them. The career of Chiang Kai-shek shows that the problem cannot be limited to such narrow terms. The truth is that great men and great events interact on each other in a subtle and close way that results in creating history. This is as true of Roosevelt, Churchill, and Stalin as it is of Chiang Kai-shek.

At this time Lattimore was still intent on proving that China under the National Government was basically democratic. In *The Making of Modern China*,[3] written in 1942 and published early in 1943, Owen and Eleanor Lattimore wrote:

China is a democratic country in the sense that the Party and the government represent what the vast majority of the people want. When we want to make up our minds whether we ought to call another country "democratic," we quite naturally begin by comparing it with our own democratic country. Has it got the same institutions that exist in our country? Has it got the same kinds of procedure for seeing that the rights of minorities are protected? If it has not, we hesitate to call it a democracy.

This way of looking at things can often lead to misunderstandings. The most important standard by which to measure progress in a country like China is not "how near have they got to our way of doing things?" but "how far have they got ahead of the way things used to be done?"

Lattimore also sought at this date to show that democratic practices were increasing in China:

The People's Political Council is an example of the way in which the Kuomintang has begun to permit political expression through channels other than those of the Kuomintang itself.

It is true that the members who stand for the provinces are also for the most part either Kuomintang Party members or are nominated by the provincial organizations of the Kuomintang; *but on the other hand the proportion of the total membership which is elected rather than appointed or nominated has steadily increased* (italics added).

Lattimore also testified at this time to the increasingly democratic practices of the Chinese Nationalist Government by saying that while the People's Political Council could not legislate "it can suggest legislation, criticize government policy, and call on all departments of the government for reports." He added that it was "noteworthy" that "an increasing proportion of the recommendations of the People's Political Council is carried into effect by the decisions of the government," and that the Chinese press was free to criticize "even the most highly placed" individuals.

But in 1949, after the Communist line had switched to all-out hostility to Chiang Kai-shek, Dr. Lattimore completely reversed himself. In *The Situation in Asia* (1949) he gave the lie to himself by contradicting his former favorable view of wartime Nationalist China:

In 1937, when the struggle for survival against Japan began, China was controlled by the Kuomintang, a party which owed nothing to elections or to representative forms of government, and which itself appointed not only the National Government but provincial governments and even the administrative officials of counties. . . .[4]

Whereas in 1942–43 Lattimore had written that Chiang Kai-shek's government was relaxing its control, so that the proportion of members elected to the People's Political Council had "steadily increased," in 1949 he said that "within Free China the Kuomintang tightened all controls, pushing its authority from the top right down into the villages."

In 1942–43 he testified concerning the increasingly democratic character of the Chinese Nationalist Government, but in 1949 he wrote that Chiang Kai-shek was influenced by "Fascist" theories and that "initiative at lower levels was regarded as subversive."

Lattimore was writing about the same historical period in all these passages. All that had changed was the Communist Party line.

Thomas F. Murphy, the prosecutor in the Alger Hiss trial,

said that since it is hard these days to find anyone who admits he is a Communist, in order to detect subversives one must observe how closely a man's opinions have coincided with the Communist Party line.

Lattimore's "shifts" of opinion paralleling those of the Kremlin were apparent long before he contradicted himself on the subject of Chiang Kai-shek and the National Government of China. During the period of the Stalin-Hitler pact, he denounced Britain, France, and the United States in much the same terms as Mao Tse-tung, Earl Browder, and other Communist leaders everywhere in the world. In December 1939 Mao Tse-tung declared that "with the liquidation of the Nazi-Soviet pact and anti-Comintern policy, the distinction formerly drawn between the fascist and democratic countries had lost its validity," and that he now "saw no difference in their positions in this war." [5]

In June 1940 Lattimore wrote in *Pacific Affairs* that he thought there was nothing to choose between the two sides in the European war. He called the war "one between the established master races and the claimant master races," and said that France and England were merely defending their possessions, not democracy, and were as responsible for the war as Nazi Germany. According to Lattimore, the causes of the war "were the wrongs done to China, Ethiopia, Spain, Czechoslovakia and Albania—not by Japan and Italy and Germany alone, but by Britain and France and the United States as well."

"It was," continued Lattimore, "because they attempted to escape the shortcomings of the old order without sacrifice to themselves at the expense of the rest of the world, including huge territories like China and Russia, as well as the geographically small nations, that they are fighting each other."

The articles published in *Amerasia* during the period of Nazi-Soviet collaboration, when Owen Lattimore was on its editorial board, were even more outspoken in denouncing the Western Powers and opposing American support of Britain and France against Hitler.

After Russia and Japan signed their neutrality treaty in April 1941, Owen Lattimore and *Amerasia,* together with the *Daily Worker* and other Communist publications, modified their hostility to Japan. The effect of this pact on their "opinions" on the Sino-Japanese War was precisely the same as the effect of the Stalin-Hitler pact on their views of the war in Europe. The Russo-Japanese pact, like the Nazi-Soviet pact, was hailed as a triumph for "democracy." [6]

The Chinese Communist Party welcomed Russia's latest pact with the aggressors as "in keeping with the interests of the working peoples and oppressed nations of the world." Owen Lattimore similarly rejoiced that the Russo-Japanese pact would isolate China, forcing the Nationalist Government to come to terms with the Communists and thus become more "democratic."

Following Hitler's attack on Russia, Lattimore again shifted his views. After June 1941 one can find no more articles by Lattimore himself, or in *Pacific Affairs* under his editorship, or in *Amerasia,* saying that the European war was one between two lots of master races and urging the United States to keep out of it. After June 22, 1941, Lattimore was all in favor of American intervention in a war which had become one to make the world safe for Stalin.

Years ago Attorney General Francis Biddle said that the clear distinction between an isolationist and a Communist was their attitude after Hitler attacked Russia. The isolationists continued to oppose America's intervention, whereas the Communists switched from shouting, "The Yanks are not coming," to all-out advocacy of American participation in the war.

If Lattimore had not been following the Communist Party line, would he suddenly have become an interventionist following Germany's attack on Russia?

One of my English friends, who like myself had joined the

Communist Party in the late twenties, and got out of it quickly after going to live in Russia and there learning the truth about Communism, said to me years later: "Draw a line from any one point to any other point and at some time or another the Party line will cross it."

This geometrical comparison is very useful because it enables us to distinguish between those who consciously followed the Communist Party line, in all its zigzags, and those whose views once, or occasionally, coincided with the Party line. If one appreciates the fundamental difference between fortuitous similarity of views at a given moment, and consistent changes of attitude paralleling those of the Communists, there can be no danger of "guilt by association" trapping the innocent.

As for the Chinese Communists, Lattimore was skillful as well as flexible. In his testimony before the Tydings Committee he made much of the fact that he had never written or said that the Chinese Communists were "agrarian reformers." Technically, this statement may be true, because Mr. Lattimore is always very careful in his choice of words. In *Solution in Asia* (1945),[7] he wrote:

During the ten years of civil war the Communists, cut off from cities and urban workers, had become a peasant party.

He then proceeds to compliment the Communist Party for limiting its membership in local governing bodies to one-third and says that this is "the most positive step yet taken in China by any party away from dictatorship and toward democracy." It is impossible to believe that Lattimore is so ignorant of Communist methods and technics that he does not know that under Communist governments, which control the press, the radio, the police, and the judiciary, non-party representatives can easily be intimidated. Was he not therefore falsely representing the Chinese Communists as democrats?

It is not wholly inconceivable that Lattimore might have

believed in the essential "democracy" of non-Russian Communists, but no one as well acquainted as he with China and Chinese-Russian relations could truthfully have stated, as he did, that in the 1930's

... the Chinese Communists were so isolated, south of the Yangtze and far inland from the coast, that they could not receive arms or any other help from Russia, while the intensity of the fight for survival made it impossible for them to slacken or strengthen their civil-war efforts in accordance with directives from either the international or the Soviet Government. . . . They were on their own.[8]

This is simply not true. The Chinese Communists were never "on their own"; they were continuously and always acting on Moscow's directions; they have followed every twist and turn of the line laid down by Moscow as obediently, or more obediently, than any Communist Party in the world; the Chinese Communist Party was recognized in official Comintern and Soviet Government publications as the most important of all the parties directed by Moscow, or at least as only second in importance to the German Communist Party before it was crushed by Hitler.

Nowhere does Lattimore refer to such documents as the Chinese Communist Party handbook, which says:

The Chinese Communist Party was born with the help of the Communist International. It grew up under the guidance of the Communist International. The Chinese Communist Party and Central Committee, with the exception of two short periods, have been loyal to the guidance of the Communist International. . . . To carry out the international line and to be loyal to the Executive Committee of the Communist International is to guarantee the success of the Chinese revolution.

Among other important official Chinese Communist Party documents concerning which Dr. Lattimore has carefully kept his readers in ignorance, was that made by the secretary of the Chinese Communist Party, Wang Ming, in which he said:

They [the people of China] regard the USSR as the country which in actual practice has shown China how it can and must transform the country . . . into one mighty and capable of defending itself, from a country poor and backward into one rich and cultural . . . into the most democratic country in the world under the banner of the Stalinist constitution.

Lattimore, ignoring such evidence, stated in *The Situation in Asia:* [9]

If the Chinese Communists gravitate toward a political center in Russia, we shall have one kind of world. If they maintain their own political center in China, we shall have a decidedly different world.

In other words, according to Lattimore as of 1949, the Chinese Communists were not already subservient to Stalin but might "gravitate" toward Moscow if America should not be friendly to them.

Similarly one can find nowhere in his writings any reference to the documentary evidence which proves that the Chinese Communists during the war with Japan were reserving their major forces for a future struggle to overthrow the National Government.

It is just as easy to misinform people by the omission of vitally important evidence, as by telling direct lies, and Lattimore's omissions are so serious that he succeeds in presenting a totally false picture for the benefit of the Soviet Union.

With complete disregard of the historical record, he wrote:

During the period of his [General Marshall's] mission, the Kuomintang kept accumulating American supplies and American transportation kept moving Kuomintang troops into North China and Manchuria.[10]

This statement is entirely false. Certainly "Dr." Lattimore as a professor of international relations, knew that General

Marshall in 1946 embargoed all arms and ammunition supplies to Nationalist China. And if he read the daily papers he must have been aware of the fact that U.S. Navy ships were prevented by the Soviet authorities from transporting Chinese Nationalist armies to Manchuria.

One could go on quoting passage after passage from Lattimore's books and articles which are as completely untrue as the ones I have already cited. Here I give only a few other examples showing his misrepresentations about aid to China.

In *The Situation in Asia*[11] he says that the coalition government including the Communists that General Marshall tried to establish, "might have been obtained if military aid to the Kuomintang had been suspended."

In March 1950, just three months before the attack in Korea, Lattimore wrote in the *United Nations World*:

It is clear that the change of power in China cannot properly be described as primarily a victory either of Communist armies or of Communist ideas. The chief phenomenon has been the moral and political bankruptcy of the National Government of China, whose 'ability' to collapse greatly exceeded the ability of the Communists to push it over. . . . This change has been so great that it could not be prevented by an American intervention measurable in money . . . by an expenditure of some three billion American dollars.

This "three-billion dollar" story took hold of the minds of the American people like a biblical commandment.

At other times Lattimore has managed to up even this high figure. In *The Situation in Asia* he wrote:

The grandiose and disastrous American attempt to determine the character and outcome of the Chinese civil war . . . proved that America does not have the kind of power that can settle Chinese issues. . . . *The American expenditure of from 2 to 4 billion dollars included both military and economic aid to Chiang Kai-shek* (italics added).

As I have shown in Chapter Two the total of military aid given to China to fight the Communists amounted to little more than a quarter of a billion dollars, and most of that came too late to prevent the withdrawal of the Chinese Nationalist Government to Formosa.

Despite all the evidence available concerning the aid Russia gave to the Chinese Communists, Lattimore in his *United Nations World* article had the effrontery to state that "Russian intervention, in the way of supplying either munitions or political advisers, was insignificant," and that Russia's strength remained "a card unplayed."

The one subject on which Owen Lattimore has shown no tendency to "shift" his views, at least since 1937, is the Soviet Union, which is consistently represented in his writings as peace-loving, progressive, powerful, and as having given the Russian workers and peasants such a happy life that they are envied by all their neighbors.

The drift of his first short popular book, *Solution in Asia* (1945) was indicated on its jacket, which stated: "He shows that all the Asiatic peoples are more interested *in actual democratic practices, such as the ones they see in action across the Russian border,* than they are in the fine theories of Anglo-Saxon democracies which come coupled with ruthless imperialism." (italics added)

And inside the covers we read, in Lattimore's own words, that

In Asia the Soviet Union has a major power of attraction, backed by a history of development and a body of precedents. . . . To all of these peoples . . . the Russians and the Soviet Union have a great power of attraction. In their eyes—rather doubtfully in the eyes of the older generation, more and more clearly in the eyes of the younger generation—the Soviet Union stands for strategic security, economic prosperity, technological progress, miraculous medicine, free education, equality of opportunity, and democracy: a powerful combination.[12]

It is hardly surprising that the Communist *New Masses* called *Solution in Asia* a "must book not only for our San Francisco delegates but for every one of us."

In it Lattimore refers to "the trend toward increased personal liberty and economic prosperity," which has contributed so largely to Russia's advantage in competing with us for the favor of the peoples of Asia, as compared with our "tardiness" in the "evolution of democratic processes." [13]

Lattimore is too clever to argue, or appear to be arguing, in favor of the Communist point of view. Instead he simply makes false assertions concerning Communism and the Soviet Union as if he were stating well-known and irrefutable facts. His smooth style, careful choice of innocuous words to describe Communist methods and aims, his pretense of not taking sides, his standing in the academic world, his erudition, and his historical distortions and omissions, all enable him to pile untruth upon half-truth upon untruth with an air of detachment and objectivity. Most of his readers are deceived into thinking that they are being given fair presentation of history and current world issues. Only those who are experts, or, at least, close observers or students of the Far East, realize that Lattimore is giving them an *ex parte* presentation and that his arguments are based on false premises. Furthermore, he appeals, with both skill and subtlety to that tolerance of Americans which is prompted by goodheartedness, and he indulges in a generosity of definition that surpasses the language grasp of all but semanticists and professors of English.

The fact that the Soviet Union also stands for democracy is not to be overlooked. Here in America we are in the habit of taking a narrow view of foreign claimants to the status of democracy. If China, or Russia, or some other alien people does not measure up to the standards of the particular American modification of Anglo-Saxon democracy, we say that it is not democratic. . . . The fact is that for most of the people in the world today what constitutes democracy in theory is more or less irrelevant. What moves people to act, to try to line up with one party or country and not with another, is the difference between what is more democratic and less democratic in practice.[14]

Lattimore here implies that the Soviet Union is more democratic in *practice* than the West. But he has carefully refrained from saying so straight out. If accused of being in line with Communist propaganda, he can reply that *he* didn't say so, but that the peoples of Asia think so.

The whole of Lattimore's arguments in favor of the Soviet Union's claims to be regarded as a "democracy" are based on false premises which he takes for granted, and which he uses his scholastic reputation and eminent position to make others accept. He does not attempt to *prove* such untruths as that the Soviet Government has greatly improved the material conditions of the peoples of the USSR and given them unlimited opportunity to better themselves. He just says it is so as if this were an incontrovertible statement of fact. He offers no proof that the peoples of the countries which are neighbors of the Soviet Union are full of admiration and envy for the happy peoples under Communist rule; he just says they are, carefully omitting any mention of the fact that thousands of people try every week to escape from the blessings of Communist rule at the risk of their lives. Nowhere in any of Dr. Lattimore's writings will you learn that according to Soviet law an attempt to "escape over the frontier" is a crime for which all the relatives of the "criminal" are punished by imprisonment, whether or not they knew of his intention to "escape" from the Soviet Union.

Nor can one find anywhere in Lattimore's writings mention of the fact that the Soviet Government holds some twelve million people as slave laborers in concentration camps, because they have failed to appreciate the benefits of Soviet rule.

Another Lattimore technique for putting across Soviet propaganda consists in overawing his critics by a display of his erudition, his knowledge of languages, and his intimate first-hand acquaintance with the sentiments and aspirations of some obscure people, or tribe, of whom his readers have never heard, and concerning whom few dare to argue with so eminent an authority as the Director of the Walter Hines Page School at Johns Hopkins University.

This particular Lattimore technique was described by Senator McCarthy in his speech to the Senate on March 30, 1950, in which he said:

One of Lattimore's subtle methods is to put his own ideas in the mouths of some hapless Mongol tribesman, or Chinese peasant, who cannot possibly refute Lattimore's assertions, and does not even know what sentiments are being ascribed to him by the learned professor. For instance, at page 140 in *Solution in Asia*, he writes: "Let us take an Uighur in Sinkiang Province ... who learns that among his near kinsmen, the Soviet Uzbeks, a poor man's children may attend, free, a school at which they are taught in their own language ... ; that they may go on to the university and become doctors, engineers, anything in the world ... then he is going to think that the Uzbeks are free and have democracy."

Incidentally, the professor is in error here. Stalin's subjects have had to pay for their high school and college education since 1941.

However, the main point is that this passage is clearly designed to batter down any doubts the reader may have by confronting him with evidence of Lattimore's unique knowledge of people such as Uighurs and Uzbeks, whose names his audience cannot even pronounce and of whose existence they have never heard. ...

The poor Uighurs are forced to act as a ventriloquist's dummy in Lattimore's writing. When he thinks that it would be advisable to have someone voice his own admiration for the Soviet Union, he drags in some Uighur tribesmen who are obviously not in a position to contradict him. Since no one else in America knows any Uighurs, Lattimore can safely ascribe to these nomads the greatest love and respect for Communist Russia. So, for instance, in his 1949 book, *The Situation in Asia*, he tells us how in 1949, he "ran into" some Uighur pilgrims on their way to Mecca via the Soviet Union, who said to him: "Haven't you heard? The Russians have democracy. They are good to Moslems."

After a perusal of Lattimore's writings, one begins to feel quite sorry for the Uighurs who have no one else to interpret their sentiments, and in all probability have no idea that a professor at Johns Hopkins has been telling the world how much they love Communism. . . .

Owen Lattimore is also adept at blaming America for what is wrong in the world and explaining away the role of the Soviet Government in these disasters. He can always find a valid excuse for Stalin's worst acts by holding America, or some other "capitalist," "imperialist" Western nation as the real culprit.

For instance, wishing to justify, or excuse the Red Army's looting of Manchuria, Lattimore writes:

[The Russians] were afraid that Manchuria, if it were left a going concern, might be turned into an American stronghold on the doorstep of Siberia. So they gutted the factories of Manchuria as they withdrew.[15]

Maybe, Lattimore says, this was a bit hard on the Chinese Communists, who were sure they could hold Manchuria, and "were loyal to Russia in all questions of common world policy." But, he remarks, "this ruthless example of the sacrifice of the interests of non-Russian Communists" has "not diminished the Russian power of attraction in Asia."

In this same book Lattimore argues that when Stalin abandons "persuasion" for compulsion he is acting under the unavoidable necessity of protecting the "socialist" world from the capitalist-imperialist United States. Thus he explains that it was the belief that the United States was "prepared to go on a war footing" which caused the Soviet leaders to "tighten up their own controls," and which led to their exerting such pressure on Marshal Tito that he broke away. He does not, however, draw the conclusion that, according to his own version of events, the way to create schisms in the Communist world is for America to show evidence of strength, not weakness.

In another passage in *The Situation in Asia* Lattimore directly echoed Communist propaganda against the United States. While the Chinese Communists were proclaiming on the radio that "the only difference between American and Japanese imperialism is that American imperialism is stronger, and that its methods appear civilized and legal on the surface," Lattimore wrote:

It took three years and from two to four billions of American money to prove the uselessness of an *American attempt to imitate this early Japanese policy in China.*

In his testimony before the Tydings Committee Owen Lattimore claimed that his support of the Marshall Plan proved he had no Communist sympathies. Louis Budenz explained this discrepancy by saying that eminent secret members of the Communist Party were permitted "certain latitude in their speeches and writings so as to prevent discovery of the Party affiliations." It would have been more pertinent to inquire why Professor Lattimore had violently opposed the Truman Doctrine, as when he wrote in *The Situation in Asia:*

The Truman doctrine originated more in out-of-date British thinking than in up-to-date American thinking. It is the child of the Fulton, Mo., speech at which President Truman sat on the platform while Winston Churchill rang down the iron curtain.

Anyone whose sympathies lie with Soviet Russia might approve of the Marshall Plan which, it should be remembered, originally offered economic aid to Soviet Russia and her satellites—so long as they rejected the Truman Doctrine promising arms aid to those resisting Communist aggression.

One could take issue too with the impudent assertion that it was not Soviet Russia, but Winston Churchill and Harry S. Truman who had "rung down" the Iron Curtain.

Being concerned, no doubt, to maintain his reputation as an objective and scholarly student of China, Mongolia, Russia, and international affairs, Lattimore, in *The Situation in Asia*, admitted a few unpleasant facts about the Soviet Union, which by that time were too well known to be denied. He went so far as to say that "No propaganda can hide the fact that there is good and bad in Russia." However, he warns that we simply have not got what it takes to resist Russia. Therefore, we had better appease Stalin if we want to avoid destruction. "Clearly," he says, "the Communist ascendancy [in China] had become so decisive that it could not be reversed."

Although the Communist bandwagon is not completely repaired, anyone who does not jump on it now is a fool who fails to realize that Soviet Russia must win, because Communism represents the inevitable march of progress. For in this book he wrote: "To be progressive in politics is to be on the side of that which is going up and against that which is going down."

Of course, he was too cautious to say this is his own belief; he said only that it is Communist theory. But he makes it abundantly clear that he believes this theory by the appeasement policy he advocates. Moreover he tells us that the Russians "are convinced of the foresight and wisdom of their leaders," and have the feeling that they are "going forward on the tide of history," when they read Stalin's "electrifying exact" formula, which Americans ought also to "study with cautious respect."

Anyone who finds it hard to understand why Alger Hiss betrayed his country, or why men like former Ambassador Joseph Davies became propagandists for the Soviet Union, and who find it impossible to believe that Owen Lattimore, or anyone else who had won an honorable position in this country could possibly have lent himself to the dissemination of ideas that parallel the propaganda of Red China, should ponder the effect of the theory that "to be progressive in politics is to be on the side of that which is going up."

Lattimore himself does not hide the fact that he not only believes that Communism is "progressive" but also that "power is the only thing which counts." Again and again, in *The Situation in Asia,* he tells us that the issue "is one of power" and that Americans are just silly to believe that moral issues are important. Besides, he tells us, we aren't really moral anyhow, since everything we do is in our own self-interest. The only reason we don't always act like imperialists is that we sometimes find it more profitable not to do so. The only reason, for instance, that we have behaved better in the Philippines than other Western Powers in their Asiatic colonies is that we just didn't need or want Philippine raw materials or sugar.

In case any Americans, inspired by Lattimore's philosophy, should start demanding that we use such power as we have to stop the Communist conquest of Asia, Lattimore hastens to add that there is just one exception to his "power decides" formula: "In China," he warns us, "moral attitudes will take precedence in deciding the future." Since, according to Lattimore, Russia is way ahead of us with respect to moral attitudes in the eyes of Asiatics, we should not imagine that we can win. Our failure so far in China is in fact due, not to Soviet Russia's design to establish her hegemony over the Chinese people, but to America's wish to do so! Soviet Russia, according to Lattimore, has succeeded because she advances by "political infiltration or persuasion which is a moral question."

Lattimore, it must be admitted, gives us some faint hope provided we will stop worrying about "moral issues," and make all the profit possible by appeasing the aggressors. In *The Situation in Asia,* he tells us that it would be very advantageous to do business with the Communists. If only

Americans would free themselves of their silly obsession with moral consideration and confine themselves to "straight considerations of sound business" by "accepting the opportunities for American enterprise" offered by the Chinese Communists, they could make large profits. Consider the fact, Lattimore says, that the USSR is not, for the moment, in a position to give economic assistance to the Chinese Communist Government, so if only you American capitalists will have the sense to "accept opportunities offered to American enterprise" and stop worrying about such unimportant considerations as moral principles, not only can you make a lot of money, but you can also prevent all Asia joining up with the Soviet Union against the United States. Here again one finds the recurring motif, as expressed in Professor Nathaniel Peffer's articles that money can buy anything.

It might be considered a little strange, by anyone who remembers how strongly Lattimore used to oppose "business as usual" with the Japanese aggressors in China, to hear him advocating good business at any price with their successors, the Russian-controlled conquerors of China. But we should, of course, bear in mind the vital distinction Lattimore would have us make between "fascist" totalitarian aggressors and Communist ones. In his view, aggression, concentration camps, terror, denial of elementary liberties, and all the rest of the paraphernalia of modern totalitarian rule are *bad* if anti-Communist, but good if they further "progressive" aims.

In *The Situation in Asia,* as shown by the above quotations, Lattimore silently abandoned his former pretense that the Chinese Communists are not "real" Communists. The admission that they are under Moscow's orders is used instead to frighten us, now that they control all of China. This in turn is used as an argument for appeasement. Briefly his argument runs as follows:

The Soviet Union is not at the moment in a position to give economic aid to Communist China, so if America will give such aid without asking for anything in return, if we will refrain from using our economic power to "force political concessions," we may be able to prevent all Asia joining up with the Soviet Union against us. But, he warns us, by 1952 the war wounds of Russia will be entirely healed—a categorical statement for which Lattimore affords no evidence. Then, he says, beware, for "the balance of the world is going to swing heavily in Russia's favor."

It is far more difficult to catch a man out in big lies, than in small ones. Big lies may be the result of illusions or lack of knowledge. But when a person lies in small matters, which can easily be disproved by evidence, the chances are he is basically untrustworthy.

This is the reason why I draw attention to one of Lattimore's small lies. In his book, *Ordeal by Slander* (1950), he repeats a lie concerning me which I have again and again, challenged and refuted, namely that in 1939 "I gave her hospitality for several weeks, and I did everything I could to get her lecture engagements and opportunities to write."

The fact is that, in 1938, not 1939, I spent *one night* at the Lattimores' house in Baltimore on the occasion of a lecture I gave to the Foreign Policy Association. In December 1939, on my return from England to the United States, I spent a few days with Dr. and Mrs. Emmett Holt in Baltimore, *not with the Lattimores,* prior to taking up residence in an apartment of my own with my five-year-old son and my mother. It is a lie that I then, or ever, accepted the Lattimores' hospitality for "several weeks." This fact is corroborated both by the Holts, and by Frederic Nelson, now an editor of the *Saturday Evening Post* (formerly with the Baltimore *Sun*), and his wife, who also gave me hospitality in Baltimore during my lecture tours before I came to live permanently in America. Obviously Lattimore intended to create the impression that I had abused the claims of personal friendship when I testified against him before the Tydings Committee. To my mind such a charge has no validity. I do not share Mr. Acheson's view that personal friendship, whether past or present, should be placed before a recognition of the truth, and before one's duty to one's country and the cause of freedom.

I shall digress briefly here to tell how I came to know the Lattimores.

I first met Owen Lattimore in April 1936 in Moscow, where I had been living for nearly six years as the wife of a Russian (a Soviet citizen but not a member of the Communist Party).[16] I was employed as a research worker in the Pacific Ocean Section of the Institute of World Economy and Politics. This Institute had become the Russian branch of the Institute of Pacific Relations a year or so earlier when the Kremlin switched over to the "Popular Front" policy, and the Communist Academy (of which the Institute formed a part) was rechristened Academy of Sciences. For the benefit of the visiting Americans, a room had been taken in another part of the town and a notice put up saying "Soviet Council of the Institute of Pacific Relations." It was here that E. C. Carter, president of the American Institute, and Owen Lattimore were first received by the leading Communists at the Institute. As I had left the Communist Party years earlier, I could not attend their private meetings. But the Americans came to the Institute for a whole day's session to consult with us on Far Eastern questions. I was astonished to see how often and completely they deferred to the Soviet viewpoint. Of them all, it seemed to me that Owen Lattimore was more independent in his attitude, since he dared to argue that it was incorrect to designate Mongol society as "feudal." [17] From this I concluded that he was not a Communist—an opinion which was fortified later, in London, when he told me he had almost lost his job as editor of *Pacific Affairs* because he had published an article by the Trotskyist Harold Isaacs.

My husband was arrested that same month of April, and disappeared into a concentration camp like so many other thousands of victims of the 1936–38 purge. I left for England in order to place our two-year-old son in safety before returning to Moscow to appeal in vain on behalf of my husband, whom I never saw again.

It was a sad and strenuous journey. I had to travel by train without a sleeping berth to Holland where I took a boat for the last lap of my return to England. As I was staggering down the steps of the ship to a third-class stateroom, carrying my son on one arm and clutching a suitcase with the other hand, Owen Lattimore suddenly appeared. He promptly relieved me of my burdens and kindly helped me put my son to bed. Subsequently in London (where I returned from Moscow to live in July 1936) he and his wife were both most generous to me, not only with their sympathy, but also by providing me with clothing for my son, from their own boy's outgrown clothes.

During that winter I saw the Lattimores often. I knew that as editor of *Pacific Affairs* Owen was closely connected with the Soviet Government. Also, I knew they were friendly to the so-called "Soviet Socialist experiment." But since they deplored the mass arrests, imprisonments without trial, and other tyrannical features of Stalin's Russia, they appeared to me to be sincere in their condemnation of the terror from which I had fled, and I believed them to be honest liberals. This was still my opinion when I came to Baltimore to live in 1940. Only then did I learn of Lattimore's defense of the Moscow blood purges in *Pacific Affairs*, his justification of them as "part of a new advance in the struggle to set free the social and economic possibilities of a whole nation and its people." I knew that he was as aware as I that hundreds of thousands of people had been arrested and sentenced to slave labor in Russia without trial. I began to realize, therefore, that he was adjusting his views to the Party line, and had abandoned his earlier misgivings. When I saw clearly that he had become an apologist for Stalin's tyranny, I broke off relations with him and his wife.

When he appeared before the Tydings Committee in 1950,

Lattimore gave clear evidence that he had not wasted the years since 1940 on any independence of thought. His testimony was a superb example of careful schooling in Communist techniques. Instead of endeavoring to disprove the charges that had been made against him, he resorted to the Communist device of abuse and vilification of his opponents.

Later, in his book of self-defense, *Ordeal by Slander,* he carried this abuse, in my own case, to the point of libel. For in characteristic Communist terminology, he accused me of having "a long record of pro-Nazi writings." Since this statement is provably untrue, only one thing is made obvious by it. No one, especially in 1950, but a Communist Party-liner would denounce anyone as "pro-Nazi" because during the war he had been anti-Communist and after the war had opposed Communist-inspired policies in Germany which could only lead to weakness rather than strength for our side.

Louis Budenz, the former Communist who edited the *Daily Worker* for many years, told the Tydings Committee that Owen Lattimore was in the same Institute of Pacific Relations—*Amerasia* Communist "cell" as Philip Jaffe and Frederick Vanderbilt Field. He said he knew this

. . . from reports received in the Politburo, and given to me officially as managing editor of the *Daily Worker.* Mr. Lattimore, when I first learned this in 1937, was connected with the publications of the Institute of Pacific Affairs. In a specific meeting to which I refer, Mr. Lattimore was commended by Frederick Vanderbilt Field and Earl Browder for the fact that he had been responsible for the placing of a number of communist writers in the organs of the Institute of Pacific Affairs, of which he was then the editor. . . . It was agreed that Mr. Lattimore should be given general direction of organizing the writers and influencing the writers in representing the Chinese Communists as agrarian reformers, or as North Dakota nonpartisan leaguers.

Budenz threw much light on Lattimore's loyalties and his influence as "the architect of our State Department's China policy" when he testified:

In 1943, at a regular meeting of the political bureau, at which Mr. Browder was present it was again officially reported that Mr. Lattimore, through Mr. Field, had received word from the apparatus that there was to be a change of line on Chiang Kai-shek. It was decided that the line was to attack Chiang Kai-shek; an article was discussed, to be put in one of the organs of the Institute of Pacific Relations; and it did so appear, by T. A. Bisson, declaring that Nationalist China was feudal China, and Red China was democratic China.

From that time on we did go after Chiang Kai-shek in the idea of a coalition government. The coalition government was a device used by the Communists always to slaughter those whom they brought into the coalition.

In 1944 Lattimore went to China as an adviser to Vice President Henry Wallace—and by the way, Mr. Wallace's trip was followed with very great care and detail by the Communist Party—Jack Stachel [18] advised me to consider Owen Lattimore as a Communist, which to me meant, because that was our method of discussing these matters, to treat as authoritative anything that he would say or advise.

Budenz also connected Lattimore with the hushing-up of the *Amerasia* case, but Lattimore denied this. The majority report of the Tydings Committee [19] dismisses Budenz's testimony, correct or not, as "in the nature of hearsay," for "his evidence against Lattimore is founded on what he states he was told, or learned from, others identified as Communists." Tydings and his Democratic colleagues seem not to have understood that a conspiracy is a *secret* undertaking, and that no underground movement could exist unless it took precautions to hide the identity of the conspirators, and that the members of a conspiracy do not get together in meetings where everyone meets everyone else. So they took the fact that Budenz had never met Lattimore as a refutation of his testimony that he had been told by higher authorities that Lattimore was to be considered as a Communist. The Committee report goes on to say that cross-examination of Budenz "revealed that he had no proof that Lattimore had given any directives to any writers or others in the alleged campaign to change public opinion on China, nor that Lattimore personally employed any of the people who wrote for the publications of the Institute of Pacific Relations." This sort of reasoning is based solely on a misunderstanding of the functions of an editor of a publication. As editor of *Pacific Affairs* and as one of the editors of *Amerasia,* Lattimore himself had chosen those writers who followed the Party line on China to write the majority of the articles he published.

Had the Committee troubled to study the evidence presented to them they would have seen that on the rare occasions when Lattimore published an article critical of the Soviet Union he invariably added some comments of his own showing that he disagreed and that the author of the article was mistaken.

The failure of the Tydings Committee to make any real effort to establish the truth concerning either Lattimore's Communist affiliations, or the effect of his writings and his advice on American policy, is illustrated by the gentle and most tolerant manner in which he was treated by the Committee's members. He was allowed unlimited time in "answering," or not answering, the questions asked him. Some of his "answers" to questions took twenty to twenty-five minutes to deliver, after which his audience knew no more than before he started. As an addendum to this chapter I quote an example of the Lattimore technique in handling the questions of the Committee.

He may not be the "architect" of the disastrous China policy pursued by the Administration, which has delivered 400,000,000 people to the Communists and placed the United States in dire peril, but there can be no reasonable doubt that the Far Eastern policy advocated, and to a large degree followed, by the Administration, was inspired by Lattimore and his disciples, protégés, and friends.

ADDENDUM

"*Mr. Morgan*. . . . I wonder, Dr. Lattimore, from your study and experience, if the word 'democracy' itself has a different meaning to the Russians from what it does to us."

"*Dr. Lattimore*. I think it does, Mr. Morgan, but I am not enough of an expert on the subject to give you a good political scientist's definition. There are many of these terms, and I have dealt with them primarily in my experience not as an expert on American domestic politics nor as an expert on Russian domestic politics. My experience has been principally in the field between the Russians and the Chinese. My most specialized studies have been on peoples like the Mongols, the various Central Asian peoples of Sinkiang Province, and so on. Now, in dealing with these people I find that very often the largest fund of factual information is in the Russian language, partly nineteenth century Czarist Russian, some older than that, of course, but very largely nineteenth century Russian, and since the Russian Revolution, Soviet Information. Now, in dealing with that information I find that over and over again, while looking toward that in the context of our daily lives you understand without any difficulty, it has to be extremely carefully handled when you are dealing with Russian political science or economic literature. It is not only the word 'democracy'; it is words like 'feudal,' 'clan,' 'tribal,' 'family,' and so forth."

"*Mr. Morgan*. When you use the word 'democracy,' Dr. Lattimore, in your writings, in which sense do you use it?"

"*Dr. Lattimore*. I am trying to recall a definition of democracy that I tried to write down for myself once not so very long ago. It may be in one of my books here, or it may be in an article that I can't lay my hands on.

"Perhaps I had better just try and recall the general thinking that led to that definition.

"I think that the essence of democracy is to be found in society where men and women may freely meet together to discuss their political ideas, and if they agree on a group of ideas, to organize themselves in the support of those ideas, and are, by the constitution or standing customs of their country, allowed to be represented in the processes of government, by freely choosing for themselves people whose ideas are like their own, to speak on their behalf in the necessarily smaller bodies that order the affairs of a community."

Mr. Morgan, at least attempting to appear to be doing his duty, then recalled Dr. Lattimore from his preoccupation with his Communist idyll, by saying: "Do you regard the Soviet System as a democratic system?"

Once again Lattimore, without interruption by Senator Tydings, rambled off into a long dissertation which excused him from answering the question. He said:

Under our definition, the definition that I have just given, certainly not. On the other hand, it would only be fair to say that so far as I know about Russia, and remember I don't know the typically Russian parts of Russia. The only parts of Russia in which I spent any time at all are these frontier districts in which very often the Russians are outnumbered by non-Russian people. In these districts which I know you might say that there exists a certain group of democratic practices which somewhat resemble an unfinished house of which the first story has been built and the second not added.

In order that I should not appear to be doing any injustice to Mr. Morgan, who was in the very difficult position of having been hired by the Democratic Administration to help Senator Tydings disprove Senator McCarthy's charges, but was a lawyer with a good reputation who could not afford to let it be said that he had helped the Administration cover up the evidence of Communist influence in the State Department, I quote further from the record:

"*Mr. Morgan.* There has been one phase of your writings brought into question here, and I would like to refer to it, since we are discussing the subject of democracy.

"In the September 1938 edition of *Pacific Affairs*, at the time when you were editor, there appears an article written by William Henry Chamberlin (I think you mention Mr. Chamberlin in your statement). In the article he is, to speak generally, critical of the Moscow trials. Thereafter, as editor, you make some observations concerning Mr. Chamberlin's criticism, and without reading it all, I want to read the concluding paragraph of your observations concerning the Chamberlin statement.

"After taking issue with Mr. Chamberlin in certain aspects of the situation, you say: 'The real point, of course, for those who live in democratic countries is whether the discovery of the conspiracies was a triumph for democracy or not. I think that this can easily be determined. The accounts of the most widely read Moscow correspondents all emphasize that since the close scrutiny of every person in a responsible postion, following the trials, a great many abuses have been discovered and rectified. A lot depends on whether you emphasize the discovery of the abuse or the rectification of it; but habitual rectification can hardly do anything but give the ordinary citizen more courage to protest, loudly, whenever in the future he finds himself being victimized by "someone in the party" or "someone in the government." That sounds to me like democracy.'

"Would you care to make any observation on that?"

"*Dr. Lattimore.* Surely. Incidentally, yesterday I spoke with Mr. Demaree Bess, who is mentioned here, because I quoted him as Mr. Chamberlin's successor as Moscow correspondent, and I spoke of this passage, and he laughed and said, 'Well, you certainly were off base that time.'

"Nevertheless, I do not think that I was off base. The point here is that, following the practice of *Pacific Affairs*, we had an article on the other side in which someone had praised the conduct of the Moscow trials, and I think there is where the phrase 'triumph of democracy' comes from. The question of 'triumph of democracy' then was not my phrase, but one which I was quoting that had come up in the course of this controversy, and I as editor was trying to close the controversy, because that was a quarterly magazine and in a magazine that comes out every 3 months you can't carry on the thing forever and ever. I stressed something Mr. Demaree Bess has published; and there were also other correspondents whom I mentioned here at that time who were reporting that since the close scrutiny of every person in a responsible position following the trials, a great many abuses had been discovered and rectified. I then emphasized the idea that when the ordinary citizen can have more courage to protest loudly whenever in the future he finds himself victimized by someone in the party or someone in the Government, that sounds to me like democracy—not like the triumph of democracy, but like democracy. In other words, I was praising what perhaps too optimistically seemed to be a change at the time from the original Russian system of authority and what I thought was the hopeful sign that people were beginning to have courage to protest when they were ridden over roughshod by party functionaries."

"*Mr. Morgan.* You still feel, therefore, that the handling of the Moscow trials sounds like democracy to you?"

"*Dr. Lattimore.* I think I was speaking there of the results of the Moscow trials. The result of the Moscow trials was that people were beginning to talk back to officials if the officials were too dictatorial. The hope did not develop, as we know. After that there were further trials, and since then the system in Russia has become more rigid, not less rigid; but what I was reacting to was what seemed to me a hopeful symptom at that time that it was becoming less rigid."

"*Senator McMahon.* It certainly was pretty rigid for the ones they stood up against a wall and shot."

10. *Time for Re-examination*

S PEAKING IN CONGRESS on July 18, 1950, Dr. Walter Judd said:

It was always fantastic to imagine we could convert our enemies into our friends by treating our friends as if they were our enemies.

Yet that is precisely what the Administration has done in China. Whether or not hidden spies and "policy saboteurs" directly influenced America's Far Eastern policy, there is no doubt, as we have seen, that it was based on a fundamental misunderstanding of Communism in general, and Chinese Communism in particular. Were this not so, the policy so aptly described by Dr. Judd would never have been followed. Even today, after most illusions concerning the nature and aims of the Soviet Government have been destroyed, a lingering belief that Communism is a progressive force when not perverted by Stalin, still activates American thinking, and prevents the adoption of a realistic Far Eastern policy.

For the most part, those who create the climate of American opinion have never been fully convinced that Communist regimes are fully as tyrannical and reactionary as Nazi Germany was, and that they constitute at least as great a danger to our civilization. Hence the fact that yesterday's "interventionists" are today's "appeasers." Hence our willingness, even today, to sit side by side with representatives of Communist governments in the UN, while boycotting Spain, whose government is at least not aggressive, and is less despotic than Tito's, not to mention Russia's or Poland's. Hence the State Department's lingering hope that Mao Tse-tung will become another Tito, in which event he would, if our present policy remains unchanged, become a desirable and preferred ally in China.

Both Roosevelt and Truman had faith too long that Stalin could be induced to become a benevolent, friendly dictator. They whitewashed his tyranny as representing the Russian people's will. They believed that, provided we made huge concessions to Stalin, were very patient, and never provoked the Russian dictator by standing up for his victims or bothering about the Four Freedoms, we could have peace in our time.

The fantastic illusions which are responsible for Communist power in the world today have perforce been abandoned as regards Soviet Russia. But they still color the views of many Americans. And with respect to China, the old fallacies concerning Communism continues to exert a powerful influence on the course of United States policy.

The White Paper shows beyond doubt that the State Department has all along considered the Chinese Communists either as "not real Communists," or as detachable from Moscow. Whether or not Mao Tse-tung would, or could, relinquish his allegiance to Moscow, in the very different geographical, military, and economic situation of China as compared to Yugoslavia is, to say the least, questionable. The main point, however, is that United States policy seems to be based on the belief that "heretical" Communists are more desirable allies than those who, like Chiang Kai-shek, have tried to uphold the principle of representative government and been uncompromising enemies of Communism.

In China we interfered at every turn to insist that the National Government should institute extensive "democratic reforms" in the midst of war and should make concessions to the Chinese Communists, if it hoped to receive our friendship and aid. But toward Communist governments the Administration's attitude has been conciliatory and based on a strict policy of non-interference in the internal affairs of the countries they rule.

Leniency toward Russia during the war can be ascribed to our pre-eminent desire to "win the war" whatever the consequences. But this aim cannot explain the partiality shown by the State Department after the war for Communist regimes such as the government of Yugoslavia, as contrasted with its continued denial of aid to the Chinese Nationalists.

Early in 1950, the State Department assured Marshal Tito that he would be given military aid in the event of a Russian attack. Nothing was said about the desirability of the reinstitution of representative government in Yugoslavia. The subjects of Marshal Tito, like the Chinese, had once been our allies, and both had been betrayed to the Communist totalitarians.

Even if the State Department chooses to take the position that the government of Chiang Kai-shek was too reactionary to deserve assistance, nevertheless the Chinese people under his rule enjoyed a far greater measure of political and civil liberties than the Serbs and Croats under Marshal Tito. But whereas there were howls of protest in the American press whenever Chiang Kai-shek's government arrested a "liberal" professor or student who was collaborating with the Communists, there was little or no condemnation of Tito's liquidation of Mikhailovitch and thousands of other liberals treated in true Stalinist fashion, or his incarceration in concentration camps of opponents of his regime.

The National Government of China gave complete religious freedom to all faiths. Marshal Tito, in his persecution of the Catholic Church, imprisoned Archbishop Stepinac and many other less eminent victims of his war on all Christians. Yet the United States Administration fails even today to demand either religious or political freedom in Yugoslavia as a condition of American aid. When, in October 1950, a drought, combined with the passive resistance of the Yugoslav peasants to Tito's tyranny, caused the Dictator of Yugoslavia to appeal to America for food aid, the State Department quickly announced it would come to the rescue. On October 29, Marshal Tito assured his hungry people that they would receive from the United States all the food necessary to prevent starvation, "without any conditions." "I can here openly say," he declared, "that the American government did not impose any conditions," in promising "all we need—wheat and sugar and other goods. . . ."

Marshal Tito was gracious enough to admit that, after the war, his country had received 430 million dollars' worth of food, machinery, and raw materials from UNRRA, but said this was only "our right" and added "We do not accept any conditions. . . . We consider that we have the moral right to ask from the United States that which we believe their leaders know that our people deserve."

To make it abundantly clear that receiving aid from America would not make his country our ally, Marshal Tito ended by saying that Yugoslavia would not abandon her declared position of neutrality and independence in the cold war between the West and the Cominform countries dominated by Russia.

Such experts on the Balkans as Leon Dennen, a frequent contributor to the *New Leader* and a correspondent of the North American Newspaper Alliance in Europe commented on the curious contrasts between the attitude of American diplomats toward corruption, graft, hunger, and misery in Yugoslavia and in Nationalist China. On a recent visit to Yugoslavia Dennen found that when he remarked upon these phenomena in Yugoslavia he was told by American officials not to hold Tito responsible, because it had always been like that in the Balkans. But in China the graft and extreme poverty and inequalities which were characteristic features of most of Asia were all blamed by the State Department on Chiang Kai-shek's government.

So, after having refused to help the Chinese National Government during its desperate fight against Soviet Russia's satellite forces, the State Department brought all its influence to bear on Congress to ensure a favorable vote on aid to Marshal Tito's dictatorship.

The extraordinary contrast between the demanding attitude of the Administration toward our declared and tested ally, the Chinese National Government, and its readiness to help and support Communist governments, provided there seems hope of getting them to join our side, or stay neutral, can be explained only on the assumption that those who direct United States foreign policy still nurture illusions about Communism. They have finally turned against Soviet Russia because of Moscow's obvious and implacable hostility to the United States. But they are still ready to help the "good" Communists, meaning anti-, or potentially anti-Russian Communists.

The argument that United States policy toward China is based on a shrewd calculation that the Chinese Communist dictatorship, given sufficient encouragement, will emulate that of Yugoslavia, takes no account of realities.

Not only is there the important difference that Yugoslavia has no common frontier with the USSR, and is in direct contact with the Western Powers, whereas China is directly subject to Russian pressure along a frontier stretching for thousands of miles in the north and to the west. There is also the important fact that China's industrial center is in Manchuria, which, thanks to the Yalta agreements, as well as to proximity, is directly under Russian control.

Politically the ties between Communist Russia and Communist China are closer and older than those between Moscow and any other Communist country, or foreign Communist Party. The Chinese Communist Party for more than two decades has proved itself in both word and deed more completely subservient to Moscow than any other. Knowing little of developments in Europe, or inside Russia, the Chinese Communists since 1928 have proved more immune to heresy than any other Communists, and are most ready to believe that the Kremlin is the citadel of the workers and of all "oppressed colonial peoples."

Nor should it be forgotten that Marshal Tito won power as the choice of the Western Powers, whereas the Chinese Communists got their weapons and military training from the Russians. Tito was supplied by the West, and enabled by the West to destroy his democratic opponents. The Chinese Communists were indirectly aided by America, but we never went to the same lengths in China as in Yugoslavia in positively supporting a Communist dictatorship. Mikhailovitch was murdered by Tito, but Chiang Kai-shek is still alive, still the head of a regime we recognize. Furthermore, it is also absurd to imagine that Marshal Tito can be trusted unless and until he restores some liberty to his oppressed people, ceases to create famine by his economic policies, and no longer emulates Stalin in his methods and aims.

A most important point ignored by Mr. Acheson is the fact that Moscow must have learnt a lesson through Tito's defection. Karl A. Wittfoegel, who is both an eminent scholar of Marxist theory and practice, and one of the greatest living experts on China and Chinese history, points out in an article in *Commentary* [1] that the very fact that China's Communist leaders are so much stronger than those of Russia's European satellite states, means that Stalin has realized that he must be especially sensitive and respectful to them, avoiding any possibility of a break.

The leaders of Communist China are obviously bound to Soviet Russia by their interests as well as by their ideology. Both the tremendous gains they can expect to win by maintaining their quarter-century ties with Russia, and the certainty that they could no more hope to survive if Soviet Russia went down to defeat, than Japan could survive the collapse of Nazi Germany, link the Chinese Communists to their Russian mentors by the strongest of all ties: self-interest and fear of destruction.

The mutual interests of the Russian and Chinese dictatorships are both positive and negative; positive as regards the tremendous power they can win together, negative in that both have to fear destruction if the free Western world triumphs. To quote Professor Wittfoegel again:

Their enmity to the forces they have partly crushed and which they intend to destroy completely establishes a tie of complicity that binds them to each other and to all those who join them in promoting the Communist system of despotic rule, managerial-totalitarianism, and absolute police terror. This tie is in turn cemented by their fear of the reprisals of a profoundly different and potentially hostile world.

In Europe today the Communists derive much of their strength from the fact that everyone knows if war comes and their country is occupied, the Communists will regard all who ever opposed them as enemies to be liquidated, whereas if the West wins, its enemies may at least escape with their lives, but its allies will gain no booty. In other words, it is odds-on in favor of an attitude favorable to the Communists. Hence one hears of businessmen in Western Europe who, while they are profiting from the Marshall Plan, are at the same time contributing substantial sums to the Communist parties to insure their personal safety in the event of Communist conquest.

Is it to be expected that the Chinese Communist leaders, who like all Communists proclaim and believe that war between the West and Soviet Russia is inevitable, will risk all their present gains and future hopes by remaining neutral? If Russia wins, they would be liquidated. If they fight with Russia against us, most of them would probably escape with their lives even if defeated. If they join our side, they cannot hope to preserve their power for long, for it is unlikely that after a victorious war against Russia, the forces of freedom would permit the continued existence of a Communist dictatorship in China. The Chinese Communist leaders have everything to win by fighting with Russia, and nothing to gain and much to lose by taking our side or remaining neutral. The odds either way are too greatly in favor of adherence to Moscow for there ever to have been much doubt of the choice which would be made by the Peiping government.

Here we must also note the fact that the power of the Soviet Union looms greater in China than in Europe. Few Chinese Communists have been in America or even in Europe, and compared with China's primitive economy Russia seems to be a modern industrialized country as well as the greatest military power in the world. Marshal Tito, who has had close contact with the West and also seen the inefficiency and backwardness of Soviet Russia, can believe perhaps that Russia is not the winning side. Mao Tse-tung is far less likely to have any doubts of Russia's victory. Furthermore, America's postwar policy in China certainly did not inspire confidence in either our ability or willingness to oppose Russian aggression. In Europe the United States soon after the war began to resist Communist expansion. In China we appeased the Communists, and the Korean war has made it even more evident that we are not prepared to drive the Communists back out of China.

One other important fact must be mentioned if we are to realize how tenuous is the basis for the State Department's hopes for the emergence of a Chinese Tito.

In 1927 the Kremlin controlled the Kuomintang (Chinese Nationalist) majority Government established in Hankow under the Presidency of Wang Ching-wei who, a decade later, was to become a Japanese, instead of a Russian, puppet. But the Comintern had not got control of the main Nationalist forces commanded by Chiang Kai-shek. Subsequent events proved that it was control of the army, not of the political apparatus, which determined the fate of China. After World War II, Stalin showed that he had learned the lesson afforded by the Comintern's failure in the late twenties to establish Russian hegemony over China. Through his trusted henchman, Marshal Malinovsky, Stalin appointed Lin Piao as commander of the Chinese Communist armies which were equipped and trained by Russia. Once assured that a man completely loyal to Moscow was in command of the crack Chinese Communist forces, Stalin no longer had any need to worry about the possibility of Mao Tse-tung, or Chuh Teh, emulating either Chiang Kai-shek in 1927, or Marshal Tito today. The proof that Mao Tse-tung, and the other former leaders of Communist China are today prisoners, or stooges, of the Kremlin, is afforded by the February 14, 1950, treaty between Communist China and Moscow.

According to Article 1 of the published text of this Treaty:

The high contracting parties undertake [sic] that they will undertake jointly all necessary measures at their disposal to prevent any repetition of aggression and violation of peace on the part of Japan or any other State which directly or indirectly would unite with Japan in acts of aggression. In the event of one of the agreeing parties being subjected to attack by Japan or any state allied with her, thus finding itself in a state of war, the other high contracting party will immediately render military or other aid with all means at its disposal.

In the preamble of the Treaty it was made yet more clear that it was directed against the United States, for it is written that its purpose is "jointly to prevent" the repetition of aggression by Japan *"or any other State which directly or indirectly would unite in any form with Japan in acts of aggression."* Since our defense of South Korea is designated as "aggression" by Moscow and Peiping it should have been clear from the beginning that Communist China, supplied and supported by Russia, would intervene in Korea. Mao

Tse-tung, in a speech he made in Moscow on December 16, 1950, made it abundantly clear that he had no intention of becoming a Chinese Tito. He said: "The most important task at the present time is to strengthen the Peace Front of the whole world which is headed by the Soviet Union."

The failure of American intelligence to appreciate the significance of this Treaty, and also its apparent refusal to give credence to Chinese Nationalist intelligence reports, is one reason why we suffered a great defeat in Korea. Both the news which now leaks through from China via Hong Kong, and the course of events, proves the general accuracy of these reports. But, as already noted in Chapter Five, the State Department forbade communication between our intelligence agencies and those of the Chinese Nationalists on Formosa.

According to a report to the UN on November 20, 1950, by Dr. Tsiang, Chinese Nationalist intelligence reports, as of June 1950, revealed that 45,100 Soviet citizens had already been sent to China, including 12,000 Army advisers and technicians, 3,000 assigned to the Chinese Communist Navy, 8,000 to the air force, 1,650 to Ordnance, and 5,000 to "the political sphere." The rest were personnel assigned to industry, agriculture, mining, and so forth.

According to Chinese Nationalist intelligence reports, duly passed on to the State Department and the Pentagon, the secret agreements signed in Moscow provided that each company in the Chinese Communist army should have assigned to it one Russian "political adviser" with a greater number of Soviet "advisers" in the higher echelons.

In its "Background Material" to Mr. Acheson's January 12, 1950, speech, the State Department took cognizance only of the "Harbin" agreement between Communist China and Soviet Russia, relating to Manchuria, proving that the Soviet Union was converting China's northeastern provinces into a Russian colony (see Appendix D). According to the State Department, Manchuria is already detached from China proper, since it has a separate currency, a separate system of economic controls, a separate railway administration and a separate trade agreement with the USSR. This, of course, means that Stalin has obviated any possibility of the Chinese Communist leaders emulating Tito, by establishing complete Russian control of her major industrial area. Moreover, it was agreed that all Manchuria's mineral, oil, forestry, and food resources were to be developed by joint commissions of Russians and Chinese. The Chinese Communist Government further undertook to continue supplying Russia with food, at the very time that a severe famine was killing off uncounted numbers of the Chinese people.

As Dr. Tsiang, the Chinese Nationalist delegate to the UN, said in one of his speeches, the Chinese Communist Government had "signed away the inalienable rights of the Chinese people in return for Soviet support."

According to an article published in the *American Mercury* in February 1951,[2] based on material supplied by Ralph Wallace (who made a trip to Formosa to obtain the evidence), and on Chinese, British, and American intelligence information, the secret agreements signed in Moscow included a proviso that there should be "complete cooperation between all persons of both countries connected with security"—meaning the domination in China of the Russian secret police which condemns to slave labor anyone suspected of opposition to the Communist dictatorship. The most hypocritical, as well as the most cruel, provision of the secret Treaty between Soviet Russia and Communist China was the provision that Russia would "help solve the economic difficulties of the Chinese" by providing "employment" for "unemployed Chinese laborers" in Russia. This meant that the Kremlin could acquire an unlimited number of Chinese slaves including all the "political undesirables" whom the Chinese Communist Government desired to liquidate. When, for instance, the 26th and 27th Chinese Communist armies rebelled in South China in 1950, revolting soldiers were shipped out to Siberian labor camps.

According to the same source, it was further agreed that should Soviet Russia be involved in war in Europe, the Chinese Communist Government would send "laborers and expeditionary forces" to serve under the Soviet High Command.

Whether or not full credence can be given to Chinese Nationalist, or other intelligence reports, concerning the secret agreements signed in Moscow by the Chinese Communist Government, the U.S. Administration would certainly have been better advised had it taken cognizance of them.

According to the *American Mercury* article, the agreements included the following:

"a. The Chinese army is to consist of 5,700,000 men.

"b. Russia was to be in control of training the Chinese army.

"c. Russia was to control: aviation, navy, radar, communications and meteorology.

"d. Russia was to begin the immediate training and equipment of fifty Chinese divisions.

"e. Russia was to transfer to China: six hundred war planes and all the Japanese naval craft awarded to Russia at the end of World War II. Russia was also to send several regiments of anti-aircraft troops to protect the Chinese airfields.

"f. Russia and China agreed to 'the intensive development of an International Army Corps with soldiers of all Asiatic nations serving in the ranks.'

"g. Russia was given twelve air bases in China, from Hami to Shanghai. Russia was also given naval bases at Port Arthur, Dairen, Yongkow, Ching-Hwang-Lao, Hu-Lu-Tao, Taku, Chefoo, Tsingtao and Lien-Yung-Kang.

"h. China and Russia agreed to operate in 'all future military operations under a joint Sino-Soviet staff'."

The fact which immediately concerns the American people is that the signing of some such agreements between Soviet Russia and Communist China was not revealed by the Administration or the press. Although the agreement that a five-million-man army had been assigned to further the Kremlin's aim to conquer the world, the U.S. Government had so poor an intelligence service, or was so determined to ignore the evidence of the complete identity of the aims of Communist China and Russia, that it failed to sound the alarm. Had this not been so, General MacArthur would not have been misled when he hopefully asserted, after our victory over the North Korean Communist forces, that our troops could expect to be home by Christmas.

Our losses in Korea prove both the disastrous consequences of our boycott of the Chinese Nationalist Government on Formosa, and of our failure to pursue a policy which is neither cynically realistic, nor based on the principles which have made America great and strong and prosperous.

Believers in *Realpolitik* can argue that the United States should have pursued a foreign policy based solely on considerations of American interests, without regard, one way or another, for the ideologies, or forms of government of other nations. But the attempt of the State Department to represent its policy as based on ethical considerations and "democratic" principles, while giving right of way to the Communists, could not but end in disaster, since General Marshall and Mr. Acheson refused to be consistent. Far from applying the principles of power politics in an unprejudiced fashion, they continually gave aid and comfort to the Communists while weakening the conservative forces, or believers in free enterprise, whom they should, logically, have considered to be our best friends.

Mr. Acheson seems never to have realized that it was illogical to refuse alliances, or arms aid, to such "people on our side" as the anti-Communist Chinese because he disapproved of their governments, while insisting on aid being given to Communist regimes, such as that of Marshal Tito, provided only that they are not dependable allies of Soviet Russia. His sentiments are echoed by such erudite but ignorant columnists as Mr. Lippmann who, in his column on February

6, 1951, urging aid to Tito, deplored America's "undiscriminating anti-Communism." Nor is it consistent to cold-shoulder Spain while still proffering the hand of friendship to Communist regimes.

It is, in any case, impossible for a government responsible to the will of the people to follow a course based on *Realpolitik*. For most of the voters will always insist on the observance of moral principles.

Consequently, the attempts of the United States Administration to pursue a Far Eastern policy based on a nice judgment of how to win Communists over to our side was doomed to failure from the start. The tug of war between the Administration and its opponents resulted in our getting the worst of both worlds. If there ever was any possibility of "detaching" the Chinese Communists from their allegiance to Moscow, it required an early and complete abandonment of the Nationalists and whole-hearted support of the Communists. But this course was politically impossible for any United States Administration, however large its majority. Consequently, we neither gave sufficient support to Chiang Kai-shek to enable him to defeat the Communists, nor transferred our support to the Communists.

Neither the Administration, nor the opposition in Congress was prepared to follow through a consistent policy to its logical conclusion. Those partial to the Chinese Communists hesitated to go all-out to appease them; and those who opposed the Administration's policy dared not face the consequences which a bold stand against Communist aggression might have entailed. The opponents of appeasement were as anxious to avoid the danger of a third world war as the present-day "men of Munich" who want to recognize Communist China and abandon our ally, the Chinese National Government. The consequence has been that neither a principled nor a completely opportunistic policy has been pursued.

A realistic view of the situation would have anticipated Chinese Communist intervention in Korea, once the Korean

Communists were defeated. But, prior to November 1950, when the Chinese Communists started killing Americans in Korea, one heard, in all quarters, that Peiping would never send its troops to fight us because it would be against the interests of the Chinese people. And even after the Chinese Communist Army had intervened in Korea, and forced us to retreat, all sorts of excuses were still being offered by those who refused to abandon old illusions. The *Washington Post* and other newspapers argued that the blame must be placed on America, rather than on Russia, because we had failed to reassure Peiping soon enough that we would, under no circumstances, destroy the hydroelectric stations on the Yalu River which supply power to Manchuria; and because we had not finally abandoned the Chinese National Government and admitted Communist China to the United Nations.

Illusions die hard, especially when reputations depend upon their preservation. General Marshall, Mr. Acheson, and the host of journalists, authors, and radio commentators who gave ill-calculated advice, based on false assumptions, to the Administration and the American people, cannot, or dare not, admit that they were wrong. Like the Bourbons, they have learned nothing and forgotten nothing. Just as formerly the majority of Americans were deluded into thinking that Stalin would be driven by Russia's interests to follow a postwar policy friendly to America, so even today, voices are still being raised to persuade us that the Chinese Communists can be induced to follow a policy beneficial to China and to the western world if we stop fighting them.

Not until this great and persistent illusion is destroyed can we hope for the adoption of a sane American policy. Until we understand that *all* Communists are animated by the same ideals, and the same drive for power and expansive urges, our strength and good will will be unavailing to avert disaster, and more and more Americans will die in more and more futile wars.

Tito's heresy has, unfortunately, greatly strengthened the

faith of the ignorant liberals who, in spite of their revulsion from the Soviet police state, continue to hope that Communism contains within it the germs of a more just social order. Ignoring the evidence that the peoples of Yugoslavia are as bowed down, hungry, hopeless, and afraid as the Russian people, they see in Marshal Tito's opposition to Moscow a hope for the evolution of the "good" Communist regime which they formerly hoped for in Russia.

There is a distinct analogy between the past and present attitude of the Truman Administration toward Communist aggression in the Far East, and that of Neville Chamberlain toward Nazi aggression in Central and Eastern Europe. Both the British Government, prior to 1939, and the United States Administration, prior to June 1950, had based their policies on the belief that an accommodation with the totalitarians was both possible and desirable, or was necessary to provide time for rearmament. And President Truman's sudden turn from appeasement, or retreat, to resistance, when the Communists attacked South Korea, is paralleled by Neville Chamberlain's abandonment of the Munich policy after Hitler marched into Prague in the spring of 1939. Up to that event Britain had been prepared to let Nazi Germany acquire *de facto* control of Eastern Europe just as Truman was acquiescent to the Communist capture of China, Korea, and Formosa. It was no more just to accuse the British Conservative Government of Nazi sympathies than to accuse the United States Democratic Administration of Communist leanings. But both Chamberlain's weakness toward the totalitarians of the Right and Truman's weakness toward those of the Left were based on a failure to understand the nature of the enemy. Neither of them offered real opposition to the expansion of the totalitarian empires so long as the dictators confined themselves to infiltration, threats, fifth column activity, or "civil war." Both were so shocked when the dictators turned to open and unashamed aggression that they suddenly reversed their policies without fully considering the consequences. Chamberlain guaranteed the security of Poland and Rumania without the means to honor his pledge, just as Truman, years later, went to war to defend South Korea without any real possibility of saving it short of all-out war against Russia and the Chinese Communists. Both of them got into a war which they were psychologically as well as militarily unprepared to fight. They failed to re-examine the premises upon which their former policies had been based, and did not change their basic attitudes. Hence the 1939–40 months of "phony war" which ended only when Germany suddenly advanced in the West and overwhelmed France. Hence, today, the fact that having got into a war with the Communists on the Asiatic mainland, the United States Administration has sought to make it one of limited liability. This explains why Truman called the Korean war a "police action," and even after the Chinese Communists intervened, continued to refuse the help of the large Chinese Nationalist forces eager to fight beside us, while waiting in vain for any substantial help from other members of the United Nations.

No government which is looking for a way to avoid a showdown with the main forces of the enemy is likely to go all-out to win. Those who believe that almost anything is preferable to war with Russia are not likely to wage war with real determination. Those who not so long ago trusted Stalin find it difficult to hate those who fight under his banner. Consequently the United States forces in Korea have been fighting with one hand tied behind their backs, continually prevented by political considerations from taking quick and effective action. While fighting Stalin's auxiliary forces, we have kept one eye cocked on his representatives and friends in the United Nations, hoping they could be induced to make peace.

Having gone to war under the auspices of the United Nations, which voted to take action to stop Communist aggression while the Russians were on one of their periodic walkouts, our military strategy is now controlled by some sixty nations, which include our enemies and the friends of our enemies as well as the advocates of peace at any price. While doing most of the fighting, we are precluded from taking the action necessary to win. Indeed, according to the French representative to the United Nations, M. Francis Lacoste, the objective of the United Nations is not to "win a war" and therefore no efforts at peaceful settlement should be omitted.[3]

As Senator Margaret Chase Smith aptly remarked in her column on January 30, 1951, the UN has become "a stone around the neck of the United States, and a stalling device for Communist Russia and Communist China."

At the same time, the United Nations provides a convenient alibi for American appeasers who would like to hand over Formosa as well as Korea to the Communists, and also give them China's seat in the UN, as the reward for their aggression, or the price for peace in our time.

The views of the Americans who hide behind the skirts of the appeasers in the United Nations were cynically expressed by Doris Fleeson in her column in the Washington *Evening Star* on January 30, 1951. Referring to the reluctance of most members of the United Nations to vote for the United States' resolution condemning Communist China as an aggressor three months after our troops were first engaged in mortal combat with them in Korea, she remarked that "we could have had the words long since had we not tried to add sanctions to them." Sanctions, meaning effective measures against the aggressors, Miss Fleeson informed her readers, are what "they will not give, lest they lead to war in Asia." One wonders what the GI's in Korea are supposed to think they are doing as they fight and freeze and die, since they are not supposed to be fighting a war in Asia.

As I write, it is as yet uncertain whether the United Nations will commit suicide by destroying all the hopes upon which it was founded. Since Americans are doing most of the fighting in Korea, the members of the "peace-loving" nations in the UN are not even called upon to commit their own people in the first large-scale engagement against Communist imperialism. True that the British and French, as well as the Turks and the Greeks, have sent contingents to fight beside us in Korea. But this has not prevented the British from continuing to supply our common enemy with huge quantities of war supplies via Hong Kong. Nor has it silenced their demand, and that of the French Government, that we abandon our friends in Asia in order to preserve our strength to defend them in Europe. It is unnecessary to dwell upon the obvious fact that appeasement of the Communists in China will embolden rather than discourage them to attack Europe. Unfortunately, however, it would seem that too many people believe that the Communist Moloch can be satiated by the sacrifice of others, or that any concessions are worth the privilege which the Cyclop offered to Ulysses: that of being eaten last.

As Ulysses escaped, so America also may avoid destruction, but there is an acute danger that the failure of our allies and beneficiaries to support us may foster such potent isolationist sentiments in America, that we shall abandon our faint-hearted European friends. In that event we may finally be overwhelmed by the Communist-directed forces of all Europe and Asia.

There is very grave danger that popular disillusionment—the realization that we *have* been misled and let down by almost all our allies—will lead to isolationist policies as disastrous as the phony internationalist policies sold to the American people during and after World War II. For how can American soldiers and marines in Korea be expected to understand why the United Nations, under whose flag they fight, should have hesitated so long to designate as an aggressor an enemy who is intent on killing them? Suppose that tomorrow India or some other member of the "Asian-Arab bloc," or the British and French who have pleaded with us not to provoke the Chinese or Russian Communists, by daring to recognize our enemy, should be attacked? Can one expect the American GI or his family and friends to feel enthusiastic about defending those who advocated appeasement until they themselves were attacked?

It is, of course, not merely the State Department or the Administration which is responsible for America's muddled policies and present hazardous situation. It is largely due to the influence enjoyed for so long by the writers and commentators who pandered to the public desire for "happy endings," or who were impelled by Communist sympathies to delude the American people with false hopes of lasting peace based on an erroneous estimate of Soviet Russia. The realists who questioned the advisability of appeasing the Communists in Europe or Asia, were silenced by affixing on them the label "Nazi" or "reactionary" or "isolationist." And even today, those who during and after World War II warned us not to trust Stalin are still in disfavor. The anti-anti-Communists who hate and fear the "premature anti-Communists," who were right when they themselves were wrong, have taken the place of the former Communist fellow travelers in vilifying those who dared to face the facts.

The sad fate of those who foretold disaster is not important in itself. The danger lies in the fact that the former avowed whoopsters for Soviet Russia are today busy creating and propagating new illusions about Communism to take the place of the old ones which the hard logic of fact has discredited.

Communist influence in America has been like a stone thrown into a pond causing circular ripples of diminishing depth and increasing extent, with the result that the majority of those affected by it were unconscious of the influence which moved them.

Not only is it hard to draw a line between those who were "real" Communists intent on furthering Stalin's interests and those who were impelled by ignorance and humanitarian sentiment to further the Communist cause. Equal weight, as we have already seen, has to be given to the fact that in order to get preferment under the Roosevelt and first Truman Administrations, it was necessary to play along with the admirers of the Soviet Union and the friends of the Chinese Communists. So today, in spite of the Alger Hiss and Remington trials and the McCarthy hearings, it is impossible to gauge the extent to which idealistic motives, as distinct from ambition, or cowardice, or secret sympathy for the Communist cause, led to treasonable activities in high places in Washington.

The only clear distinction which can be made is that between the hidden Communists and their sympathizers and those who left the Communist Party while honestly proclaiming their former membership, once they realized that the aims of the Communists were incompatible with their desire for liberty and justice. Those who, like Whittaker Chambers, have endeavored to atone for their past mistakes by telling the truth, even at the cost of losing their jobs as well as their reputations, and with the certainty that they would be vilified by the time-servers of all political parties, must be accounted as honorable men. They are certainly both braver and more honorable than the crypto-Communists who denied their Communist affiliations, in order not to risk losing good jobs in the Administration, while endeavoring to provide for their future well-being by secretly and subtly playing Moscow's game. The most despicable are those who continue to pose as champions of liberty while assisting the Communists to destroy us.

Summing up the evidence available, the verdict of an impartial jury would be that the delivery of China to the Communists, with what amounted to the blessing of the United States Administration, was due to ignorance, refusal to face facts, romanticism, and political immaturity or a misguided humanitarianism, and the influence of Communist sympathizers and the careerists who staked their reputations on a pro-Soviet policy.

As I conclude the writing of this book, evidence accumulates that the Chinese people have themselves created something like a second front against our enemies and theirs. There are reports from American correspondents in Hong Kong that the revolt against Communist tyranny is spreading all over China. Hungry farmers, forced to pay more to the Communist authorities than to the landlords, usurers, and tax-collectors under the Nationalist government, and also compelled to give their sons to fight for Russia in Korea against the United Nations, are staging food riots and storming the strongholds of Communist power, although their only weapons are hoes and scythes. The Communists themselves have not denied that more than a million guerrillas are up in arms against them. So great is the menace of internal revolt that Peiping, according to a *New York Times* report dated March 10, 1951, has decreed the death penalty, or life imprisonment, for anyone who in any way opposes the Communist government. Thus already the Chinese people are endeavoring to overthrow Moscow's satellite forces, and in China today, as long since in Russia, mass liquidation of all who strive for freedom is the order of the day. Whether or not Chiang Kai-shek's government-in-exile on Formosa is still the only rallying point of the resistance in China, we should resolve to give help to our Chinese friends who have regained hope, thanks to our courageous stand in Korea.

Great men admit their errors and seek to rectify them even at the cost of tarnishing their reputations. Little men pretend they have always been right. The vanity and lack of true patriotism of small men of limited understanding and high ambitions, constitutes a greater danger to the Republic than all the Communists in America. For it is only because of their cleverness in taking advantage of human weaknesses that the Communists are able to influence policy. The tragic fact that their tactics have given them control over a large part of the world should impel us all to re-examine the policy we have so disastrously pursued in the past so that in the future we may conduct ourselves in such a way as to avoid further humiliation and unnecessary defeat. As Confucius said: "A man who knows he has committed a mistake and does not correct it is committing another mistake."

Whatever the reasons for the mistakes of the past, we must join hands now with our Chinese friends in their struggle against those who masqueraded so successfully for so long as democrats and as the saviors of humanity, while seeking to destroy us.

Appendices

Appendix A

*Personal Statement by the Special Representative
of the President (Marshall) January 7, 1947*

THE PRESIDENT has recently given a summary of the developments in China during the past year and the position of the American Government toward China. Circumstances now dictate that I should supplement this with impressions gained at first hand.

In this intricate and confused situation, I shall merely endeavor here to touch on some of the more important considerations—as they appeared to me—during my connection with the negotiations to bring about peace in China and a stable democratic form of government.

In the first place, the greatest obstacle to peace has been the complete, almost overwhelming suspicion with which the Chinese Communist Party and the Kuomintang regard each other.

On the one hand, the leaders of the Government are strongly opposed to a communistic form of government. On the other, the Communists frankly state that they are Marxists and intend to work toward establishing a communistic form of government in China, though first advancing through the medium of a democratic form of government of the American or British type.

The leaders of the Government are convinced in their minds that the Communist-expressed desire to participate in a government of the type endorsed by the Political Consultative Conference last January had for its purpose only a destructive intention. The Communists felt, I believe, that the government was insincere in its apparent acceptance of the PCC resolutions for the formation of the new government and intended by coercion of military force and the action of secret police to obliterate the Communist Party. Combined with this mutual deep distrust was the conspicuous error by both parties of ignoring the effect of the fears and suspicions of the other party in estimating the reason for proposals or opposition regarding the settlement of various matters under negotiation. They each sought only to take counsel of their own fears. They both, therefore, to that extent took a rather lopsided view of each situation and were susceptible to every evil suggestion or possibility. This complication was exaggerated to an explosive degree by the confused reports of fighting on the distant and tremendous fronts of hostile military contact. Patrol clashes were deliberately magnified into large offensive actions. The distortion of the facts was utilized by both sides to heap condemnation on the other. It was only through the reports of American officers in the field teams from Executive Headquarters that I could get even a partial idea of what was actually happening and the incidents were too numerous and the distances too great for the American personnel to cover all of the ground. I must comment here on the superb courage of the officers of our Army and Marines in struggling against almost insurmountable and maddening obstacles to bring some measure of peace to China.

I think the most important factors involved in the recent breakdown of negotiations are these: On the side of the National Government, which is in effect the Kuomintang, there is a dominant group of reactionaries who have been opposed, in my opinion, to almost every effort I have made to influence the formation of a genuine coalition government. This has usually been under the cover of political or party action, but since the Party was the Government, this action, though subtle or indirect, has been devastating in its effect. They were quite frank in publicly stating their belief that cooperation by the Chinese Communist Party in the government was inconceivable and that only a policy of force could definitely settle the issue. This group includes military as well as political leaders.

On the side of the Chinese Communist Party there are, I believe, liberals as well as radicals, though this view is vigorously opposed by many who believe that the Chinese Communist Party discipline is too rigidly enforced to admit of such differences of viewpoint. Nevertheless, it has appeared to me that there is a definite liberal group among the Communists, especially of young men who have turned to the Communists in disgust at the corruption evident in the local governments—men who would put the interest of the Chinese people above ruthless measures to establish a Communist ideology in the immediate future. The dyed-in-the-wool Communists do not hesitate at the most drastic measures to gain their end as, for instance, the destruction of communications in order to wreck the economy of China and produce a situation that would facilitate the overthrow or collapse of the Government, without any regard to the immediate suffering of the people involved. They completely distrust the leaders of the Kuomintang and appear convinced that every Government proposal is designed to crush the Chinese Communist Party. I must say that the quite evidently inspired mob actions of last February and March, some within a few blocks of where I was then engaged in completing negotiations, gave the Communists good excuse for such suspicions.

However, a very harmful and immensely provocative phase of the Chinese Communist Party procedure has been in the character of its propaganda. I wish to state to the American people that in the deliberate misrepresentation and abuse of the action, policies and purposes of our Government this propaganda has been without regard for the truth, without any regard whatsoever for the facts, and has given plain evidence of a determined purpose to mislead the Chinese people and the world and to arouse a bitter hatred of Americans. It has been difficult to remain silent in the midst of such public abuse and wholesale disregard of facts, but a denial would merely lead to the necessity of daily denials; an intolerable course of action for an American official. In the interest of fairness, I must state that the Nationalist Government publicity agency has made numerous misrepresentations, though not of the vicious nature of the Communist propaganda. Incidentally, the Communist statements regarding the Anping incident which resulted in the death of three Marines and the wounding of twelve others were almost pure fabrication, deliberately representing a carefully arranged ambuscade of a

Marine convoy with supplies for the maintenance of Executive Headquarters and some UNRRA supplies, as a defence against a Marine assault. The investigation of this incident was a tortuous procedure of delays and maneuvers to disguise the true and privately admitted facts of the case.

Sincere efforts to achieve settlement have been frustrated time and again by extremist elements of both sides. The agreements reached by the Political Consultative Conference a year ago were a liberal and forward-looking charter which then offered China a basis for peace and reconstruction. However, irreconcilable groups within the Kuomintang, interested in the preservation of their own feudal control of China, evidently had no real intention of implementing them. Though I speak as a soldier, I must here also deplore the dominating influence of the military. Their dominance accentuates the weakness of civil government in China. At the same time, in pondering the situation in China, one must have clearly in mind not the workings of small Communist groups or committees to which we are accustomed in America, but rather of millions of people and an army of more than a million men.

I have never been in a position to be certain of the development of attitudes in the innermost Chinese Communist circles. Most certainly, the course which the Chinese Communist Party has pursued in recent months indicated an unwillingness to make a fair compromise. It has been impossible even to get them to sit down at a conference table with Government representatives to discuss given issues. Now the Communists have broken off negotiations by their last offer which demanded the dissolution of the National Assembly and a return to the military positions of January 13th which the Government could not be expected to accept.

Between this dominant reactionary group in the Government and the irreconcilable Communists who, I must state, did not so appear last February, lies the problem of how peace and well-being are to be brought to the long-suffering and presently inarticulate mass of the people of China. The reactionaries in the Government have evidently counted on substantial American support regardless of their actions. The Communists by their unwillingness to compromise in the national interest are evidently counting on an economic collapse to bring about the fall of the Government, accelerated by extensive guerrilla action against the long lines of rail communications—regardless of the cost in suffering to the Chinese people.

The salvation of the situation, as I see it, would be the assumption of leadership by the liberals in the Government and in the minority parties, a splendid group of men, but who as yet lack the political power to exercise a controlling influence. Successful action on their part under the leadership of Generalissimo Chiang Kai-shek would, I believe, lead to unity through good government.

In fact, the National Assembly has adopted a democratic constitution which in all major respects is in accordance with the principles laid down by the all-party Political Consultative Conference of last January. It is unfortunate that the Communists did not see fit to participate in the Assembly since the constitution that has been adopted seems to include every major point that they wanted.

Soon the Government in China will undergo major reorganization pending the coming into force of the constitution following elections to be completed before Christmas Day 1947. Now that the form for a democratic China has been laid down by the newly adopted constitution, practical measures will be the test. It remains to be seen to what extent the Government will give substance to the form by a genuine welcome of all groups actively to share in the responsibility of government.

The first step will be the reorganization of the State Council and the executive branch of Government to carry on administration pending the enforcement of the constitution. The manner in which this is done and the amount of representation accorded to liberals and to non-Kuomintang members will be significant. It is also to be hoped that during this interim period the door will remain open for Communists or other groups to participate if they see fit to assume their share of responsibility for the future of China.

It has been stated officially and categorically that the period of political tutelage under the Kuomintang is at an end. If the termination of one-party rule is to be a reality, the Kuomintang should cease to receive financial support from the Government.

I have spoken very frankly because in no other way can I hope to bring the people of the United States to even a partial understanding of this complex problem. I have expressed all these views privately in the course of negotiations; they are well known, I think, to most of the individuals concerned. I express them now publicly, as it is my duty, to present my estimate of the situation and its possibilities to the American people who have a deep interest in the development of conditions in the Far East promising such an enduring peace in the Pacific. *

---
* White Paper, p. 686.

Appendix B

FROM "China Presents Her Case to the United Nations," Item 68 of the Agenda of the General Assembly, Fourth Session, of the United Nations, pp. 17-18.

"In addition to Japanese arms and ammunition captured by or surrendered to the Soviet Army, which were transferred in large quantities to the Chinese Communist forces in Manchuria to assist them in their armed rebellion against the Chinese National Government, the Soviet Union supplied the Chinese Communist forces with arms and ammunition manufactured in the Soviet Union itself. Some samples of these captured equipment are listed as follows:

(a) Thirteen cases of explosives manufactured in the Soviet Union captured on October 4, 1946, when the Chinese Communists were dynamiting the railway near Kungchiachiao between Hailung and Meihoko.

(b) Soviet-manufactured rifles captured during the campaigns north of Changchun between November, 1946, and March, 1947.

(c) Soviet-manufactured rifles captured during the fifth Szepingkai campaign, June 10-30, 1947.

(d) German-type Soviet-manufactured rifles captured during the Szepingkai campaign.

(e) Soviet-manufactured air-cooled type heavy machineguns captured during the Szepingkai campaign.

(f) Soviet-manufactured light machineguns captured during the Szepingkai campaign.

(g) Soviet-manufactured artillery shells captured July 1949 in North Hunan and the Northwest theater.

(h) Soviet-manufactured Sikcarlof machineguns captured during battle of Hsinhsien, Shansi Province, August 1946.

(i) 27 machineguns of the same type as (h), captured at the battle along the Chengting-Taiyuan Railway, April 28, 1947. (Photographs of the above items are available for inspection.)

. . . Soviet military aid to the Chinese Communists also included military training which was openly done by Soviet authorities. Soviet instructors were on the staff of Chinese Communist military schools, especially in artillery and mechanized warfare training, at various points in Manchuria. The main school was located at Kiamutse, where a large number of Soviet instructors were concentrated. Soviet instructors also helped in the training of the Chinese Communist air force, with one center at Tsitsihar, in north Manchuria, and another center at Khabarovsk, in the Soviet Union itself. The Chinese Consulate General in Khabarovsk reported that, on June 23, 1948, a group of some 50 Chinese wearing Communist air force uniforms were sighted on Marx Street in Khabarovsk.

In addition, large groups of Chinese youths were sent to the Soviet Union for military training. For instance, the Chinese Ministry of National Defense reported that a group of some 300 graduates of secondary schools, all natives of Manchuria, passed through Suifenho in Manchuria on April 27, 1948, on their way to Spask in the Soviet Union, to receive Soviet training in navigation and in amphibious warfare. Another group of 350, composed of students from the North China provinces of Shansi, Chahar and Hopei, passed through Ulam Bator, capital of Outer Mongolia, on July 4, 1948, for advanced training in the Soviet Union. Still another group of 300, from Inner Mongolia, Suiyuan and Chahar, was reported to have gone to the Soviet Union for training in motorized warfare."

Appendix C

Extracts from General Wedemeyer's report of 1947 as given in Annex 135 of White Paper on China.

"I WAS ASSURED by the Generalissimo that China would support to the limit of her ability an American program for the stabilization of the Far East. He stated categorically that, regardless of normal encouragement or material aid received from the United States, he is determined to oppose Communism and to create a democratic form of government in consonance with Doctor Sun Yat-sen's principles. He stated further that he plans to make sweeping reforms in the government including the removal of incompetent and corrupt officials. He stated that some progress has been made along these lines but, with spiraling inflation, economic distress and civil war, it has been difficult to accomplish fully these objectives. *He emphasized that, when the Communist problem is solved, he could drastically reduce the Army and concentrate upon political and economic reforms. I retain the conviction that the Generalissimo is sincere in his desire to attain these objectives* . . ." (italics added)

"Soviet actions, contrary to the letter and spirit of the Sino-Soviet Treaty of 1945 and its related documents, have strengthened the Chinese Communist position in Manchuria, with political, economic and military repercussions on the National Government's position both in Manchuria and in China proper, and have made more difficult peace and stability in China. The present trend points toward a gradual disintegration of the National Govern-

The Chinese Communists constantly foster anti-American feeling in areas under their control, picturing the United States as an imperialistic power which has as its objective the enslavement of the world. Their ruthless tactics of land distribution and oppression of the Christian missionary movement have made for them bitter enemies among many Chinese in the rural areas. Some sources say that Communist land reforms have benefited the poor peasants who comprise the majority of the rural population and who, therefore, support the Communists, while other sources say that Communist terroristic tactics have alienated the vast majority of peasants. Where local government, regardless of ideology, is competent, honest and humane, there is no local revolt. Whether by suasion or by intimidation, the Communists have in many areas been successful in organizing the countryside against the National Government."

"The Soviet Union has assisted the Chinese Communists in Manchuria by the timing of the withdrawal of Soviet troops and by making available, either directly or indirectly, large quantities of surrendered Japanese military equipment. . . ."

General Wedemeyer in fact proposed a realistic and intelligent China policy for the United States. He admitted, indeed emphasized, all the weaknesses and shortcomings of the Chinese National Government, and his criticisms on this score are quoted with approval in the White Paper's text. But Wedemeyer was so well aware of the vital security needs of the United States that, instead of writing off China as the State Department had done, he proposed measures which could have led both to reform and Communist defeat. Specifically he recommended both arms aid to China and China's acceptance of American advisers "as responsible representatives of the United States Government in specified military and economic fields to assist China in utilizing U. S. aid in the manner for which it is intended."

General Wedemeyer's repudiation of the State Department's policy was emphatically stated in the recommendations he made to President Truman. In the section of his suppressed report headed "Implications of 'No Assistance' to China or Continuation of 'Wait and See' Policy" he wrote:

"To advise at this time a policy of 'no assistance' to China would suggest the withdrawal of the United States Military and Naval Advisory Groups from China and it would be equivalent to cutting the ground from under the feet of the Chinese Government. *Removal of American assistance, without removal of Soviet assistance, would certainly lay the country open to eventual Communist domination.* It would have repercussions in other parts of Asia, would lower American prestige in the Far East and would make easier the spread of Soviet influence and Soviet political expansion not only in Asia but in other areas of the world. (italics added)

"It is possible that the adoption of a 'wait and see' policy would lead to the Generalissimo's finally carrying out genuine reforms which in turn would enable the United States to extend effective aid and which themselves would furnish the best answer to the challenge of Communism. Because of an inevitable time lag in its results, however, such a policy would permit for an appreciable time the continuation of the process of National Government disintegration. At some stage of the disintegration the authority and control of the National Government might become so weak and restricted that separatist movements would occur in various areas now under Government control. At this point, it is conceivable there might emerge a middle group which would be able to establish a modicum of stability in the areas under its control. It would then be possible for the United States to extend support, both moral and material, to any such group or combination of groups which gave indication of ability to consolidate control over sizable portions of the country and whose policies would be compatible with our own. This, however, represents conjecture regarding a possible future course of events in China. There is the further possibility that such a policy would result at some point in the Generalissimo's seeking a compromise with the Chinese Communists, although it is likely that he would not do so until his position became so weak that the Communists would accept a settlement only on terms assuring them a dominant position in the government. At worst, under a process of continued National Government disintegration it may be expected that there would be a long period of disturbance verging on chaos, at the end of which the Chinese Communists would emerge as the dominant group oriented toward the Soviet Union."

General Wedemeyer, who so exactly foretold the dire consequences to the United States of denying aid to the Chinese National Government, now commands the Sixth Army with headquarters at San Francisco. The general opinion in Washington is that he was shelved on account of his opposition to the State Department's and General Marshall's China policy, instead of being made Chief of Staff.

Appendix D

CENTRAL NEWS AGENCY, reported from Tokyo October 16, 1949, the terms of the two secret agreements concluded between the Chinese Communists and Moscow, known as the *Harbin Agreement* and *Moscow Agreement,* respectively:

The Harbin Agreement, it is reported, contains the following provisions:

(1) The Soviet Union undertakes to give complete support to the Chinese Communists in diplomatic and military affairs.

(2) The Soviet Union and the Chinese Communists shall cooperate in the development of the economy of Manchuria.

(3) The Chinese Communists recognize that the Soviet Union enjoys special privileges with regard to land and air communications in Manchuria.

(4) The Soviet Union shall assist in the supply and maintenance of fifty planes of the Chinese Red Air Force.

(5) The Soviet Union shall return all arms and equipments surrendered by or captured from the Japanese, such arms to be returned to the Chinese Communists in two installments.

(6) The Soviet Union shall sell to the Chinese Communists, at a fair price, all the military installations and supplies in Manchuria now under Soviet control.

(7) The Chinese Red Army may retreat into the Soviet Union via North Korea in case of emergencies.

(8) The Soviet army shall secretly assist the Chinese Red Army in case of amphibious attacks by the Kuomintang army in Manchuria.

(9) The Soviet Union shall permit the Chinese Red Army to establish air training stations in Chita and North Korea.

(10) The Chinese Communists shall supply the Soviet Union with intelligence regarding the Kuomintang and American activities in China.

(11) The Chinese Communists shall supply the Soviet Union with Manchurian products, including cotton, soybeans, and other strategic materials, the percentage to be retained for local consumption to be determined later.

(12) The Soviet Union shall assist the Chinese Communists in gaining control of Sinkiang.

(13) Special areas in the Manchurian provinces of Liaoning and Antung are reserved for the stationing of North Korean troops, these areas to be incorporated into Korea at a subsequent date.

The Moscow Agreement:

(1) The Soviet Union shall have priority in the exploitation of mines in the territory of China. A Sino-Soviet Company to be known as the China Commerce Company, is to be established to determine and execute the steps by which such mining rights are to be transferred.

(2) The Soviet Union shall have the right to station troops in Manchuria and Sinkiang.

(3) In the event of the outbreak of a Third World War, the Chinese Red Army shall fight alongside the army of the Soviet Union. The Commander of the Joint Forces to be nominated by the Soviet Union and the Deputy Commander to be nominated by China.

(4) The Soviet Union shall assist in the establishment of a joint Sino-Soviet Air Force.

(5) The organization of the Chinese Communist Party shall be expanded, and the Far Eastern Cominform shall be located in China.

(6) In the event of an outbreak of war in Europe involving the Soviet Union, the Chinese Communists shall send an expeditionary force of 100,000 men and a labor force of one million to assist the Soviet Union in the prosecution of the war.

(7) The Soviet Union shall as a matter of urgency train and equip eleven divisions of the Chinese army.

Notes and Index

Notes

CHAPTER ONE

1. According to the testimony of General Bonner Fellers, Roosevelt before he left for Yalta had received from General MacArthur unofficial Japanese peace overtures amounting to an acceptance of unconditional surrender, with the sole reservation that the Emperor should not be deposed. General MacArthur had recommended negotiations, but Roosevelt brushed his suggestion aside. This is corroborated by Rear Admiral Ellis M. Zacharias (retired), *Behind Closed Doors* (New York, G. P. Putnam's Sons, 1950), p. 63.
2. It is necessary to recall that the Chinese Communists, true to the principle of "Russia First," welcomed the Russo-Japanese Neutrality Treaty of 1941 and the even more important treaty Stalin made with the Japanese in 1944 and denounced as "craven tricksters" the Chinese, who were dismayed at Soviet Russia's recognition of Japan's puppet state of "Manchukuo." It must also be noted that after signing its 1944 Treaty with Russia, the Japanese Government felt certain enough of immunity from Russian attack to send seven divisions of the Kwantung Army guarding Manchuria to Central China to launch Japan's last big offensive against the Chinese Nationalist forces.
3. For fuller discussion, see Chapter Three.
4. See White Paper on China, Annexes 61 and 62.
5. In a dispatch from Mukden dated May 6, 1946.
6. White Paper, p. 88.

CHAPTER TWO

1. In his "Letter of Transmittal" to the White Paper on *United States Relations With China,* 1949.

2. This figure was confirmed by General W. O. Reeder, now a deputy assistant chief of staff and former Foreign Liquidation Commissioner in the India–Burma theater. See column of Peter Edson, Scripps-Howard newspapers, February 3, 1951.
3. White Paper, p. 887.
4. In a dispatch published in the Washington *Daily News,* September 24, 1947.
5. New York *Times,* June 22, 1947.

CHAPTER THREE

1. *Documents on the Problem of the Chinese Communist Party.* Presented to the People's Political Council, March 1941. Published in Chungking 1944 by the Supreme National Defense Council.
2. For a fuller discussion of this historical background, see the author's *Last Chance in China* (Indianapolis, Bobbs-Merrill, 1947).
3. White Paper, p. 832.
4. See *World Politics,* Vol. II, No. 4, July 1950.
5. Report on the Proceedings of the Tydings Committee, Vol. 1, p. 446.
6. It can be argued that in *China's Destiny* Chiang Kai-shek expressed a semi-Leninist or conventional Asiatic view of Western imperialist "exploitation" of China in the nineteenth century. Nevertheless, his preference for the West against Russian Communist imperialism is as clear in his writings as in his actions.
7. White Paper, p. 263.
8. Pp. 817–22.
9. Pp. 891–94.
10. The surprise attack of September 18, 1931, when the Japanese army seized Mukden, Changchun, and other Manchurian cities.

CHAPTER FOUR

1. *The Situation in Asia,* p. 97. Lattimore in this book admits that there has been some "land reform" in Korea, resulting in "a large increase in the number of owners of land." He says, however, that there hasn't been any progress because control of the land "through the political, administrative, and tax machinery" is in the hands of "politicians." Presumably he wants a one-party dictatorship eliminating "politicians" from control of the government.
2. On January 19, 1950, a majority of the Republican members of the House of Representatives joined sixty-one Democrats in rejecting the "Korean Aid Bill" which provided *only for economic assistance* because they believed that without military assistance

both to Korea and "other critical areas in Asia" the proposed grant would merely "enhance the prize dangled before the Communist aggressors" by the Administration spokesmen who professed themselves uninterested in the fall of China, Korea, and Formosa.

3. According to the *New York Times* and *New York Herald Tribune* reports of his speech, Dean Acheson said that Japan, Okinawa, and the Philippines were the American line of security in the western Pacific, and that with bases on this line our position would be impregnable, that he would not speak for the Joint Chiefs of Staff, although he gave the impression that he knew something of their views. He strongly reaffirmed President Truman's stand against sending military forces or military advice to the Chinese Nationalists on Formosa, and added that he alone was responsible for the State Department's confidential guidance message of December 23, telling its officials abroad to prepare for the loss of Formosa to the Communists.

Acheson said that several important problems had come to a head since Congress adjourned three months ago. One of them was possible American recognition of Communist China. On this point he reminded Senators that the Communists now control all of China except a few isolated areas, which the Administration saw no need for haste in recognizing. He said American recognition would depend on future events, including assurances that Chinese Communists would protect the safety of American citizens and obey international law. He distinctly stated that beyond the line laid down the United States could not assure the rest of the Far East against attack.

4. *New York Times*, December 10, 1950.

CHAPTER FIVE

1. Foreigners usually refer to the three large cities of central China situated at the confluence of the Yangtze and Han rivers, 300 miles above Shanghai, as Hankow, which is only one of them. The Chinese call all three the Wuhan cities. They consist of Hankow on the north bank of the Yangtze, Wuchang on the south bank, and Hanyang, which faces Hankow across the narrow Han River.

2. This stupid but understandable, even if inexcusable, misunderstanding of mine concerning the motives of the Chinese Communists, led me to write as follows in my book, *China At War* (1939):

"Moreover, the Chinese Communist Party long ago abandoned the dream of establishing its own dictatorship. Now that social basis is amongst the peasants of the most backward provinces in

China, and amongst the middle-class youth and the liberal reformers, its aim has genuinely become social and political reform along capitalist and democratic lines. The Chinese Communists have become radicals in the English nineteenth century meaning of the word."

In writing this passage I was endeavoring to be fair and objective, and not let my hatred of Stalin's tyranny blind my judgment of the character and aims of the Chinese Communist Party. I was terribly mistaken, and I have less excuse for my mistake than the many writers who propagated this same myth without having received my "education" in Russia. However, wrong as I was, I cannot conceive how Owen Lattimore, who persisted in propagating the same error for so many more years, could decently have quoted this passage against me before the Tydings Committee. I at least had, long since, admitted my mistake. He had continued to pretend that my statement was true.

3. In his testimony before the Senate Foreign Relations Committee, 1946.
4. White Paper on China, report dated November 7, 1944, p. 573.
5. *Loc. cit.*
6. *Ibid.*, pp. 575–76.
7. "Can Truman Be Educated?" in the *New American Mercury*, December 1950.

CHAPTER SIX

1. September 30, 1950.
2. *The Situation in Asia*, p. 96.

CHAPTER SEVEN

1. In the following paragraph appearing on p. 374 in the 1938 edition (Random House), the italicized portion, critical of the Soviet Union and the Chinese Communists, was left out of the editions published in 1939 (Garden City Publishing Company) and in 1944 by the Modern Library, which is owned by Random House.

"And finally, of course, the political ideology, tactical line, and theoretical leadership of the Chinese Communists have been under the close guidance, if not positive *detailed* direction, of the Communist International, *which during the past decade has become virtually a bureau of the Russian Communist Party. In final analysis this means that, for better or worse, the policies of the Chinese Communists, like Communists in every other country, have had to fall in line with, and usually subordinate themselves to, the broad strategic requirements of Soviet Russia, under the dictatorship of Stalin."*

Another omission from the revised edition was the italicized portion of the following quotation:

"The three periods of Sino-Russian relationship mentioned above accurately reflect also the changes that have taken place in the character of the Comintern during recent years, and its stages of transition *from an organization of international incendiaries into an instrument of the national policy of the Soviet Union* . . ."

Other typical changes were the elimination of Snow's original reference to the Comintern as "a kind of bureau of the Soviet Union" and "glorified advertising agency" for Communism.

2. A few quotes:

"Soviet policy in the East, like Soviet policy in Europe, requires the skillful, active promotion of political forces friendly to the Soviet Union and likely to help improve its security."

"Today Moscow views the Kuomintang regime with only slightly more confidence than it ever placed in the Polish government in exile."

3. For a fuller discussion of this subject, see the article by Irene Kuhn entitled "Why You Buy Books That Sell Communism," in the *American Legion Magazine,* January 1951.
4. See, for example, page 120.
5. Re Philip Jessup, it is interesting to note here that he was the oldest member (in length of service) of the Board of Trustees of the Carnegie Endowment for International Peace that appointed Alger Hiss its president. He was also the only member thoroughly acquainted with Hiss's State Department background.
6. Subsequently Joe Barnes served on the New York *Star* (successor to *PM*) and has recently become elevated to the influential position of Executive Editor of Simon & Schuster. (Simon & Schuster, it may be remembered, made a big thing of Joe Davies' *Mission to Moscow,* a by-no-means objective account of his ambassadorship in the Soviet Union.) Barnes was named by Louis Budenz before the Tydings Committee in 1950 as a Communist.

CHAPTER EIGHT

1. Seth Richardson is a law partner of Joseph Davies, former Ambassador to Moscow, author of *Mission to Moscow.*

2. Senator McCarthy showed his fundamentally liberal convictions when in 1949 he insisted upon a re-examination of the cases of the Germans accused of complicity in the Malmédy massacre, whose "confessions" had been extorted by torture. He took the position that due process of law must be upheld.
3. Remarks of Senator Hickenlooper, *Congressional Record*, April 5, 1950, pp. 4957–58.
4. Senate Resolution 231. 81st Congress, Second Session.
5. See, for instance, Alfred Friendly's article in the August 1950 issue of *Harper's*, in which this Washington *Post* correspondent's main argument against McCarthy is the discrepancy in his total figures of subversives in the State Department. The article makes no mention of all the evidence presented against the principals accused by McCarthy, and in the case of Owen Lattimore omits entirely the evidence concerning his Communist sympathies afforded by his writings, quotations from which were presented to the Tydings Committee. In the same issue *Harper's* printed Eleanor Lattimore's defense of her husband.
6. See, for instance, Alex Barth's *The Loyalty of Free Men*, in which it is argued that it is not the function of Loyalty boards to discover spies and that the danger from Communist political subversion is negligible.
7. Furthermore, McCarthy claimed, even those files which the Senators were permitted to see had been stripped of any material which supported the charge that they had Communist affiliations.
8. *Proceedings of the Tydings Committee*, p. 780.
9. *Ibid.*, p. 732, as follows:

"Mr. Field, I have no desire to pursue the matter, but to take you completely into my thoughts, so that I may now hope to get an answer.

"If you were to say that you didn't know, first of all, these individuals whose names have been brought out here, who are working for the State Department, of course that would be one thing. In the event that you said you did know them, I would like to ask you the question as to whether or not you know them to be members of the Communist Party, or know them to be disloyal to the Government of the United States.

"Now, it does seem to me that you might reconsider, with your attorney, that area, because I can see nothing in that particular situation which, if it stopped there, would involve you; and may I point out to you that if you don't answer the question all sorts of inferences can be drawn, some favorably, some unfavorably to

the individuals concerned. So, I would ask you if you wouldn't consult with your attorney again to see whether, to the extent I have outlined, and to the men I have named, who are now employed, you couldn't find it possible to give this committee the benefit of your testimony."
10. The official transcript of the hearings does not, of course, describe gestures and tones. One had to be present to appreciate the significance of Senator Tydings' broad smile and the warmth of the tone in which he thanked Field for his "evidence" in favor of the accused.
11. The fact that he did not cease to be a trusted Soviet agent was shown when he was appointed Moscow's representative for the sale of Communist literature in America immediately after his "expulsion" from the Party.
12. *Proceedings of the Tydings Committee,* p. 701.

CHAPTER NINE

1. *White Paper on China,* p. 573.
2. *Proceedings of the Tydings Committee,* Part 2, Appendix.
3. P. 185.
4. P. 136.
5. In an interview with Edgar Snow published in the *China Weekly Review* January 1950.
6. In the June 1941 issue of *Pacific Affairs,* Lattimore wrote: "In China a right-wing government can stand if it has a certain amount of foreign support and approval, but if foreign attack overweighs foreign support, it must get on without it. The second of these lessons applies particularly to China. It will become more obvious if the effect of the Russo-Japanese Neutrality Pact is to increase the isolation of China, forcing the Government to rely less on foreign support, and to come to terms with the people by making the methods of government less authoritarian and more representative and more democratic."
7. P. 108.
8. *Solution in Asia,* p. 94.
9. P. 164.
10. *The Situation in Asia,* p. 147.
11. P. 152.
12. P. 134 and p. 139.
13. P. 150.
14. *Solution in Asia,* p. 139.
15. *The Situation in Asia,* p. 89.

16. For the story of my life in Soviet Russia, see my book *Lost Illusion* (published in England as *The Dream We Lost*), Philadelphia, Fireside Press, Inc., 1948.
17. In his latest book, *Pivot of Asia* (1950), Lattimore speaks of "feudal" Mongol society.
18. A leading member of the American Communist Party.
19. *Proceedings of the Tydings Committee,* p. 56.

CHAPTER TEN

1. October, 1950, "How to Checkmate Stalin in Asia."
2. "Untold Facts in the Korean Disaster" by William Bradford Huie.
3. *New York Times,* January 29, 1951, report of United Nations debate.

Index

Acheson, Dean, 14, 15, 30-31, 38, 66, 85, 86, 95, 96, 117, 189, 210, 224, 228, 231
  opinions on Communism, 125-138
  speech at U.N. General Assembly, 129
  speech to National Press Club, 93
All-China National Assembly, 16
Amerasia case, 158-163, 183, 213-214
American Defense Grant, 78
American Youth Congress, 152
American-Chinese Agricultural Mission, 64
American-Russian Institute, 152
Andrews, Bert, 174
Arms embargo, 13-14, 33, 36
Atcheson, George, 120-121
Atlantic Charter, viii, xi

Baldwin, Hanson, 101
Barbey, Daniel E., 7
Barnes, Joseph, 151
Barr, David G., 42-43
Belden, Jack, 142
Bentley, Elizabeth, 117
Berkey, Russell S., 45
Berle, Adolph, 136
Bess, Demaree, 217-218
Bevin, Ernest, 17
Biddle, Francis, 152, 195
Bielaski, Frank B., 159-160
Bisson, T. A., 152, 153-154, 213
Boas, Franz, 153
Bodine, Cornelius, 50
Bridges, Styles, 78-80, 164
Browder, Earl, 178-180, 194, 212
Buck, Lossing, 64
Budenz, Louis, 178, 179, 181, 205, 212-213

Bullitt, William C., 41, 61, 78
Butterworth, William W., 120
Byrnes, James F., 17, 27-29, 72, 169

Carlson, Evans, 107, 157
Carter, Edward C., 151, 156, 210
Chamberlain, Neville, 234
Chamberlin, William Henry, 217
Chambers, Whittaker, 239
Chang Chia-ngau, 70
Chang Chih-chung, 84
Chefoo, 53
Chen Cheng, 52
Chennault, Claire L., 144
Chen-yi, 99
Chengteh, 12
Chiang Ching-kuo, 69-70
Chiang Kai-shek, 4, 8, 11-13, 48, 56, 65, 141, 142, 189, 191, 213, 221
  appeal to President Truman, 25-26
  attitude towards Russia, 52
  loyalty to the West, 68, 72-74
  offer of troops for Korea, 133
  opposition to Communism, 22
  peace proposals, 16
  problems, 58-59
  request for American officers, 61
Chihfeng, 11
China Aid Act, 27, 34, 38
Chinese Central News Agency, 50, 52
Chou En-lai, 10-12, 16, 105, 143
  influence on General Marshall, 11
Chuh Teh, 142, 227
Chungking, 10, 120
Churchill, Winston, 45, 114, 205, 206
Clark, Worth D., 78
Clark-Kerr, Archibald, 106-107

INDEX

Communism, Chinese, character of, 197
  intervention in Korea, 97
  relations with Russia, 12-13, 224-225
  Russian aid to, 53
  U.S. aid to, 5, 10
Communism, spread of, 135
Communist Academy, 210
Communist Party, Chinese, character of, 10-11, 43
  hostility towards U.S., 15
  refusal of UNRRA aid by, 50
  training of Korean troops by, 51
Connally, Tom, 31, 94
Creel, George, 145
Currie, Lauchlin, 36, 117-118, 154

Dairen, 7, 53, 69, 119
Daniels, Jonathan, 27
Davies, John Patton, 107, 109-113, 118, 150, 189-190
  opinion of Chinese Communism, 113
  report from Chungking, 112
Davies, Joseph, 206
De Toledano, Ralph, 184
Dean, Vera Micheles, 153
Dennen, Leon, 222
Dewey, Thomas, 48, 181
Division of International Security Affairs, 121
Dodd, Bella, 180-182
Dondero, George A., 164
Donovan, William J., 160
Dorn, Frank, 107
Drumright, Everett F., 123
Dulles, Foster R., 154
Durdin, Tillman, 53, 143

Eastman, Max, 124, 148
Emerson, John, 109
Epstein, Israel, 147
Executive Order No. 9835, 186

Faculty Advisory Board of the American Law Students Association, 152
Fairbank, John K., 144, 146
Field, Frederick Vanderbilt, 151, 156, 177-178, 213
Fisher, Francis F., 142
Fleeson, Doris, 236
Foreign Policy Association, 149, 209
Forman, Harrison, 145
Formosa, 61, 85, 95, 134, 228, 236

Gallup Poll, 174

Gayn, Mark, 148, 158, 160, 161
Gillem, A. C., 77
Green, Theodore F., 167, 177, 185
Greenberg, Esther, 154
Greenberg, Michael, 154
Grew, Joseph, 116, 118, 119, 120, 161

Hankow, 104
Hanley, Joseph, 181
Hanson, Haldore, 178
Harbin, 15
Hazen, Charles A., 174
Hickenlooper, Burke, 166, 182, 185
Hiss, Alger, 121, 136, 137, 153, 164, 165, 175, 186, 206, 238
Hitchcock, Robert M., 161
Hitler, Adolf, ix, 197, 234
Hodge, John R., 51
Holland, William L., 155
Holmes, Julius, 160
Holt, Emmett, 209
Hornbeck, Stanley, 123
House Un-American Activities Committee, 136
Hulutao, 7
Hurley, Patrick, 27, 110, 113
Hutchinson, Claude B., 64

Institute of Pacific Relations, 149, 155-156, 210
Institute of World Economy and Politics, 210
Isbrandtsen Line, 96
Isaacs, Harold, 210
Ives, Irving M., 181

Jacoby, Annallee, 144, 145, 146, 147
Jaffe, Philip J., 158, 159-162, 183, 212
Jehol, 11
Jessup, Philip, 81, 150, 151-153, 172, 173, 183, 189
Johnson, Joseph E., 121
Judd, Walter, 33, 164, 219

Kalgan, 52
Kennan, George, 127
Kenyon, Dorothy, 176, 179
Kizer, Benjamin, 155
Knowland, William F., 85, 164
Korea, 86, 87-102, 227, 232-233, 236-237
  postwar aid to, 88-92
  President Truman's policy on, 131-133
Korean Aid Bill, 92
Korean troops, trained by Chinese Communists, 51, 52, 74
Krock, Arthur, 187

INDEX

Kung, H. H., 67
Kuomintang, 55-56, 192-193

La Follette, Robert M., 174
Lacoste, Francis, 236
Land reform, in China, 64-65
Larsen, Emmanuel, 114, 158, 160, 161, 162, 184-185
Lattimore, Eleanor, 192
Lattimore, Owen, 65, 88, 89, 141, 144, 145, 146-147, 152, 154, 156, 168, 173, 174, 181, 185, 187, 188-218
  as *Amerasia* contributor, 194-195
  education, 190-191
  opinion of Soviet Union, 200-202
  recommendations on Korea, 189
Lauterbach, Richard, 144, 148
League Against War and Fascism, 152
Leahy, William D., 27
Leber, Amadora, 143
Lehman, Herbert, 181
Lenin, Nicolai, 65
Levine, Isaac Don, 184, 185
Li Tsung-jen, 82-83, 85
Lie, Trygve, 189
Lin Pao, 98-99, 227
Lippmann, Walter, 150, 151, 231
Lodge, Henry Cabot, Jr., 167, 183, 186
Loyalty Review Board, 165, 186-187
Lucas, Scott, 166
Luce, Henry, 148
Ludden, Raymond, 109, 113-114, 150

MacArthur, Douglas, 23, 97-98, 119, 146, 154, 231
  on defense of Formosa, 134
Malinovsky, Rodion, 70, 227
Manchuria, capture by Communists of, 7
  looting by Russians, 204
  loss to China, 52, 228-229
  seizure by Japan, 56
Mao Tse-tung, 56-57, 86, 110, 122, 194, 220, 226, 227-228
Marley, Sheppard, 155
Marshall, General George, xi, 7-10, 78, 96, 198-199, 231
  appeasement policy of, 60
  cooperation with Chinese Communists, 13-14, 49
  friendship with Stilwell, 111
  mission to China, 18-21
  testimony before Armed Services Committee, 27-29
Marshall Plan, ix, 49
Marx, Karl, 63, 128

Marxian philosophy, 135
McCarthy, Joseph, 97, 118, 151, 152, 153, 163, 164-176, 177, 183-184, 186, 203, 238
McMahon, Brian, 167, 179, 181, 218
Mikhailovitch, Drazha, 221, 224
Mitchell, James, 162
Mitchell, Kate L., 156, 158, 160-161
Molotov, V. M., 17, 21
Moody, L. B., 34-36, 45, 46
Morgan, Edward P., 78, 182, 215-218
Morgenthau Plan, ix, xi
Morris, Robert, 169
Moscow Conference, 24
Mukden, 14
Mundt, Karl E., 164
Murphy, Thomas F., 193

Nanking, 41, 84, 104
National Committee on Democratic Rights, 152
Nationalist First Army, 50
Nationalist Government, Chinese, American aid to, 31-38, 44-45
  intelligence service, 98
  need of ammunition, 38-40, 50
  task of, 55-56
  Truman boycott of, 13-14, 33
Nelson, Frederic, 209
Newspaper Guild, 174
Newton, William H., 50
Nimitz, Chester, 99
Nixon, Walter, 164

Overpopulation, of China, 64

Pai Chung-hsi, 51-52, 83
Pauley, Edwin W., 130
Pearson, Drew, 99
Peffer, Nathaniel, 144, 145, 147-148, 208
Peiping, 50
Port Arthur, 7, 53, 69
Potsdam Agreement, ix
Powell, John B., 144-145, 148

Quebec Conference, x

Rand, Christopher, 53
Remington, William, 186, 238
Rhee, Syngman, 87, 93
Richardson, Seth, 165
Ringwalt, Arthur G., 120
Roosevelt, Franklin D., viii, x, xi, xii, 3-5, 68, 189, 220
Roosevelt, Theodore, 4
Roschin, Nikolai V., 73, 83

INDEX

Roth, Andrew, 158, 160, 161, 162
Rusk, Dean, 121-122
Russia, post-war position of, x, xi

Sabbath, Joseph, 169
Salisbury, Lawrence, 150
Service, John Stewart, 109, 113, 115-116, 118, 135-136, 148, 150, 158, 160, 173, 178, 180, 183, 191
Shanghai, 96
Sherwood, Robert E., x-xi
Shub, Anatole, 127
Silvermaster, Nathan G., 117, 179
Sinkiang, 84
Sino-Soviet Treaty, 69, 229-230
Slatekovsky, 70
Slave labor, 229
Smedley, Agnes, 106-107, 142, 146
Smith, Margaret Chase, 236
Snow, Edgar, 140-142, 144, 145, 147, 157
Soong, T. V., 67, 139
Soong family, 67
Sprouse, Philip, 120
Stachel, Jack, 213
Stalin, Joseph, vii, ix, xii, 4, 8, 63, 121, 191, 220
  attempt to win Chiang Kai-shek, 69-71
  Chinese policy, 227
Steele, A. T., 11, 76, 143-144
Stein, Gunther, 145-146, 152, 154, 156
Stettinius, Edward R., Jr., 3, 160
Stewart, Maxwell, 153
Stilwell, Joseph, 5, 11, 105, 109, 110
Stolypin, Peter A., 65
Stone, William T., 154
Strong, Anna Louise, 154
Stuart, Leighton, 38, 40
  letter to General Marshall, 47-48, 75
Sun Fo, 68-69
Sun Li-jen, 61
Sun Yat-sen, 57, 64
Sun Yat-sen, Madame, 139
Szepingkai, siege of, 52-53

Taber, John, 164
Taft, Robert A., viii, 95, 130
Thompson, Dorothy, 101
Tientsin, 96
Tito, Marshall, 114, 131, 204, 221-224, 226, 234
Tolun, 12

Truman, Harry S., 8-10, 13, 17, 25-27, 28, 46, 78, 127, 160, 187, 205, 206, 220
  Korean policy, 92, 96, 130, 132, 234
Truman Doctrine, ix, 49, 205
Tsiang, T. F., 40, 229
Tydings, Millard E., 167, 169, 174, 177-180, 181
Tydings Committee, x, 65, 148, 151, 163, 176-187, 214

Uighurs, 203
United Nations, action on Korea, 99-100
  failure of, viii, 236
United States Military Mission, 41
UNRRA aid to China, 49
Uzbecks, 203

Van Beuren, Archbold, 159
Vincent, John Carter, 68, 116-118, 119, 178, 180
"Voice of America," 54

Wallace, Henry, 118, 189, 213
Wallace, Ralph, 229
Walsh, J. Raymond, 161
Walter Hines Page School of International Relations, 190, 203
Wang Ching-wei, 226
Wang Ming, 198
Wang Shih-chieh, 72
Ward, Angus, 123
Watts, Richard, Jr., 154
Wedemeyer, Albert C., 5, 6, 36, 55, 61, 74-75, 76, 110, 114
  report to Senate Appropriations Committee, 78-81
White, Theodore, 144, 146, 147, 148
White, William S., 174
White Paper on China, 9-10, 16, 18-19, 31, 32, 73, 76-78, 220
  Davies reports, 113
  on the Wedemeyer report, 81-82
Withers, Garret L., 166
Wittfogel, Karl, 63, 224, 225
Woltman, Frederick, 159
World Affairs Council Conference, 121

Yalta Agreement, ix-x, 1-5, 68, 81
Yalu River, 137
Yeaton, Ivan, 114
Yenan, 114, 140
Yingkow, 7
Yu Ta-wei, 77